THE WAY TO EXECUTIVE SERENITY

THE WAY TO EXECUTIVE SERENITY

How to Achieve the Satisfying Life-style of the Philosopher-Executive

R.G.H. Siu

A Cole-Beren Book

BTB
BEECH TREE BOOKS
A QUILL EDITION
New York

Library of Congress Cataloging-in-Publication Data

Siu, R.G.H. (Ralph Gun Hoy), 1917–
The way to executive serenity.

Reprint. Originally published: Transcending the power game. New York : Wiley, c1980.
Bibliography: p.
Includes index.
1. Executives. 2. Stoics. I. Title.
HD38.2.S58 1985 650.1′3 85-19959
ISBN 0-688-05054-9 (pbk.)

Printed in the United States of America

First Beech Tree Books/Quill Edition

1 2 3 4 5 6 7 8 9 10

BTB

The word "book" is said to derive from *boka*, or beech.
The beech tree has been the patron tree of writers since ancient times and represents the flowering of literature and knowledge.

To
Ramsey Clark

PREFACE

Our previous book, *The Craft of Power,* was addressed to executives and readers concerned with the acquiring, maintaining, and expanding of personal power.

This companion volume is written for those interested in an alternative life–style. Not one which denies the necessity of power and progress. But one which fosters a kind of executive serenity, that simultaneously satisfies society and the inner being. That liberates from the heroic spells of bullying and bruising others, yet immunizes against the antiheroic trances of nihilism and the absurd within oneself. That wilts not in the heat of competition, kowtows not before persons of power, mopes not at being apparently niched at a plateau without a promotion in sight. That succors, savors, muses, and laughs; leading others to succor, savor, muse, and laugh. In sum, a life perfused with a deeper meaning, which serves the people, serenes the soul, gets the job done, and provides the groceries at the same time.

As a counterpoint to the executive of power, we now add the philosopher–executive with a Stoic–Taoist melody.

R. G. H. Siu

Washington, D. C.
November 1979

CONTENTS

THE WAY TO EXECUTIVE SERENITY

I OVERALL COMPOSURE

One of the principal qualities that blossoms from transcending the game of power, which is what this book is essentially about, is relative serenity. But we would find it rather difficult to specify what brings serenity into a person's life. Serenity is rather shy. Determined pursuits and bold strokes are repellent. The more forward the person's desires and actions, the farther serenity retreats into the distance. There are indications that serenity is attracted to a milieu of uncontrived reasonableness and graciousness, with a natural forgetfulness about its presence. Experience indicates that it leaves the moment the host takes pains to recognize it. To be sensible about the situation, then, we have no alternative but to go about nurturing a conducive composure, leaving it to come and go as befits its private preferences. After all, life can still be quite tolerable and even satisfying without it.

Two intuitive predispositions are necessary to this state of composure. The first is a living of each instant as the steady focus of one's total life, including the last wave of goodbye. The pithy brevity of this Part I has been adapted to stimulate this grasping of the totality at one glance as it were. The second is a sensing of things that are not heard and not seen and of things that cannot be heard and cannot be seen. It is out of these unnameables and indescribables that various manifestations exhibit themselves, like straws on the surface of the river. What are written in books are only straws; what is to be remembered is the river. Hence, as an introductory exercise, the style of presentation—at times allusive, epigrammatic.

The following approach to Part I has proved effective for many readers. You may wish to try it. Pick up the book on a relaxed occasion, when you can devote forty minutes or so to it. Ignore the bracketed numbers for the time being and leisurely go over the part in one sitting. In the process, allow the words to enter your eyes fully and freely, without being concerned as to what they may mean in particular. Let your thoughts and sensations emerge and recede as they will. Then lay the book aside for several days or more. Return to it at another relaxing opportunity. Give Part I a "once over quickly" from beginning to end. After that, peruse at random here and there within it—muse, contemplate, think as you please, but do not argue. Now lay the book aside for another week or more. Finally, proceed with the entire book in whatever way comes naturally. You would then have been suitably prepared to get the most out of the essential elements in Part II as well—to note the cross-linkages of the various facets of meaningful living; to learn from the voids, the contradictories, and the strangenesses; to criticize, modify, and embellish what has and has not been written; and to assimilate whatever is enriching into your being.

SEEING BEYOND THE EXECUTIVE SUITE

1 Ever since the days of the Pharaohs, organizations have assumed the shape of the pyramid. The higher in the hierarchy, the fewer the incumbents.

So it remains today. For every hundred eager aspirants among you crossing the junior executive threshold, 99.9 never get to the top. They level off at various echelons. Most farther below the peak than closer. Most rather young in the prime of their managerial potential.

The higher prizes, for which they have been striving, lie—it has now become probable—forever beyond their reach.

2 The spectre looms: a dispirited drifting, a treadmill routine, an emptiness.

How can they relieve their frustrations?[1]* Where can they look for firm emotional footing? For a feeling of lasting meaning? They search their surroundings for answers.

None comes forth.

3 Those of you at or near the apex have anxieties of your own. Harpoons sunk deep in your troubled psyches by persons of power. Harnesses strapped tight on your weary backs by institutions. The thrill of jousting no longer satisfies.

Is there no way to soften the competitive stresses? No loosening of the entanglements? No semblance of serenity? They, too, search their surroundings for answers.

None comes forth.

*Numbers in brackets in Part I refer to essential elements in Part II beginning on page 33.

4 None is and none will ever be forthcoming from those quarters.

All of you have been constrained by the masters of power to whirl your gears in the institutional world created by them. Institutions use you like you use a wrench, so there is no feeling for you. They maintain you like you maintain a washing machine, so there is no caring for you. Does a wrench ask for meaning? Does a washing machine ask for serenity?

Institutions do not answer. They do not understand. They do not hear.

5 Perhaps the more inclusive civilization itself might oblige.

But what can be expected of this culture of ours, which has preached God's love for, lo, 2000 years, while leaving a trail of blood and misery; which has exalted humanism, while presenting as the flower of its genius the Bomb of Hydrogen?[2] Does the aimless violence throughout the world signify that twilight of personal freedom is at hand?[3] Will new behavioral patterns evolve, which will wash these globals ills away?

Alas, civilization takes decades for major changes in mores. You'd be long gone before they can make any significant difference in dilemmas like yours. And if they do, it might even be for the worse.

6 Then how about turning away from the grand headlines of the tabloids and the academic gymnastics of the textbooks to sources within your immediate self?

As you do, you hear the self-same sweet seductions of unseen sirens that had been beckoning you hither and yon for the past decades. Repeatedly do you attempt to penetrate the thick and aromatic smokescreen beclouding your view[4] and break out of the cuirass encasing your person.[5]

Yet again and again, no answer comes forth.

7 The outcome is not unexpected. For the voices with the answers have long since been muted in our age of institutions and precluded from our executive suite.

They belong to the likes of Lao Tzu, with his sensitivity to the natural, the ineffable, and the spontaneous[6]; Chuang Tzu, with his whimsical wisdom and musing laughter[7]; Epictetus, with his transcendence over misfortunes[8]; and Marcus Aurelius, with his depth of experience as the philosopher-king[9].

If you would but step out of your office, lift your head, blank your mind, and cock your ear in their direction, you would hear a faint but clear chorus: "Be more of a philosopher-executive!"

BEGINNING WITH GIVENS

8 Begin not with the oughts but always with the givens.

Hoodwink yourself no longer that people that are, are not. That you yourself that are, are not. That things that are, are not. That all that are not, actually are.

Face reality as clearly as a still pond reflects the sky on a sunny day.

9 Sooner or later, things go awry. Computers get confused; basements get flooded; people get mugged. Hunger among poor people, cancer among the rich, betrayal among friends.

Whimper not in adversity and complain not over evil; questioning evil does no good. Hide not behind excuses and seek not blame; imputing blame ameliorates no pain.

Accept the givens[10] and do some good while advancing forward.

10 The superior person, who disapproves of the state of affairs but cannot do anything about it, does not become defiant and scornful. Defiance and scorn lend no dignity to one's stance; they only preclude creative solutions.

The superior person, who is oppressed but cannot do anything about it, does not seek martyrdom. Martyrdom lends no justification to one's despair; it only precludes recovery.

Refine the art of doing nothing.[11]

RECOGNIZING THE DEMON

11 The predicament of most executives lies in large degree in allowing themselves to come under the spell of The Demon and imprisoning themselves in one of his cramped nooks, under the illusion of its being an important universe. They worship Him as society and sacrifice themselves in his temples called institutions.

Being terribly possessive of His subjects, He refuses to share them with Nature, which alone can sustain their selfs in their wholeness. He wants them all to Himself.[12]

His ministers are cunning and His disciples tireless in recasting all communicants like you in the sweaty molds of modules.[13]

12 Activity, capacity, creativity. Progress, success, avidness. More, more, more.

For the greater glory of The Demon. The Devouring Demon. The Demon of Disjunction.

His kingdom come.[14]

13 Observe the cormorants.[15]

Would they be fishing day and night with rings round their necks in rowboats were they not so gluttonous for fish, so skilful in the catching, so devoted to the job?

There may be an object lesson here worth mulling over.

14 More than anything else, acquisitiveness[16] is The Demon's open sesame!

Your heady acquisitiveness of power, possession, and prestige has so involuted upon itself that power, possession, and prestige has now exercised a tandem acquisitiveness of you. The more of them you acquire, the more of you they acquire—like an ocean swallowing a drowning swimmer.

You have acquired so much that you are enjoying a not insignificant store of power, possession, and prestige. They, too, have acquired so much that they are enjoying a not insignificant store of you.

15 The bartering of self for gain accounts for the heightened hollowness that follows each triumph. A piece of you had to be offered The Demon for each acquisition.

By now, you are much diminished and fragmented.

You need be whole again.

DELINEATING OPTIONS

16 What, then, are the practical options?

Essentially four—with their various combinations.

Forging ahead as a person of power, operating within assigned responsibilities, escaping from the world of affairs, and superseding The Demon.

17 The path of power involves contention with The Demon Himself.

The struggle is over the domination of human destinies. It is not what people believe, feel, or do that matters, but that they believe, feel, or do as the person of power personally desires. The final test of one's greatness as a person of power is his taming of The Demon Himself to become the loyal lieutenant for the implementation of his commands.

Then will the people worship him in His stead as a god on earth.

18 The path of the faithful institutional operator begins with a vow of obedience to The Demon within His Empire of Anxiety[17].

Having been well indoctrinated in the attendant dogmas and rituals, the agent gladly commits his self to His service toward the efficient functioning of His schools, corporations, labor unions, banks, churches, governments, and other institutions as measured by their self-proclaimed criteria.

His primary mission is not to see that The Demon's directives are beneficial for those under his purview, but that they be carried out.

19 The path of escape from the world of affairs is made up of many trails to suit diverse personalities.

The spiritually minded retreats into the cave of the religious recluse. The intellectually inclined hides in the cloister of the scholar. The jaded pouts in the nihilism of the cynic[18]. Because of the small numbers involved, The Demon is quite willing to leave them unmolested. But having been regimented for so long, they feel lost in their newly asserted freedom.

So they each conjure up a little guardian demon, specially equipped to spur their respective isolations along.

20 The path of superseding The Demon consists of two major approaches: That pointing to eternal rewards in the afterlife is exemplified by the worshipper supplicating God[19]. That pointing to peace of mind is exemplified by the Stoic-Taoist[20].

The Demon is rather clever in dealing with these deviants. Under the pretense of protecting their individual liberties, He coopts most of them into aggregations of churches, schools, and philosophies. A little demon is then anointed within the respective congregations and coteries to inspire them through reverberations of mutual adulation back into His Empire of Anxiety.

Those who succeed in regaining their selfs are not only sufficiently strong-willed to supersede The Demon, but also sufficiently perceptive to see through His recurring felicitations and lures.

21 Of the four principal options, the path of power precludes the composure most people seek. That of institutional operator is inhibitory, while that of escape is overly self-oriented to be balanced and complete. Only the path of superseding The Demon holds promise.

The most widely followed variant of the last option is the other-worldly one. We shall leave this to the revered ministers and eloquent theologians, who have long ago preempted the field.

Because executives are predominately dealers of earthly affairs, we shall concentrate our attention on the this-worldly way of the Stoic-Taoist.

CLARIFYING PARAMETERS

22 Hectic is the life of the executive.

Cases overflowing the in-baskets. Phones ringing without surcease. Committee meetings chewing away the hours. Conflicting pressures coming from all directions. Incompetence and venality fouling the operations.

And he or she, with only ten hours a day to navigate through them all.

23 In the frenzy of the drill, the executive can easily be distracted from the essential purpose—from the bottom line, as the jargon of the workplace would put it.

To ensure that the institutions' interests not be overlooked, their agents have made them explicit: more profit for corporations, more victories for armies, more souls for churches. Not necessarily better and better and better, but bigger and bigger and bigger.

That is clear enough from the institution's point of view.

24 But the bottom line for the institution can rarely be the same for the individual[21].

The institution can neither live the individual's life nor die his death. He must do it alone.

What bottom line have you drawn for yourself? As determined by what coordinates?

25 The value-reality-power coordinates may be a useful framework.

One's values as a person of Nature are alloyed with his values as an executive of institutions along one axis. The reality of things are modified in his perceptions of them along the second. His power as a maker and shaker is attenuated by the power of other makers and shakers and that of The Maker and Shaker Himself along the third.

The mobile of life keeps moving continuously like a glider in the sky.

26 If one is sensitive to the invisible currents and feathering with one's hands on the rudder, the chances of one's trajectory of life being on compass, smooth, and satisfying can be raised immeasurably.

For the full development of this reflex responsiveness, one needs to mature an absentminded nonattachment to the fruits of one's efforts[22] and an intuitive apprehension of the ineffable[23]. The relevant questions then emerge unsolicited and the appropriate answers follow undistorted.

The montage of composure, it seems, includes the gentle and the gracious, the good and the tranquil.

27 How can one be gentle[24], if one is anxious over maximal gains? Consider the magnanimous man[25].

His aspirations are relatively simple[26]. He rises above the petty bickerings that saturate office politics and the trivial cheatings that permeate commercial traffic. What does it matter if he is occasionally swindled out of his rightful due? The loss does not amount to much in any case; there's more than ample left for his own requirements. Granting that bad people also have a right to happiness, he stays as affable as ever. After all, they are but robots automated by The Demon's apostles. His services not being sales, he's in no need of gratitude; his honor not besmirchable, he's in no need of vengeance. Being tolerant of others' failings, he is never hurt; being unselfconscious of his own virtues, he is always true.

Magnanimity is central to the life of gentleness.

28 How can one be gracious[27], if one is sputtered by one's own exertions, far beyond his natural capacities? Slow down your pace according to a sensible plan.

A person travels farther, lasts longer, and acts more equably if he taxes himself at a fraction of his capabilities. Because of the resulting large reserve, he is not apprehensive over possible emergencies. His body is not fatigued and his mind not numbed. He dwells in the midst of difficulties, feeling no despair; brings his goals within ready reach, regretting no rewards passed over. There is no need for sycophancy before superiors, nor abuse before subordinates. His is an easy-going discipline, a genial demeanor, absorbing attention. He induces an airiness of festive calm. His presence is a pleasance.

Cruising is prerequisite to the life of graciousness.

29 How can one be good, if one is inattentive to the suffering of man and beast? Judge evil with a commensical scan.

How can anything be evil, if it brings no pain? And how can pain itself not be an evil? The minimizing of pain, then, is the basic measure of morality. Contrary rationalizations belong more with the luxuries of ethics and the inducements of institutions. Of all of God's creatures, man uniquely can greatly magnify or palliate the pain for one and all. Man's latitude for good and evil continues to widen with awe-inspiring potential.

Compassion[28] is basic to the life of goodness.

30 How can one be tranquil, if one is blown off one's feet by every gust of ill wind? Revive your anchorage of infinite span.

The child addressing birds and trees, the artisan regretting fallen tiles, the bystander pitying the bleating sheep in slaughtering stockades—a few of many signs revealing mutualities within the one of Nature. That is the totality from which one comes at birth, to which one returns at death. It is the web of ageless interlacings, which damp the viciously vicissitudinous assaults and perturbations of The Demon's minions.

The union of the self with Nature is integral to the life of tranquility[29].

RECTIFYING SELF

31 Much of the progress of man-made civilization is generated by the continuing creation of virtual presences and their elevation to divinities. Although their substance is imaginary, their effects on human beings are real.

The real courtiers control through the authority of the Almighty Virtual Gods[30]; the believing followers meekly obey in the interminable War of the Virtual Gods. "Slave!" they command, and the people slave. "Kill!" and the people kill. "Die!" and the people die.

Stay with the good and wise, who turn aside and stroll along the moonlit gardens. Returning—bury the dead, console the wounded and ease their pain, and sweep up the trash.

32 The Virtual Gods feed on litanies of intellectual discourse and insecure obsessions.

The urban centers offer these abundantly.

'Twas thus that they became the Great Virtual Valhalla[31].

33 You scurry at the beck and call of the courtiers of the Virtual Gods, forsaking family[32] and self.

Why addiction to the ceaseless chase?

Why not deliverance?

34 Deliverance need not be burlap-sacked. Sweets abound all around[33].

Enjoyments, too, inexpensive to boot: convivial dining, friendly chats, lovely music, engrossing reading, delightful musing[34].

Lace your life with laughter[35].

35 Courtiers spout a stream of enticements to rejoin the thralldom.

You've heard them many times before. You've preached the same encouragements so many times before. You've practiced the same tricks of the trade yourself, oh, so many times before[36].

Come now, what is the point of playing games against yourself much longer[37]?

36 Imagine how the very presence of the Real God would threaten the survival of the courtiers of the Virtual Gods.

Understand why He has accordingly been banished from their midst[38].

The deprived populace, adrift, is now maintained in compliant narcosis through effusions of the virtual.

37 Heal your own incompleteness with a shared consciousness.

Keep an open passage to the realm of the real.

Reforge your primal links to Nature on the outside[39].

BELONGING WITH NATURE

38 A human being is fairly judged by the integration of his net impact on others[40].

The practical expression of brotherhood is that others are better off for one's having been around—a broader smile, a lighter burden, a more contagious zest for life.

Preserve that warmth against the calculating guiles of the marketplace.

39 In relating with others, open first your eyes to the universe and squint at your own insignificance.

Recall the 1976 earthquake outside Peking that killed 700,000 people; would it have been averted had you been present? Recall the last institution you left; did your departure make a scintilla of difference to it?

We would smile at an amoeba trying to become a little man. Would we not laugh at a man trying to become a little god?

40 Your own finiteness leaves much lack for nurturing by others.

The more extensive the input, the more complete your self.

Open the portals wide.

41 To absorb the full enlightenment from the greater community, one must immerse oneself in its all-embracing unity.

To sustain one's responsive belonging, one must reciprocate with contributions of one's own as an identifiable nexus[41].

Subsume yourself and resonate[42].

42 A creature in pain is more pain than creature. To remove the pain is to restore the self.

There can be no greater good than that a man or beast be given back his self.

Let the reduction of suffering be the foundational expression of your relating to others on earth.

43 Science has long taught us that the beasts in the field are kindred to us in the office.

Yet, witness the widespread fratricide.

So cruel.

44 Behold the ways how man enjoys himself at the expense of dumb animals.

Clipping ears and tails of dogs for appearance, skinning minks and raccoons for decorative clothing, maiming mice and monkeys out of intellectual curiosity, plunging swords and lances into bulls for entertainment.

So unnecessarily cruel.

45 Many are those who hunt and fish.

How can one gain harmony with Nature by stalking and killing her tigers and lions, elks and moose, foxes and wolves, ducks and doves, pheasants and quails, et cetera and et cetera?

How can one become attuned to one's fellow beings by fashioning fish lures and other deceptive devices to their premature death?

46 Fewer are those who collect butterflies.

Even so, how can one be in communion with Nature, while scooping her creatures from their carefree flutterings, gassing them in chloroform bottles, and sticking pins through their thoraxes?

How can he be so insensitive as to call these sepulchres a beautiful collection?

47 It is no wonder that human fratricide is so common and even commended as expressions of the highest devotion and justice.

Man's cruelty to his fellow men has been well paved through reinforcing practices of cruelty to his fellow creatures. Having become unmoved by the twitchings and cries of his fellow creatures, it is a relatively easy transition to become unmoved by the twitchings and cries of his fellow men.

How can any meaning to life emerge from such a progression?

48 Infuse yourself with the vast infinitude of Nature away from the gruesome sports of the day.

Hike among the fragrances of springtime, saunter through the red leaves of autumn, and watch the glowing disk descend beneath the desert sun. Sense how the glen embraces the fern, behold how alive are the rocks, and see how the waters wave goodbye to the snows.

Free your associations of ulterior motives[43].

49 Leaven your activities with the artlessness of the cracking of the frozen rivers in spring thaw, the hissing seethes of seas, the soughing of the breeze through the trees, the flap-flapping of wild ducks, the golden carpeting of asphalt streets by gingko leaves of fall.

Experience the soles of your feet as one with the earth, the retina of your eyes one with the sky, the cells of your trachea one with the air.

Plant trees so birds can sing in freedom for generations to come.

50 Reflect this kin-tie to Nature in your doings.

Ask of your plans: Will they contribute positively to men and beasts under your care? Will they minimize suffering at large? Will they restrain, within the limits of essentiality, all forms of environmental blight?

Then act conformably.

51 Freshen this bond from time to time in that solitude, in which your inner stillness merges with that of Nature[44].

Engage in the intimate conversation of the Whole, as Silence listens and Silence speaks.

The last vestige of meaningless loneliness is then dissipated as the feeling of broadly based belonging gradually comes over you.

BEHAVING AT WORK

52 Notice your immediate associates[45], continually measuring themselves in being measured by others—not in mere accomplishments, but in the most demanding. When they succeed, they dread the animosity of others. When they fail, they dread the disappointment in themselves. And when they neither succeed nor fail, they dread the stress of yet another facing down.

Their suspicion turns into insincerity. Their impatience over progress tosses caution overboard to risk anew. Their fear of slipping over the zenith drives them blindly after the *big* killing.

Purge yourself from these neurotic aspirations[46].

53 Straightway, remove the greatest obstacle to a serene composure. Pay the necessary price: the pursuit of fame and promotion[47].

Should unsought fame and promotion come your way, they will be doubly sweetened. Once because they are free from the bitterness of past strife; twice because they are free from the anxiety of more strife to come.

Your performance excels simply because your concentration is not distracted by extraneous concerns. Your jobs are well executed simply because doing so feels right.

54 With that bugaboo out of the way—and only with it out of the way—your relations with your fellow workers take on a refreshing complexion from their point of view as well as yours.

Like the great river accepting the clear and muddy waters from large and little streams with equal ease, your cooperation is indiscriminately wholehearted. You make one and all look their very best, especially before their respective bosses.

You compete no more, but only perform.

55 You become sympathetic of the battle-scarred persons of power.

No longer do you joust for the power they crave so much, for such power is only over externalities and does not touch your real self. No longer do you hustle among them for credit, for that does not diminish the good that is being accomplished. No longer are you irritated by their pomp and arrogance, for these do no harm to anyone else.

It takes so little on your part to make quite a few people at least transiently happy. So why not?

56 You become understanding of the overstressed actors, struggling for an upper-middle class income and a little renown to live up to their sense of self-importance.

Understanding their problems, you begin to appreciate their relative assistance to others. Appreciating their relative assistance to others, you begin to realize that work is much more than paycheck and prestige.

Work then assumes a genuine sharing with your fellow beings.

57 The incessant undertow of tension and contention within The Demon's Empire of Anxiety is taken in stride with firm footing.

You deal with it unemotionally. Much as you would heat in the summer and cold in the winter. There is no sound reason to add more heat and cold yourself.

You bank instead on reasonableness[48] and pliancy[49].

58 Note how hypnotically The Demon has cast the spell of work commitment[50] over His executives.

The greater their achievements at work, the more tenaciously they cling with a religious fervor. To them, leisure is a cloying vacuity.

Shake the spell and welcome leisure as release from serfdom.

59 Work is an honorable and, for most people, a necessary means of livelihood.

But institutionally sponsored work, especially that for which one gets paid, can be neither a free nor a natural expression of the self that truly is.

Look to an avocation[51].

60 Do not try to be a hero.

If you happen to be one or will be one in the normal progression of things, you are merely being yourself. But should you try to become a hero by force-fitting yourself into a superhuman status, you will most likely be rebuffed and saddened by what you will have to absorb along the way.

To be natural is not heroic; so it's easy. To be heroic is not natural; so it's hard.

61 After a series of setbacks, many executives grow embittered, cynical of flesh and cynical of spirit.

They quote reporters on the falsity of leaders, chroniclers on the corruptibility of churchmen, and writers on the absurdity of life. They turn self-doubt into mocking face.

Do you yourself not fall into this sulking drain.

62 Unless proper precautions are taken, those special talents of yours may well become a source of friction in your dealings with your associates.

Your insight may be so much keener than theirs and your mental agility so much quicker that they may have considerable difficulty trying to keep up. What they do not comprehend, they suspect; what they cannot approximate, they fear.

Avoid the overwhelming display of your ability. Dilute your expertise with the solvent of patience[52].

63 Sustain an atmosphere of considerate civility around your person and office.

Ensure that your programs on the reduction of occupational stress for the workers are real and positive in effect[53]. Dispense the little thoughtfulnesses[54]. Purify your humor of scornful trace and your deliberations of adversarial sting[55]. Prepare the way well for your successors[56].

And always, keep the doors and windows to the outside ajar for those within your jurisdiction.

64 If you plant for a season, plant budgets. If you plant for a decade, plant reorganizations. If you plant for a century, plant people.

Be prudent therefore in the guidance of the young proteges with respect to their accommodations to institutional expectations[57].

In so doing, realign your own perspective.

65 Begin with the art of getting things done[58].

No squeaking frictions, no extraneous motions, no forcing tactics[59]. Unobtrusive, pleasing, elegant.

Encourage that kind of knowledge expressed in action[60].

66 Emphasize a perceptiveness in one's relations with people.

Expound a genuine acceptance of the humanness of one's fellow workers as they are, to be enjoyed in their stronger suits and understood in their weaker. Most are productive collaborators and good company. Some are not, such as the thirty-two-year-old viper of contentious venom, the urban smoothie of ephemeral enthusiasms, the intellectual with gnawing neuroses, and the hard-pressed plodder of congenital inadequacies[61]. Explain how cabals connive and flourish when the supervisors are weak. Charge them to remain aloof, guard their flanks, and respond to their natural feel-rightness in the event of an unavoidable confrontation[62]. Clarify the differences among professional acquaintances, connections, and friends. Acquaintances are identifiable names, which appear and disappear without a ripple in one's life. Connections are instruments of use, which cease to be when they deliver no more. Friends are persons who are together in mutual assistance without invitation or explanation[63]. Admonish your fellow workers not to pass up the institutionally marginal employee[64], nervously awaiting some unbegrudging help. See that they acquire the intuitive reflex of extending aid to people in deep distress without becoming exasperated by the ill-humor that often is encountered[65]. Undue suffering is to be mitigated without requiring proof of deservedness[66] or thrusting oneself rudely on the scene[67]. But quench their eagerness at straightening out the world. Their butting into other people's business leaves their own undone. Their contradicting associates in public embarasses more than edifies. Their evangelizing for major changes from subordinate positions disrupts more than constructs. Supplant these tendencies by decorum[68].

As they begin to rise in the ranks, pass on the ten proverbs for executives[69].

67 Transmit the sense for when, where, and how much of which what is propitious to a given situation.

There is a proper time to demonstrate their wares and one to hide them. There is a proper place for public and for private growth. There is a proper level of aggressiveness and of diffidence. There is a proper time and place and emphasis for the rote responsiveness that supervisors demand and for the living reciprocity that Nature offers.

This gut-feeling fitness will turn out to be one of their most important attainments under your tutelage.

68 Finally, assist your proteges in laying the foundation for a lifelong peace of mind.

This is reflected in the setting of dual-tracked objectives. As they enter the work force, it may be stated as: become a supervisor, yet remain in harmony with Nature while so doing. At thirty years of age: become a project leader, yet remain in harmony with Nature while so doing. At fifty years: become a senior official, yet remain in harmony with Nature while so doing.

In this way, the essential continuum of harmony with Nature

is preserved in the midst of professional advancements throughout their lives, as they relish each ongoing moment in the present[70].

69 As an overall policy in your managerial positions, buffer efficiency with harmonious propriety[71] and blend beneficence into the workings of the institutions.

Hold tight reins on the competing stallions within your authority; protect those to whom Fate had parceled only one thin, measly talent from the unbridled tramplings by the more gifted. Ensure precise directives, when ambiguities may lead to contentions and harm; speed decisions when delay means interim anxiety in your associates. Mete just penalties, but cast no shame. Tempt no Judases, for crimes thus gotten off the books aren't crimes controlled but crimes caressed, enlarging people's distrust of people and spewing new dishonors through the land. In prosperous times, think first of saving the reputation of your subordinates; in hard times, think first of saving their jobs. At all times preserve self-respect among the staff and pay generously.

Within the permissive interstices of power, persistently and quietly nudge the institutional centroid in the direction of de facto human caring[72].

COOPERATING WITH THE INEVITABLE

70 Superseding The Demon comes rather easily during retirement.

Until then, assuage the wrath of The Demon by burning appropriate incense in His temples of institutions.

But initiate now a progressing enlargement of your narrow focus of a career into the expanse of life and death itself[73].

71 Attune yourself first psychologically, as you lessen your longing for esteem.

Liquidate all debts and forget old wounds. Adjust investments. Routinize health habits. Absorb the mood for leisure and express yourself more in your avocation[74]. Nurture friendships.

Shape your plans for retirement readiness, emotionally and financially.

72 Anticipate the day when you genuflect for the last time in the shrines of The Demon.

He abruptly releases all claims on you and takes back all the trappings on loan to you. His ministers promptly forget you and His disciples have no further use of you.

You are free at last—but on the outside[75].

73 See yourself as elder[76]—a gentleperson of generosity.

You do not sell.

You give.

74 You resort to neither contrivance nor effort in bringing joy to others.

You live simply and freely, allowing the felicities to spill over from your own oneness with the living and the after-living[77].

Your glow brightens time's gratuity.

75 As a practical matter, attend to the ten don'ts:

Don't risk your health. Don't overload yourself. Don't dip into reserve unless essential. Don't dispense the bulk of your own fortune while still living. Don't succumb to bargain traps. Don't vie. Don't kibitz. Don't cocoon yourself. Don't be a burden to others unnecessarily.

And finally, as you witness the heated contests over evanescent values, don't take sides[78].

76 As well as the ten dos:

Be on your own. Ensure your self's continuing union with Nature. Adopt criteria of choice that match your age. Put finances in order and remain within a budget of nine-tenths of current income. Keep a well-written will, which having cared for your beloved ones, includes some token to those charities alleviating suffering directly, unaffiliated with powerful institutions. Square outstanding obligations, heal past injuries to others, and make your peace with the world at large. Choose multipurpose leisure interests. Regard loss as natural. Be intimate with Nature through your avocation.

And finally, as you are freshened by the cool of the night air and hear the tolling of the church bells, know that everything is transitory until the great transition[79].

77 Why should people feel that death is so frightening and saddening?

It is scheduled at birth. Every birthday is a reaffirmation of deathday.

Death comes as naturally as the finale of a play and the end of a day.

78 Yet there is something unique about the instant of death. What a person is at that instant, he is forever.

Fear at death is fear forever; peace of mind at death is peace of mind forever.

Tune your wavelength to this final beacon[80].

79 A quick rule of thumb is the running ledger of right living.

Each action is assimilated as an ingredient of a pool, which integrates the happiness one has rendered into Nature less that he had drawn, and the suffering he has eased in Nature less that he has inflicted. Since death is possible at any moment, a favorable balance is to be maintained at all times.

The good life is like a self-renewing poem, with a new stanza being melded with each action, giving rise to yet another ever sharper reflection of the beautiful.

80 Whether you believe in an afterlife or not, do not let the promise of heavenly reward color your activities on earth. Be bighearted in thoughts and deeds simply because it is the natural right-feeling thing to be. Searching for other reasons is bargaining. And bargaining bespeaks of a stingy soul.

Do not die expecting something, for then the ending which characterizes your self forever is the thought of Nature owing you something. A permanent incompleteness cut off on a sour note.

Die a part in harmony with the whole.

81 Life is the One's affirmation of His Love for His own part—accept with love. Death is the part's affirmation of his love for his own whole—accept with Love. That is all there is—to All.

In the meantime, let us subsume ourselves in Nature, resonate with our fellow creatures simply, reasonably, and graciously if we can, and muse over utopias like

The Land of Keikitran and Eleevan[81].

II ESSENTIAL ELEMENTS

The manner of presentation in Part I was fashioned in an attempt to condense the broad range of relevant issues into a sufficiently short span of attention to heighten the sense of an harmonious wholeness of life and death in each present moment of living. Because of the brevity, it might have appeared nebulously cryptic.

Part II consists of commentaries on many of the essential elements. It is divided into nine sections covering the spectrum from the self through the workplace to Nature. The way in which these elements fit into the overall scheme of things is summarized in the respective introductions.

Besides providing realistic counsel on practical techniques with philosophical grounding, the text seeks to convey a feel for the very roots of the satisfying life of the philosopher-executive.

SEEING BEYOND THE EXECUTIVE SUITE

More often than not, being lost is a long and gradual affair of pursuing incidentals and forgetting the primary points of reference in the process. This initial section describes how it is that you are perplexed over the meaningfulness of your present situation and why it is that the missing compass cannot be found by searching within yourself or your immediate surroundings. The section also points to the kind of sources from which enlightenment might come and samples their suggestions.

1* **Frustration** Even executives at the highest levels of society are frustrated. In his letter to a New York State Republican national committeeman, dated January 18, 1979, Nelson A. Rockefeller wrote about the vice-presidents of the United States. Mentioning that he had personally known every one of them since Henry A. Wallace (1940–1944), the former vice-president added that "I think it is fair to say that all of them were frustrated."

2 **Turmoil of the times** In sizing up the turmoil of the times, we see people maiming people, lies brooding lies, nihilism amplifying nihilism. We become even more dismayed as we look back over the past several centuries in an attempt to see what had led to the current state of affairs.

The scene that flashes back is a strange montage: eloquent doctrines of love, impressive advancements in economic status, vast strides of the intellect, generous programs of public charity, and other fruits of the Christian culture. At the same time, white Christians were enslaving the blacks and browns of Africa, decimating the polynesians in the tropics, lording over the yellow people in the East, depriving the red men of their lands in America, and persecuting the Jews in Europe. Christians were fighting Christians in bloody wars,

*The item numbers here correspond to the bracketed reference numbers within the items of Part I.

cheating each other in commercial operations, and burning each other in religious controversies. After several hundred years of hate and strife, Irish Catholics are still killing Irish Protestants and vice versa on the streets of Belfast during the late 1970s, while the Pope in Rome and the Archbishop in Canterbury continue to preach Christian brotherhood.

As persons of practical affairs, we do not separate theory from action, doctrines from effects. A Christian is what a Christian does, and a Christian culture is what a Christian people do. Imperceptibly, a terribly mushy meaninglessness seems to fog over this professedly great civilization of ours.

3 Decay of freedom Institutions have long been the reservoir of culture. They preserve the knowledge, transmit the dogmas, indoctrinate the members, and punish the transgressors. The degree to which these institutions condone departures from their own prescriptions determines the amount of freedom enjoyed by the individual. What can be expected from a great civilization is that its institutions are relatively more disposed toward the welfare of the members as persons and toward a wider latitude for private choices.

But having been agents of institutions, we have no doubt that institutions are destined to become progressively more dominant over the lives of individuals for centuries to come. The coordination of individual actions had always been necessary since people began to live together. When the stone ax was replaced by the bronze model over 5000 years ago, specialization and organization entered the picture. The casting of bronze became an industrial art and commerce was established for the import of the ingredients, for copper and tin were often mined in widely separated regions. What is different in the impact of institutions on people's lives in our own time is its pervasiveness. There is practically no activity and time left in a person's waking day that is not institutionally provided for. The overt and insistent pressures are continuously exerted to consume more and more of one's personal time to the point where the actual option is not whether a person is going to spend an hour of his spare time as a free individual or as an extension of the institution, but as to which institution it is going to be.

Whereas prehistoric man might have chosen to roll a few stones in front of his cave or draw a bison on the rock wall for entertainment, modern man is more likely to choose between institutional alternatives, such as watching football in the stadium or listening to the opera on the radio. Whereas prehistoric man might have gazed in awe at the sun or grunted in supplication to some celestial phenomenon in worshipping a superior presence, modern man is more likely to choose among institutional alternatives, such as the Methodist or Mormon Church.

Now and then a feverish campaign erupts to stem this encroachment of the institution on the individual. The promoters begin pure enough, delivering the message face to face from one person to another. They soon become disappointed, however, with the negligible influence being made by this personal approach. So they organize an effort—an anti-institution crusade. The net result is another institution in the social galaxy. Personal liberty, besides being chewed away by the existing institutions, is now being nibbled by yet another new one.

This appeal to institutions for individual liberation from institutions shows how institutionally usurped modern man has become. The decay of modern freedom is differentiated from that of former decades by just this voluntary surrender of the self.

4 Superstructures With such a sobering train of impressions, one can't help feeling childish about having indulged so excitedly in heated debates over abstractions and uncontrollables.

Instead of arguing whether revolutions and imperialisms are morally justifiable or not, one should simply note that most governments had come into being through revolution and most institutions are aiming at becoming larger. Instead of getting lathered up over the intrigues of chiefs of state, saturated with nuclear power and intoxicated with the thrill of the gigantic poker game in which they have conditioned 500 million bodies to acquiesce as stakes, trying to stare down each other across miniaturized oceans, one should simply note that even if the initial intentions are honorable, it is unlikely that their practical embodiment will turn out honorable in the political outcome. Instead of trying to come up with ingenious rationalizations for the existence of evil, one should simply note that the most vociferous apologists go about postulating an all-powerful and all-good Being and insulting Him with the veiled condemnation of allowing evil to exist or of not being as all-powerful in the all-good fashion He is supposed to be.

The ease with which a person can be sidetracked from the fundamental purpose of things reminds me of the legend about the Persian prince who built a magnificent mausoleum to house the sarcophagus of his deceased wife, whom he had dearly loved.

The most gifted architect, builder, and artisans were assembled to complete this wonder of marble and alabaster towers and minarets around the sarcophagus. Decades were spent perfecting the memorial. But somehow the prince was not satisfied with the result. Some aesthetic flaw kept eluding him. One day, as the prince was standing in the gallery overlooking the great hall and the main aisle, he realized what was disturbing the majestic harmony of the place. He pointed to the sarcophagus, which was now dwarfed by the grand edifice, and said to the architect: "Take that away!"

5 The encasement As an exercise in introspection, let your mind meander over your past life, meeting and joining the events of your recollection.

Recall how your mother and father had brought you up to be a God-fearing young person. You attempted to walk in the path of the Bible. For some reason, the wars, the persecutions, the meannesses, and the other bad things in the chronicles never made a lasting impression. It was the virtues, the life of the early saints, and the love of Jesus that did.

All through grammar school and high school, you had been taught the secular virtues of hard work, progress, and success. The this-worldly saints were paraded before you. First were the military conquerors of history: Alexander, Caesar, Napoleon. Then came the financial and economic tycoons: Rothschild, Krupp, Ford. Finally, the intellectual giants: Plato, Shakespeare, Einstein.

As you went through college and strayed beyond the watchful eyes of your parents, you began to learn that many of those less laudible practices as recorded in the Bible but glossed over when you were a child turned out in fact to be more representative of your own contemporary society. You became disappointed with the hypocrisy of the world. You were appalled at the lethargy of the older generation. You vowed to yourself that when the time came for you to have your say, you would straighten things out the way they ought to be. Your idealism was reinforced as you listened to the inspiring commencement speaker on graduation day.

Your first job gave you an introduction to the actualities of your society. The prophets of expansion and power presided over the proceedings. You were initially reluctant about paying tribute at their altars. But this was short-lived.

By your late twenties, you came to respect the rude facts of life: you had to earn enough to pay the rent and entertain the friends. To gain this, you had to go along with the doings of the day. So with token resistance, you shoved the lofty enthusiasms of your youth onto a neatly walled-off back-burner of your mind. You will come back to it when the proper occasion presents itself—so you told yourself.

Before long, you were caught up in the swing of the setting. At thirty you became reconciled completely to the essentiality of an institutional platform for the realization of your ambitions. Your energy must be spent on useful things, and utility was defined as that quality appreciated by society in terms of money, power, and prestige.

You saw through the befogging double-talking of your former professors about the unimportance of money. Why is it then, you asked yourself, that the president of the university and the deans are forever courting the wealthy? How does it come about that most of the outstanding scholars happen to be members of the richest colleges? How long would the Nobel Prize continue to attract international admiration if its honorarium of $190,000 in 1979 suddenly dropped to $1000? To your way of thinking, money paves the way for prestige and power. This was repeatedly confirmed in the daily papers, such as the news about the storming of the Gasre Prison in Teheran in February 1979. A Texas millionaire claimed that it was he who, contrary to American law, sent the money and cadre to foment the riot, which led to the liberation of thousands of prisoners, two of whom were his own employees, who could not be freed through any other way.

The quickest path to more money for you at that stage of your career was to please the institution. You became its effective instrument, growing impressively versed in the tactics of competition. Soon, you emerged a full-fledged protector of institutional prerogatives. Personal ethics was subordinated to institutional doctrines. Personal scions were grafted to the institutional stock. Your responsibility was to make the dependency of the followers as absolute as possible in the sphere of interest staked out by your institution. To your way of thinking, qualified dependency on the part of your subordinates constituted a cardinal sin. You smiled with satisfaction as you overheard someone remark that you were a most forceful leader.

As you approached forty, you were initiated into the secret of great success. You seized upon it, which sped you upward. The thing you observed among the most admired leaders of society was their ability to complex the gods of society with their own persons, so as to command the obeisance of the masses. They were the personal representatives of God, of the nation, of the corporation. Obedience to God meant obedience to *them.* Majesty in the nation meant majesty in *them.* Profit for the corporation meant profit for *them.*

By then you had come to relish the nectar of power. Might was right—so often had the statement been confirmed in your experience, as you witnessed weak nations crushed under the war machines of their mighty neighbor. You were reminded by the preacher that the basis for right is not might but the moral law of God. But you also heard the same preacher constantly referring to God as the most powerful of all. He it was who suppressed the Lucifer revolt in Heaven. You mischievously asked yourself: what if Lucifer had actually won and fabricated the biblical account? But that just can't be, for God was the most powerful. So the mightiest was the rightest, after all.

The mightier you became, the righter you felt you were. The righter you felt you were, the more compellingly you exercised your might. The more compellingly you exercised your might, the more the subordinates said you were right. The more the subordinates said you were right, the more you felt you were.

At forty-five, the emoluments of your position became the fabric out of which your spouse and children tailored their lives. The routine was set. You finally carried on like a steadfast warrior—fully encased in your institutional cuirass.

6 **Lao Tzu** Lao Tzu (c. 604–531 B.C.) was a native of Chu (in present Honan province) who rose in the ranks within the court of Chou to become custodian of the imperial archives. At that time, the Chou dynasty was in decline. Externally, enemies were increasing and intensifying their raids. Internally, intrigues ran rampant and morality was at a low ebb. As legend tells it, Lao Tzu retired in discouragement over hopes for reform. As he went into the desert to die, he was persuaded by a gatekeeper to write down his thoughts for the betterment of posterity. Whereupon he composed the *Tao Te Ching,* which became the foundation for the philosophy of Taoism.

The complete text of the *Tao Te Ching* is only about 5000 words. You may wish to read it in its entirety. The following nine representative excerpts provide a flavor of his message.

On the ineffable: "The Tao that can be told is not the true Tao. The Name that can be named is not the true Name."

On weakness in management: "To be frivolous is to lose one's anchorage; to be restless is to lose one's self-mastery. . . . People are cheated because the rulers are cunning; they starve because the rulers eat up too much tax-grain; they are rebellious because the rulers govern too much."

On greatness in management: "To create and nourish without possessing, to inspire and lead without dominating—this is the Mystical

Quality. . . . Of second-rate rulers, people speak respectfully saying, 'He had done this, he had done that.' Of first-rate rulers, people do not say this; they say instead, 'We had done it all ourselves.' "

On far-sighted actions: "The master confronts major difficulties when they are but minor ripples. In so doing he achieves the greatest of things by doing the littlest and the easiest."

On excesses: "Fill the carrying pail to the brim and water will surely spill over; sharpen the blade overly much and the edge will soon dull. . . . He who stands on tiptoe does not stand firm; he who stretches his stride does not walk gracefully. . . . He who knows when to stop encounters no dangers."

On economy of effort: "The skillful traveler leaves no tracks; the eloquent speaker makes no slips; the polished accountant uses no tallies. The well-shut door requires no locks, yet cannot be opened by others. The well-tied bundle requires no strings, yet cannot be loosened. And so it is that the sage is gifted at saving all people and therefore abandoning no one; he is adept at saving all things and thereby rejecting nothing."

On credit: "The sage gets things done but claims no credit. Because he claims no credit, credit cannot be taken from him. . . . When the objective is attained, withdraw into obscurity, for such is the way of Heaven."

On contentment: "Fame or self, which is loved more? Self or wealth, which is valued more? . . . Because the Sage forgets himself, his self is preserved. ... He who is contented with enough will always have enough."

On kingliness: "Empty yourself of concerns and treasure that tranquility that ensues. All things return to their root of stillness after the luxuriant phase. He who grasps this eternal pattern is empathetic of others. Being empathetic of others, he acquires a king-like character. Being king-like in character, he draws ever closer to being at one with the Tao."

7 Chuang Tzu Chuang Tzu (c. 335–275 B.C.) was Lao Tzu's greatest exponent. The old master's simple, natural, and social harmony was expanded into a sophisticated and enlightened freedom from the kind of personal desires that thwart the harmonious movement with the all-encompassing mystical Tao. At the same time, he was a man of this world with a keen appreciation of the relativity of things, refraining from quarrels and befriending those who, like him, have penetrated the illusions. He had served as a minor government official and refused a premiership that had been offered. As a philosopher, he was somewhat special—he laughed.

Even though most of his writings involved a serious and rigorous development of Taoism, we believe that you would be more attracted at this point to his anecdotes and parables. Nine representative ones are repeated in the following paragraphs.

On illusions: Chuang Tzu once dreamt that he was a butterfly fluttering among the spring flowers in the field. Suddenly he awoke. Whereupon he asked himself, "Am I a man who had just dreamt he was a butterfly or am I a butterfly who is now dreaming that it is a man?"

On institutional blinders: The Spirit of the Ocean once told the Spirit of the River, "You cannot speak of the ocean to a well-frog—the creature of a narrower sphere. You cannot speak of ice to a summer insect—the creature of a season. You cannot speak of Tao to a pedagogue—the creature of a limited scope. But now that you have emerged from your narrower sphere and have seen the Great Ocean, you know your own insignificance and I can speak to you of the Great Principles."

On freedom: A lovely sea bird which had flown into the country was caged and taken by the Duke of Lu to his temple. There the bird was given the choicest delicacies from the royal sacrifice and serenaded with music by the royal orchestra. The bird stared in sorrow, without eating a single morsel or drinking a single drop. Three days later, it died.

On visionary concepts: A cicada and a wren had heard someone mentioning birds capable of flying hundreds of miles without resting. "This is impossible," said the wren. "We know very well," agreed the cicada, "that the farthest that one can reach with even the greatest of effort is that elm tree over there. And even this cannot be achieved with certainty. One often drops to the ground long before reaching it. All these claims about flying hundreds of miles without stopping are sheer nonsense."

On interdependency of things: "A little while ago, you were moving around," said the Shade to the Shadow. "Now, you're standing still. A little while ago, you were sitting down. Now, you're getting up. Can't you make up your mind?" "I have to depend on others to be myself," replied the Shadow. "Others have to depend on still others to be themselves. I am like the shell of a cicada and the cast-off skin of a snake. How can I explain why I do this or why I do that?"

On the value of being useless: The cinnamon tree is edible, so it is chopped down. Ch'i oil is useful, so the ch'i tree is gashed. But there was an old sacred tree, which was totally good for nothing and was spared on that account. It appeared to the axman in a dream one night and said. "For a long time I have been learning how to be useless. I nearly failed on several occasions and was nearly destroyed. But now I have finally succeeded in being completely useless, which is of greatest use to me. People come from hundreds of miles to admire and worship me. If I were useful, could I have become so great?"

On the allaying of suspicions by persons of power: The Prime Minister of Liang heard rumors to the effect that Chuang Tzu was after his job. Whereupon Chuang Tzu visited him and said, "Are you familiar with the great phoenix? It flies from the South Sea to the North Sea, alighting only on the wu-t'ung tree? It eats nothing but the fruit of the bamboo and drinks nothing but the purest of spring water. As this great phoenix was flying high overhead one day, an owl clutching a rotting mouse on a scrub oak screeched at it. Are you screeching at me for fear of losing your ministry?"

On the transcending of competition: Chi Sheng-tzu had been training fighting cocks for the king for some time. One day the king inquired as to whether a particular cock was ready. "Not yet," replied Chi. "He is still impulsive and vain." Ten days passed and the king again inquired. "Not yet," came the same reply. "He continues to react to the sounds and shadows from the other birds." To the third inquiry after another ten days, Chi said, "Not yet. He still has that angry look and is still full of fight." Finally after the fortieth day, the trainer passed judgment that the cock is just about ready. "He does not react when the other cocks crow. He looks like a cock of wood. His character is now nearly complete. No other cock will dare fight him but will run away instead."

On desirability of high posts: Two representatives of the Prince of Chou caught up with Chuang Tzu fishing on the River P'u and conveyed the prince's invitation to become the Premier. Without turning his head, Chuang Tzu said, "I have heard that there is a 3000-year-old turtle enshrined in a chest in the Prince's ancestral temple. Do you think that this turtle would rather be dead and thusly venerated or alive and wagging its tail in the mud?" The two envoys surmised the latter. "Then begone," cried Chuang Tzu. "I too would rather be wagging my tail in the mud."

8 **Epictetus** Epictetus (c. 60–100 A.D.) was a Greek, who spent most of his life in Rome as a slave, a lame freedman in poor health, a minister of Emperor Nero, then an exile with other intellectuals by order of Emperor Domitian, and finally returned to Nicopolis in Epirus. There he spent the rest of his life teaching and establishing his school of Stoic philosophy.

His statements were sincere and lofty, based on keen observations on human behavior. Considerable emphasis was placed on the distinctions between what is within one's control and what is not, between what is an actuality and what is an illusory judgment. He pointed repeatedly to the act of will and self-control toward mastering oneself and contributing to the good life of one's fellow men. Nine exemplary admonitions, as translated by P. E. Matheson, are presented below.

On harmony with Nature: "When you are about to take something in hand, remind yourself what manner of thing it is. If you are going to bathe put before your mind what happens in the bath—water pouring over some, others being jostled, some reviling, others stealing; and you will set to work securely if you say to yourself at once: 'I want to bathe, and I want to keep my will in harmony with Nature,' and so in each thing you do; for in this way, if anything turns up to hinder you in your bathing, you will be ready to say, 'I did not want only to bathe, but to keep my will in harmony with Nature, and I shall not so keep it, if I lose my temper at what happens.' "

On offense and hatred: " 'Ought not this robber and adulterer to be put to death?' Nay, say not so, but rather, 'Should I not destroy this man who is blinded not merely in the vision which distinguishes white and black, but in the judgment which distinguishes good and evil?' If you put it this way, you will recognize how inhuman your words are; that it is like saying, 'Should I not kill this blind man, or this deaf one?' For if the greatest harm that can befall one is the loss of what is greatest, and a right will is the greatest thing in everyone, is it not enough for him to lose this, without incurring your anger besides? Man, if you must need harbor unnatural feelings at the misfortune of another, pity him rather than hate him, give up this spirit of offense and hatred: do not use these phrases which the back-biting multitude use, 'These accursed and pestilent fools.' "

On contentions: "The good and noble man does not contend with anyone, and to the best of his power does not suffer others to contend. . . . Look at the *Symposium* of Xenophon and see how many contentions he has reconciled, and again how patient he was with Thrasymachus, with Polus, with Callicles, and patient always with his wife, and with his son, when his son tried to convict him of fallacious arguments. For he remembered to hold fast the truth that no man is master of another man's Governing Principle. Therefore he wished to do nothing that is not his own. What does that mean? Not to move other people to act naturally, for that is not his to do: but to let others act for themselves, as they think fit, and himself none the less to live and spend his days in accord with nature, only doing his own business in such a way that they, too, should follow nature."

On the casting of blame: "What disturbs men's minds is not events but their judgments of events. . . . And so when we are hindered, or distressed, let us never lay the blame on others, but on ourselves, that is, on our own judgments. To accuse others for one's own misfortunes is a sign of want of education; to accuse oneself shows that one's education has begun; to accuse neither oneself nor others shows that one's education is complete."

On anxiety: "When I see a person in a state of anxiety, I say 'What can this man want? If he did not want something which is not within his power, how could he still be anxious?' It is for this reason that one who sings to the lyre is not anxious when he is performing by himself, but when he enters the theater, even if he had a very good voice and plays well; for he not only wants to perform well, but also to win a great name, and that is beyond his control."

On losses: "Never say of anything, 'I lost it.' but say, 'I gave it back.' Your child died? It was given back. Has your wife died? She was given back. Has your estate been taken from you? Was this also not given back? But you say, 'He who took it from me is wicked.' What does it matter to you through whom the Giver asked it back? As long as He gives it to you, take care of it, but not as your own; treat it like passers-by treat an inn."

On conduct during illness: "What hinders you in a fever from keeping your Governing Principle in accord with Nature? Here is the test of the matter, this is how the philosopher is proved. For fever too is a part of life, like walking, sailing, traveling. Do you read while you are walking? No. Nor do you in a fever: but if you walk aright, you have done your part as a walker; if you bear your fever aright, you have done your part as a sick man. What does bearing fever rightly mean? It means not to blame God or man, not to be crushed by what happens, to await death in a right spirit, to do what you are bidden; when the physician comes in, not to be afraid of what he may say, and if he says, 'You are doing well,' not to be overjoyed: for what good is there in that? What good had you when you were in health? It means not to be disheartened if he says, 'You are doing badly'; for what does 'doing badly' mean? It means drawing near the dissolution of the soul from the body. What is there to fear in that? If you do not draw near now, shall you not draw near later? Is the world going to be turned upside down by your death? Why then do you coax the physician? Why do you say, 'Master, if you will, I shall get well?' Why do you give him occasion to lift his brow in arrogance? As you give the shoemaker his due in regard to the foot, the builder in regard to the house, why do you not give the physician his due (and no more) in regard to the paltry body, for the body is not mine and is naturally dead? This is what the moment requires from the man in a fever: if he fulfills these requirements, he has what is his own."

On duty: ". . . when it is your duty to risk your life with friend or country, do not ask the oracle whether you should risk your life. For if the prophet warns you that the sacrifice is unfavorable, though it is plain that this means death or exile or injury to some part of your body, yet reason requires that even at this cost you must stand by your friend and share your country's danger. Wherefore pay heed to the greater prophet, Pythian Apollo, who cast out of his temple the man who did not help his friend when he was being killed."

On magnanimity: "Which of us does not admire that saying of Lycurgus the Lacedaemonian? For when one of his young fellow citizens had blinded him in one eye and was handed over to Lycurgus by the people to be punished as he chose, he did not punish him but educated him and made a good man out of him, and brought him before the Lacedaemonians in the theatre, and when they wondered he said, 'This man, when you gave him to me, was insolent and violent; I give him back to you a free and reasonable citizen.' "

9 Marcus Aurelius Marcus Aurelius Antoninus (121–180 A.D.) was the last of the great line of Antonine emperors. His twenty years as emperor was filled with crises. He had to deal with earthquakes, pestilences, and revolts at home. Externally, he had to repulse the German invasion of Northern Italy, restore the Danubian frontier, and pacify the Syrian provinces. Burdened and wearied by his public responsibilities, he had longed for retirement to some quiet country life. But the opportunity never came, as he died in Vienna at the age of fifty-nine.

His basic philosophy was practically identical to that of Epictetus, although tempered somewhat by the humanism of his friend Fronto and his practical experience as an executive. The brotherhood of man was a recurring theme, as manifestated through wisdom, justice, moderation, and fortitude. The following nine passages were taken from his *Meditations,* as translated by G. Long.

On the good life: "Everything harmonizes with me which is harmonious to thee, O Universe. Nothing for me is too early or too late, which is due time for thee. Everything is fruit to me which thy seasons bring. O Nature: from thee are all things, in thee are all things, to thee all things return."

On knaves: "When thou art offended with any man's shameless conduct, immediately ask thyself, Is it possible, then, that shameless men should not be in the world? It is not possible. Do not, then, require that which is impossible. . . . Let the same consideration be present to thy mind in the case of the knave, and the faithless man, and of every man who does wrong in any way. For at the same time that thou dost remind thyself that it is impossible that such kind of men should not exist, thou will become more kindly disposed towards everyone individually."

On obstructionists: "As those who try to stand in the way when thou art proceeding according to right reason, will not be able to turn thee aside from thy proper action, so neither let them drive thee from thy benevolent feeling toward them, but be on thy guard equally in both matters, not only in the matter of steady judgment and action, but also in the matter of gentleness towards those who try to hinder or otherwise trouble thee. For this also is a weakness, to be vexed at them, as well as to be diverted from thy course of action and to give way through fear; for both are equally deserters from their post, the man who does it through fear, and the man who is alienated from him who is by nature a kinsman and a friend."

On fame: "But perhaps the desire of the thing called fame will torment thee. See how soon everything is forgotten, and look at the chaos of infinite time on each side of the present, and the emptiness of applause, and the changefulness and want of judgment in those who pretend to give praise, and the narrowness of the space within which it is circumscribed, and be quiet at last. For the whole earth is a point, and how small a nook in it is this thy dwelling, and how few are there in it, and what kind of people are they who will praise thee."

On rewards: "Have I done something for the general interest? Well then I have had my reward. Let this always be present to thy mind, and never stop doing such good."

On the unnecessary: "Occupy yourself with few things, says the philosopher, if thou wouldst be tranquil. But consider if it would not be better to say, Do what is necessary, and whatever the reason of the animal which is naturally social requires, and as it requires. For this brings not only the tranquility which comes from doing well, but also that which comes from doing a few things. For the greatest part of what we say and do being unnecessary, if a man takes this away, he will have more leisure and less uneasiness. Accordingly on every occasion a man should ask himself, Is this one of the unnecessary things? Now a man should take away not only unnecessary acts but unnecessary thoughts, for thus superfluous acts will not follow after."

On one's place in the scheme of things: "This thou must always bear in mind, what is the nature of the whole, and what is my nature, and how this is related to thee, and what kind of a part of it is of what kind of a whole; and that there is no one who hinders thee from always doing and saying the things which are according to the nature of which thou art a part."

On tranquility: "Remember to retire into this little territory of thy own [principles stemming from good ordering of the mind], and above all do not distract or strain thyself, but be free, and look at things as a man, as a human being, as a citizen, as a mortal. But among the things readiest to thy hand to which thou shalt turn, let there be these, which are two. One is that things do not touch the soul, for they are external and remain immovable; but our perturbations come only from the opinion which is within. The other is that all these things, which thou seest, change immediately and will no longer be; and constantly bear in mind how many of these changes thou hast already witnessed. The universe is transformation, life is opinion. . . . Take away the opinion, and then there is taken away the complaint, 'I have been harmed.' Take away the complaint, 'I have been harmed,' and the harm is taken away."

On death: "Think continually how many physicians are dead after contracting their eyebrows over the sick; and how many astrologers after predicting with great pretensions the deaths of others; and how many philosophers after endless discourses on death or immortality; how many heroes after killing thousands; and how many tyrants who have used their power over men's lives with terrible insolence as if they were immortal . . . Add to the reckoning all whom thou hast known, one after another. One man burying another has been laid out dead, and another buries him; and all this in a short time. To conclude, always observe how ephemeral and worthless human things are, and what was yesterday a little mucus tomorrow will be a mummy or ashes. Pass then through this little space of time conformably to nature, and end thy journey in content, just as an olive falls off when it is ripe, blessing nature who produced it, and thanking the tree on which it grew."

BEGINNING WITH GIVENS

The philosopher-executive operates with calm firmness and evenness of mind and action that is not easily perturbed or disturbed. This section describes two foundational abilities. The first is the acceptance of the reality of the here and now as givens, from which all progressions are to begin. The second is the mastery of the art of doing nothing as an essential complement to that of doing something.

10 **The givens** Life is a succession of ups and downs. Much of our anxieties stem from a refusal to accept the latter as given, as natural in the cycle of things.

Having been inculcated with the desire for honors and adulation, the educated class in general can be rather easily embarrassed and insulted. Not many have taken Francois de la Rochefoucauld to heart when he wrote: "Few have the wisdom to prefer useful blame to treacherous flattery." Three pieces of advice have been offered by Russell Lynes, which are pertinent.

With regard to flattery and compliment, he suggested: "Never accept flattery as though it were a compliment, and never treat a compliment as though it were a flattery." With regard to insults: "The only graceful way to accept an insult is to ignore it; if you can't ignore it, top it; if you can't top it, laugh at it; if you can't laugh at it, it's probably deserved." With regard to success and failure: "Always accept defeat as though it were defeat and success as though it were success, but never take either for granted; neither as permanent."

Some individuals can not even accept their own faces as given. In February 1979, the director of the New York Facial Plastic and Reconstruction Group, Ralph Dicker, spoke of the significant increase in facelifts among businessmen. "Ten years ago we would hardly ever see a man in the waiting room," he said. "Now, of every ten patients wanting a facelift, two or three are men."

Many people simply refuse to admit that expediency, corruption, and insatiate power are widespread in the world, as they actually are. They do not see that the persons on the rise during certain phases of history are inferior in character. They wish to blanket unbearable reality as untrue, even though they continue to witness the repetition, over and over again, of the reply of the Athenian emissaries to the defeated weaker Melians, who appealed to the victors on the basis of justice and fair play. As recorded by Thucydides, "we will not make a long and unconvincing speech, full of fine phrases, to prove that our victory over Persia justifies our empire, or that we are attacking you because you have wronged us. . . . You know and we know, as practical men, that the question of justice arises only between parties of equal strength, and that the strong do what they can, and the weak submit."

There are times, of course, when everything seems to go wrong. The tribulations continue at an almost despairing intensity. Robert Louis Stevenson advanced the following comment for such conditions: "Anyone can carry his burden, however hard, until nightfall. Anyone can do his work, however hard, for one day. Anyone can live sweetly, patiently, lovingly, purely, till the sun goes down. And this is all that life really means." Your equable bearing of suffering and harsh adversity in itself constitutes a major springboard toward earliest possible recovery. It means that your spirit has not been eroded, like that of many others under similar ordeals, into a complaining and whimpering derelict. With your alert dignity intact, amelioration remains only a matter of time when Nature in her ever-changing ways comes around with the conducive permutation of factors. Not having been alienated from her realities, your response to the favorable upturn is immediate.

But things seldom reach such extremities. Ordinarily dilemmas are not as bad as the person makes them out to be. By moping in his self-pitying strains, he or she fails to see the many outlets for opportunities still present. This recalls the story of the prime minister who was suddenly fired from his post in the fourth century B.C. As the deposed Ch'u P'ing sat emaciated from dejection on the banks of a river, a fisherman recognized him and rowed up to him, inquiring what he was doing there. Whereupon Ch'u replied, "The whole world is corrupt; I alone am clean. The whole world is drunk; I alone am sober. That is why I was dismissed." "A sage is not the slave of circumstances, but follows them, acts in accordance with them," said the fisherman. "If the whole world is filthy, you must jump in the muddy water and splash about in it. If all men are drunk, you must drink with them. What is the good of meditating so deeply and academically?" But the former prime minister continued on, "I have heard that when a man has washed himself, he dusts off his hat, and when a man has bathed he shakes his clothes. How can a person who has purified himself put on his old clothes again? I would rather jump into the river and feed myself to the fishes. I will not be sullied by the dirt of the world." The old fisherman rowed away from the shore and, keeping time with his oar, said, "If the water of the river is clear, I will wash the ribbon of my hat. If it is dirty, I will wash my feet." And he was gone.

On many an occasion my own father had reemphasized the acceptance of the given to me as a youngster. One series of lessons that made a lasting impression took place at the dinner table. As is customary in Chinese family dinners, each person has his own pair of chopsticks and bowl of rice. The common dishes of meats, fish, and vegetables are placed at random in the center of the round table. One reaches for a piece of food among them and eats it with some rice from his own bowl. Table etiquette dictates that a person select pieces only from the sector of the respective common dishes directly facing him.

As the eldest son, I sat next to dad. When I was not completely trained in the good manners of group eating, I was often tempted by some boneless morsel of meat in someone else's sector. Thinking that nobody was watching, I would make a quick stab at it with my chopsticks. But father was indeed watching. And down would come his knuckles on my head. After a few knucklings, without a word of explanation, I learned the secret of contentment that he was trying to pass on: All the pieces that Fate happens to place within one's sector of life are edible and many of them quite delicious.

11 Wu-wei As a participant in the free-enterprise competitive system, you believe in action. "If you don't know what to do," so you have been trained, "*do* something." We would commend the contrasting option: "If you don't know what to do, do *nothing*."

How can you clear a muddy pond? Certainly not by stirring it up. Just leave it alone and the mud will settle on its own. How can you resolve a heated controversy? Certain not by adding more shouting. Just keep quiet and the tempers will cool on their own.

The practical value of deferring action shows up quite often in our daily decisions in the office. R. L. Katz reported the case of the Pacific Coast sales manager, who had a reputation for decisiveness and positive action. One day he was asked by his chief to pick an understudy from among his several well-qualified assistants. To everybody's surprise, he did nothing about it, as several months went by. Finally, "it became clear that the sales manager had very unobtrusively been giving the various salesmen opportunities to demonstrate their attitudes and feelings. As a result, he was able to identify the strong sentiments for one man whose subsequent promotion was enthusiastically accepted by the group." By doing nothing, he allowed the cream to float to the top.

Especially important is the cultivation of that which harmonizes one's self with the Tao. This is the principle of wu-wei or "having-no-activity." A more practical translation is "doing-lessness." Rather than resorting to "over-doingness" and artificialities, one outgrows crises by living in accordance with oneself. The world takes care of itself as the necessity of circumstances works itself through the natural evolution of things.

Determined inactivity or "stonewalling," as the Washingtonian phrase expressed it some years ago, is not the conducive inaction of which we speak. The art of wu-wei involves letting things happen. This can not be achieved through the conscious act, for conscious acts never just let things happen. "Consciousness is forever interfering, helping, correcting, and negating, and never leaving the simple growth of the psychic processes in peace," explained Carl G. Jung. "The conscious mind raises prolific objections, in fact it often seems bent upon blotting out the spontaneous fantasy-activity in spite of real insight, even of firm determination on the part of the individual to allow the psychic processes to go forward without interference."

The story by Charles Kingsley may be worth retelling in this connection. Two mullahs were trying to convince the Khan to adopt their respective gods. Said the first: "O Khan, worship my god. He is so powerful that he made all things!" Then spoke the second: "O Khan, worship my god. He is so wise that he makes all things make themselves!" The Khan chose the second.

RECOGNIZING THE DEMON

To free yourself, you need to know who the jailer is and the nature of the chains he uses. This section identifies The Demon Himself, who is behind the entire enterprise, and delineates the basic techniques for enslaving people like you.

12 **Methods of enslavement** Society has its own ideas as to your place on this earth in the furtherance of its purposes. It began working on you the moment you were born.

The formula for enslavement is primarily fourfold: (1) You are surrounded by the agencies of society, called institutions. (2) An array of desires is aroused in you, which are intensified through repeated reinforcement until life becomes hollow without their fulfillment. (3) You are encouraged through partial success but never complete realization of your aspirations without adding further unfulfilled desires, thereby precluding a breakdown in your persistence of pursuit. (4) Conditions are maintained such that potential satisfactions can most readily be achieved through channels devised and approved by society.

By means of this technique, society interposes itself between you and Nature and fixes the boundaries within which you are expected to conduct yourself. You are led to accept the world that it offers as the milieu of your activities and the god that it presents as the object of your worship.

Once these parameters are embraced by you as a member of the community, enforceable rules are then promulgated that are internally self-consistent. These cannot be challenged with any rational force unless appeal is made to principles that transcend the limits of that particular community. Since the members of that community have already been well anchored in their belief in the superiority of its own methods and mores, the social patterns attain a sanctity supported by the might of consensus and the body of scholarship matured under that fenced philosophy. The machinery thereby becomes self-perpetuating.

A selection follows in the kinds of human relations to be promoted. Those that advance the interests of the institution are fostered. Those that threaten are banned. Those that do neither are ignored. Family, ritual, entertainment, and other activities are shaped accordingly. All vectors point to the institution as the focus of loyalty. By intensifying the interactions, a degree of fanaticism is fanned, thereby providing one of the essential factors for institutional strength. The formidable following of controlled fanatics suffuses the membership at large with the bolstering exhilaration of belonging.

As far as the institution is concerned, communicating with its members means working on them to promote institutional objectives. Heroes are made and unmade toward that end. Actions to the contrary are labeled as selfish disregard of the public welfare. To be considered normal and psychologically balanced is to mesh smoothly into the subassemblies allotted by the society of institutions and to turn one's gears synchronously with the rest.

General acquiesence is facilitated through a system of behavioral definitions and laws. Killing a person, for example, is not permitted except as directed by institutions. Because of this necessity, institutions are continually encroaching on the intellectual and spiritual allegiances of the members, even though the professed aims may have little to do with moral or religious matters. To remain dominant, all institutions must become religious in part and prevail over that segment of faith and ethics that are critical for their survival and growth. National governments show no hesitancy in exercising practical veto over its internal churches in the waging of wars, the oppressing of minorities, and the exploiting of masses.

There is a continuous intrusion of the institution in little as well as big issues. The resulting responses may or may not be of important consequences in themselves, but collectively they constitute the principal means of keeping the institutions in their precedence and authority. You are required to sign a loyalty oath each time you take a new post in the government, even though you have already affirmed your fealty ten times before. You are required to refrain from eating stipulated meats as a member of a particular religion. You are required to stand, bow, and address high officials according to the prescribed manners of deference. You are required to subscribe openly to assertions that go contrary to convictions of your own. You are required to wear uncomfortable dress. By forbidding this and directing that throughout your daily activities, you are lashed quite securely by these innumerable behavioral strings to the institutional framework.

The welfare of human beings as individuals, therefore, is not the decisive factor in modern institutional decision making, although it may constitute a significant local consideration when the survival or expansion of the institution is not at stake. Speaking as an institutional leader, President Abraham Lincoln felt compelled to spell out his plan and motivation unmistakably in his letter to Horace Greeley during the Civil War. "If there be those who would not save the Union unless they could at the same time save slavery, I do not agree with them. If there be those who would not save the Union unless they could at the same time destroy slavery, I do not agree with them. My paramount object in this struggle is to save the Union, and is not either to save or destroy slavery. If I could save the Union without freeing any slaves. I would do it; and if I could save it by freeing all the slaves, I would do it; and if I could save it by freeing some and leaving others alone, I would do that."

During the long development of civilization from informal groups to organized bodies, there has been a continuous weeding out of those characteristics of the individual that go contrary to the social objectives of the collectivity. The less compatible individuals gave way to the more compatible. Social norms became progressively less personal in values and increasingly more impersonal in transactions. The transition over the centuries has been so gradual, yet pervasive and penetrating, that most people have almost come to feel that the interest of the person and that of the institution coincide.

There is something magnetic about the entire process. People compete fiercely for the role of being used by institutions. Enthusiasms are fanned to the pitch of the beverage executive who proclaimed during the 1960s: "For many of us who work in Cola, it's gotten to be almost a religion." A former assistant to an American president described his own commitment in these words in 1970: "To devote every ounce of one's energy and intellect to the highest endeavors of statecraft can be every bit as satisfying as to devote those same resources to a passionate love affair. . . . Most of all, there is the ecstasy for the man who finds himself turned into a creative instrument for his nation."

This servitude to institutions, so eagerly sought by the individual, is the modern form of the *maya* illusion, against which the Hindu gurus had so emphatically warned a thousand years ago.

13 The temple of higher learning Much of the debate over the activist role of the university in social affairs centers around the issue as to whose interest it is to serve primarily. There is a strong feeling to the effect that, wittingly or unwittingly, the university serves the interests of those in power within the social order. Two quotations, 2000 years apart, suffice to indicate the historical persistence of this view.

One is by Aristotle (384–322 B.C.): "But of all things which I have mentioned that which most contributes to the permanence of constitutions is the adaptation of education to the form of government. . . . The best laws, though sanctioned by every citizen of the state, will be of no avail, unless the young are trained by habit and education in the spirit of the constitution, if the laws are democratic, democratically; oligarchically, if the laws are oligarchical."

The other is by Nikolai Lenin (1870–1924): "The more cultured the bourgeois state, the more subtly did it lie when it declared that the school could stand above politics and serve society as a whole. As a matter of fact, the school was turned into nothing but an instrument of the class rule of the bourgeoisie. Its purpose was to supply the capitalists with obedient lackeys and intelligent workers. . . . We publicly declare that education divorced from life and politics is a lie and hypocrisy."

Many leading contemporary educators insist, however, that these assertions do not apply to a university. Sidney Hook stressed the "other dignities" of the "pursuit of truth—the cultivation of friendship, of courage against odds, of shared joys and contained grief."

Taking a broader look at the contributions of the educational system, we can see without too much difficulty that the schools are the principal transmitters of the underpinning cultural know-how. The basic skills of reading, writing, and arithmetic are imparted early. These are supplemented by advanced studies in the literature, arts, science, and crafts. Throughout the period, the personality is being psychologically readied to function smoothly within the institutional apparatus. For over a decade during the most formative years, lesson over lesson, example over example, game over game, there is an incessant subliminal drumming of the urgency and loftiness of the three fundamental motivations behind social prosperity—ambition, progress, success. The fanfare is never on limited satiety, but on unlimited appetite. Long since have the schools silenced the voice of Epicurus (341–270 B.C.), who expounded the serene life as the greatest good, that "It is not the stomach that is insatiable, as is generally said, but the false opinion that the stomach needs an unlimited amount to fill it."

The university provides the final step in the long shaping process. It transforms the persons in their wholeness into standardized specialists to fill the modular replacement needs of society.

Many professors have deplored this trend toward the fragmentation of life. Experts from different departments have pooled their talents to form interdisciplinary teams. Yet here again, each member continues to view the totality in terms of his thin sliver of a specialty. Just as the student is being taught today, he has also been taught to conceive reality as a composite of viewpoints of specialists. The outcomes of these interdisciplinary efforts, more often than not, remain artificial, nonviable Rube Goldbergs of alternative force-fitted subassemblies.

The sense of a student riot can never be obtained from listening to a theologian on the action of God's grace in people's lives, then listening to a physicist on the equation of force, an economist on the pressures of inflation, a psychologist on the meaning of the gestalt, a lawyer on the constitutionality of violence, and so on. The thousand and one, out of the infinite, facts related to man may be analyzed in the thousand and one academic courses. But a human being cannot be appreciated as a human being through endless repetition of the same recitation.

A major introspection among American colleges regarding the undergraduate curriculum has been sparked by Harvard University during the late 1970s. It may be that one of these days an innovative university might make a concerted effort to establish a required four-year course for the explicit purpose of sensing, appreciating, and communicating the condition of man, as lived in the person and in the social group, as well as described in books. In this setting, life as lived is the prime reference. The instructors do not lecture on the psychological facets of human actions, later on the social facets, then on the economic facets, and still later on the religious facets, and so on in a sequential fashion. No, the masters pass on what has been experienced as living. They are the intuitive teachers with a feel for individual anguish and joy and a grasp of how things actually happen in man and masses. The new professors show their affection for Nature unabstracted. They speak to the wholeness of the human being and his surroundings. They transform the transmission of techniques and facts into the enhancement of human beings. But the chances of this coming to pass within the reasonable future are rather slim.

All this must have been foreseen by Johann Fichte, who declared that the purpose of education is to destroy free will. The student emerges thinking generally the way his teachers teach, as indicated by the grades, and the teachers emerge teaching generally the way the institutional leaders approve, as indicated by the donations and appropriations.

There is no way around it. The university is just another of the many temples dedicated to society's entrapment of the person.

14 **Lassos** The more refined enticement toward social conformity assumes the form of guidelines for social respectability. It is hinted that you ought to afford a house two and one-fourth times your annual gross income. This, despite the fact that the federal and state tax offices had already taken half off the top. The church asks ten percent for its share. The welfare drive suggests one percent for one of the main local charities. The alma mater presses for its thousand-dollar club. Investment services during your lifetime are offered for appropriately bequeathing codicils to your will. And so on.

To lull you into further arrears, society presents convenient arrangements of credit cards, installment buying, insurance policies, lump-sum loans, and pledges. Throughout your life, you are continuously exposed to a well-designed regimen of verbal and emotional conditioning, reconditioning, and fortifying. These culminate in the pathological restlessness and dissatisfactions of the modern mind. In the meantime, inflation keeps shrinking your emergency savings. Success and greater success for money and more money offer the only apparent solution to your dilemma. As Charles Dickens depicted the typical American of a couple generations ago, "All their cares, hopes, joys, affections, virtues, and associations, seemed to be melted down into dollars. . . . Men were weighted by their dollars; life was auctioned, appraised, put up and knocked down for its dollars." It seems that times have not changed much since his day.

For those less enticeable by dollars, society throws out the psychic lassos. The most honored recognitions bestowed on individuals are institutionally based—not only in the sense that they are awarded by institutions but also in the more significant sense that a person has little chance without being a member of and having the support of an institution or an organized effort of some kind. It is doubtful whether any more than a rare few of the Nobel prizes will be awarded in the future in the fields of chemistry, physics, medicine, economics, and peace to an individual who has worked entirely on his or her own resources. There may be more exceptions among the literature laureates. Even here, assistance in the form of public relations by the communications media, staging of new plays by producers, and translations by publishing houses leaves much room for institutional contribution. To gain institutional rewards, it is best to be allied with institutions.

The more institutionally vatted one becomes, the more of his personality is leached away. When one achieves the position of chief executive officer, he is transformed, to borrow the phrases the newly appointed president of Yale University, A. Bartlett Giamatti, applied to himself in May 1979, into "one of the symbolic containers" of "the essential core of values and traditions and hopes the place has." The reshaped "public person" then speaks and writes "in a style that I suppose you might call High Institutional."

Even the most respected of personal desires, such as a good name, is socially conferred. There is nothing unseemly about an outstanding reputation per se. It is only natural to be pleased with being held in high esteem by the community and to be associated with famous peers. Professional thieves look down on the snatch-and-grab, the boot-and-shoe, and other amateurs of the trade. Big time practitioners do not socialize with the shoplifter, the sneak, and other small-timers. The person becomes enslaved, however, when reputation becomes a matter of personal necessity. Since society has preempted the dispensing of major recognitions, the individual must do its bidding if he is to realize this kind of renown.

It takes an uncommon equanimity and self-mastery not to be excited over insults upon one's stature and competence. The Zen Buddhist, Bankei, possessed this in tranquil measure. While he was preaching one day, he was repeatedly interrupted by a Shinzu priest. So Bankei finally stopped and invited the priest to say what he had on his mind. "The founder of my religion," announced the priest, "stood on one bank of a big river, while a disciple stood on the other bank, holding a sheet of paper. Yet the founder was able to write the holy name of Amida on the paper through the air. Can you perform such a miracle?" "No," replied Bankei. "I can work only little miracles, such as: When I am hungry, I eat. When I am thirsty, I drink. And when I am insulted, I forget."

People like Bankei are few and far between.

15 **Cormorants**

Cormorants have been used for fishing in China and Japan for centuries. A man in a rowboat with a small number of birds, each with a ring around its neck, moves slowly among the waters. On sighting a fish, the bird swiftly dives into the water and unerringly comes up with it. Because of the ring around the neck, however, the bird is unable to swallow the fish, which remains caught in the throat. The fisherman then picks the bird up by its legs and squeezes out the fish through the cormorant's mouth. The bird again dives for another and yet another with repetitious alacrity until it is too old and worn out. Whereupon it is replaced by a much younger cormorant with the eager glint in its eye—good for at least 150,000 more dives.

16 Acquisitiveness Acquisitiveness is a natural characteristic of all living things. At any given moment there exists a biological or psychological lack within each of us. Acquisitiveness is the drive to fill this lack.

The oak spreading its roots through the earth and the young baboon challenging the king have long laid the prototype expressions for human acquisitiveness. But man has gone much further in his unique ways. The human being became the first of the creatures to be driven by an open-ended self-accelerating acquisitiveness. This ensued on the evolutionary development of a novel trait not present in previous species—imagination.

The real biological lack is now augmented with an imagined psychical lack. With the infinite range of the imagination, the law of diminishing returns no longer operates to moderate people's drives.

When society found techniques of harnessing this individual trait into a group drive, it became an acquisitive society. When the acquisitive society found techniques of stimulating this natural trait to unnatural excess and siphoning the differences for institutional purposes and social progress, it began to prosper. When the prosperous society found techniques for subordinating man's nature to its prosperity, it became established as The Demon.

DELINEATING OPTIONS

There are four practical options available to you for dealing with the dilemma imposed by The Demon. The first option of pushing ahead as a person of power has been covered in our previous book, *The Craft of Power*. With respect to the second option of a dedicated institutional manager, this section discusses the state of anxiety in which he usually finds himself. With respect to the third option of withdrawal, this section comments on the cynicism that often descends on people treading this path. With respect to the fourth option of superseding The Demon, this section touches upon two variants, namely, those of the theist and of the Stoic-Taoist.

17 **Anxiety** It is not clear how much of the rampant anxieties of the twentieth century is induced by institutions through their pressures on individuals and how much is congenital and personal in origin. It is certain, however, that there are more things over which a person can be anxious today than during past centuries. There are many more tightly organized institutions vying for greater shares of the individual's attention and commitment. There is much less resignation to the fact that certain things just "can't be helped." W. H. Auden called these times "The Age of Anxiety." People's personalities are being squeezed out of their being by the pressure toward conformity, leaving them in pulpy loneliness, "unattached as tumbleweed."

In *The Meaning of Anxiety* Rollo May interpreted the observations of the Lynds on the social transformation of Middletown between the 1920s and the 1930s as one from covert to overt anxiety. The dominant symptom of covert anxiety, recorded in the first study, was represented by "the compulsive work," such as frantic chasing about to make money; "the pervasive struggle to conform, the compulsive gregariousness," such as the urge to join clubs; and "the frantic endeavors of the people in the community to keep their leisure crammed with activity . . . however purposeless this activity might be in itself," such as motoring. In the words of one of the citizens of Middletown, who sensed the underlying apprehension, to his neighbor: "These people are all afraid of something: what is it?"

A different situation was detected by the Lynds eight years later. It had now become one of overt anxiety. The feeling of insecurity in the midst of a complex world was clearly discernible. The individual was visibly confused as to his role in the scheme of things. In Lynds' description, he "is caught in a chaos of conflicting patterns, none of them wholly condemned, but no one of them clearly approved and free from confusion; or, where the group sanctions are clear in demanding a certain role of a man or woman, the individual encounters cultural requirements with no immediate means of meeting them." May felt that this "chaos of conflicting patterns" in Middletown "is one expression of the pervasive social change occurring in our culture, which are intimately connected with the widespread anxiety of our times. The Lynds observe that since 'most people are incapable of tolerating change and uncertainty in all sectors of life at once,' the tendency in Middletown was toward a retrenchment into more rigid and conservative economic and social ideologies."

Many explanations have been attempted for the range of symptoms of anxiety from diffused thinking to terror. To Samuel Butler in 1903 in *The Way of All Flesh,* life is nothing more than the process of accommodating one's changing self to the changing context. When "we fail in it a little we are stupid; when we fail flagrantly we are mad; when we suspend it temporally we sleep; when we give up the attempt altogether we die. In quiet, uneventful lives the changes internal and external are so small that there is little or no strain in the process of fusion and accommodation; in other lives there is great strain, but there is also great fusing and accommodating power; in others great strain with little accommodating power. A life will be successful or not, according as the power of accommodation is equal or unequal to the strain of fusing and adjusting internal and extreme changes."

Much more complex theories have been advanced since Butler's time. Sigmund Freud suggested that anxiety results from one's inability to either discharge or master an overwhelming excess of stimuli. Harry Stack Sullivan stressed the anticipated disapproval from people important in one's life. Frieda Fromm-Reichman spoke of the "lack of freedom for self-realization and the feeling of stagnation and 'nothingness' that goes with it, this sense of psychological death." Paul Tillich emphasized the anxiety of fate and death, the anxiety of emptiness and meaninglessness, and the anxiety of guilt and condemnation as among the principal obstacles standing in the way of attainment of the courage to be, which is "the ethical act in which man affirms his own being in spite of those elements of his existence which conflict with his essential self-affirmation."

Institutions, however, do not theorize; they just make use of whatever is handy to expedite their purposes. Anxiety is the raw stuff of greatest utility. Institutions tense people up to the point where they frantically seek relief. And lo and behold, the only apparent channel of relief from the unbearable anguish is that offered by the institutions themselves. In this way social entrapment takes on the mien of beneficence. The masses sing their hallelujahs, forever and ever. Amen.

18 Cynicism Infectious cynicism permeates the urban upper class. Debunking is a popular sport among writers. Literati who dwell on the bleakness of life are applauded.

The 1970 Nobel laureate in literature, Samuel Beckett, emphasized "the useless predicament of life," in which his heroes are constantly going downhill to nowhere. In his novel *Murphy* the hero refused the life of this world. When he accidentally died through his own doing, his will directed that his ashes be flushed down the toilet in Dublin's Abbey Theater. But even then things went wrong. The man carrying his ashes got into an argument and threw the packet of ashes at the other fellow. It missed and hit the wall. And Beckett added: "By closing time the body, mind and soul of Murphy were freely distributed over the floor of the saloon; and before another day-spring greyened the earth had been swept away with the sand, the beer, the butts, the glass, the matches, the spits, the vomit."

The individual usually does not notice his own slide from idealism to cynicism. In the initial phase it is hardly distinguishable from the process of maturing. He or she begins by seeing the facts of life as they are, the reality of evil and the limitations of the forces for good. This, after all, is the door of wisdom.

But many let the disillusionment grow out of hand. Thousands of young Americans had gone through a recent collective disillusionment of that kind. They had perceived the North Vietnamese officials during the 1960s and early 1970s as gentle and kind people, who were being oppressed by Western powers. So they demonstrated against their own government's incursion into South Vietnam to prevent the North's conquest of the South. Their protests succeeded in discouraging the president from seeking reelection and in causing the American army to suffer its first military retreat in history. With a feeling of moralistic optimism, they looked forward to the peace-loving North Vietnamese settling down to rebuild their war-torn country in genuine brotherhood with the neighbors. But without even so much as catching their breath, the officials dominated the Laotians, who had given them the supply route connecting the North and the South during the Vietnam War; sent their army into Cambodia, which had furnished them military sanctuary during the war; broke off relations with China, which had provided Ho Chih Minh, Vo Nguyen Giap, and the Vietminh the essential operational base and military and economic aid to overthrow the domination of the French, Japanese, and Americans; drove hundreds of thousands of Vietnamese out of the country with thousands perishing at sea; and caused the starvation unto death of tens of thousands of Cambodians. A mist of cynicism descended over their youthful idealism.

After several cycles of expectation-and-disappointment, a degenerative process of the spirit often sets in. As described by Edward Bergler, "Slightly forlorn, and for the time being desperately bewildered, wondering what hit him and whether the effort he puts into his daily drudgery pays off, he finally rebels." But the unfortunate victim does not foresee that his revolt is destined to end "in submission, or in trouble surpassing in magnitude the difficulties of the situation he rebelled against." He emerges from being "buffeted, browbeaten, and at last unconditionally defeated . . . with a precious souvenir; a martyr complex." He had been an "injustice collector" all along.

19 **The perennial god** History has long confirmed man's ineradicable faith in a supernatural being of some kind. The earliest gods took on tangible appearances. Primitive Mongols bowed to *Tengri,* the sky, as the controller of rain. Others worshipped the sun as the source of living energy. Women prayed to the moon, regarded as a male god who blessed them with menstruation by the grace of seduction.

Before long these inanimate gods and goddesses assumed the form of living creatures from the Egyptian scarab to the Hindu elephant. In time, they gave way to human personifications, such as Zeus and Yahweh.

At first there was no qualitative distinction between gods and men. To the Greeks the gods were their ancestors. As the competition between religious spokesmen developed, succeeding gods transcended all human limitations. They became progressively more powerful and more appealing, yet more fearsome, than their predecessors. Then they became exclusive. Each spokesman presented his own god as the one and only true god, the most powerful, the most wise, and the most good. This god, according to the spokesman, is represented on earth solely by him and his institution and is to be defended to the death, if necessary.

The real God is always there as He is. What man says He is, of course, is something else. Since man tends to listen to himself more than to anyone else, he has come to forsake the perennial God for the ephemeral idol. Therein may lie one of the greatest sacrilegious confusions and a prime source of human unease.

20 **The Stoic-Taoist** As can be gathered from the quotations in the earlier Essential Elements 6 to 9, there is much in common between the philosophical orientations of the Taoists, Lao Tzu and Chuang Tzu, and the Stoics, Epictetus and Marcus Aurelius. All four rest their systems of thought on the same foundation, namely, the primacy of Nature and one's keeping in harmony with Nature.

In some respects we may refer to Lao Tzu and Chuang Tzu as neo-Stoics and to Epictetus and Marcus Aurelius as neo-Taoists. Since Lao Tzu lived two centuries before Zeno, the founder of Stoicism in 308 B.C., the latter nomenclature would chronologically be more appropriate. But since the two schools were never in touch during their formative years, either practice would be justified. But the underlying philosophy of life remains the same:

Accept the given and cooperate with it. Life and death are one; good men and bad men are all men. Freedom from the man-made world with its illusions is the prelude to true virtue. Master the passions and actions, as the Stoic would put it, in conformity with the law of Nature, or as the Taoist would put it, in conformity with the way of the Tao.

At a fundamental level, the religious worshipper of God is also giving expression to the same intuitive feeling of the Stoic-Taoist. They all sense that the more the institutions screen people from Nature's whole and separate them from each other, the greater is the yearning across the gaps. This yearning is the paining cry of Love. Love's diminution is the genesis of suffering; its absence Evil. Buddha's minimizing of suffering becomes Lao Tzu's embracing the Tao and John of the Cross's uniting with the Mystical. All seek the Good through the return of Love, shredded by the partitioning devices of The Demon of Disjunction.

CLARIFYING PARAMETERS

Composure involves the feeling-rightness of the infinite factors that impinge on your life at a particular point in time. We cannot point to a single parameter or a group of parameters that can be said to be sufficient to assure this condition of meaningful repose. By refracting it through a relatively small number of selected prisms, however, you can come to a fair apprehension of its essential character. After emphasizing the matter of quality rather than quantity in one's own life, the prerequisite of nonattachment to the fruits of one's efforts, and the sensitivity to the ineffable, this section elaborates on the essences of gentleness, magnanimity, simplicity, graciousness, compassion, and tranquility.

21 **Tiffany** When thinking about satisfaction in living and progress as a person, you need to subordinate size to quality. Once you confound meaning with size, you are on the road to abandoning your self to the institution, for institutions are primarily respected for their size. It is the larger organization swallowing the smaller in business mergers in order to get still larger that is admired, rarely the reverse. We are reminded of what had recently happened to Tiffany and Company, the prestigious Fifth Avenue jewelry store. Its very name, "Tiffany," had come to be the American byword for premier quality. Yet in 1979 it was taken over as a subsidiary by Avon Products, Inc., the world's largest cosmetics and costume jewelry company. The highest symbol of excellence was gulped down by the purveyor to the masses. As an executive, you must be doubly vigilant about letting this institutional habit degrade your personal quality of life.

The blue-collar workers in America appear to be making faster progress than the educated class in recent years as far as independence from institutional domination and inducements is concerned. They are much more conscious of their personal fullness of living. Long have they become, in the words of Douglas Fraser, the president of the United Automobile, Aerospace and Agricultural Implement Workers of America, "suspicious of institutions, including their own institution—the union. This is a general malaise from which our whole society is suffering. People don't trust their leaders." Referring to the changes in the life ethic of workers in 1979, he reported that young people were turning their backs on a double-time Sunday of $18 an hour for eight hours. Workers now "got different priorities. . . . different interests in life. . . . not as materialistic."

Though short of book learning, modern workers seem not short of horse sense.

22 Nonattachment, accomplishments, and satisfaction

Satisfaction in life comes from accomplishments—so we have been repeatedly taught. We are adjured to set objectives, far-reaching ones, and seek the attendant rewards, which come from winning over others in the competitive free enterprise system. As the coach of the Washington Redskins professional football team bemoaned after a defeat during the 1970s, "losing is like dying." For over a decade he had been trying desperately to gain the Super-Bowl Championship without success. He pursued the prize with such intensity that losing had indeed become like dying to him. His distress continually flared internally as ulcers and externally as confrontations with the owners of the club.

In reality, deep satisfaction does not rest on accomplishments as such. Accomplishments attained through questionable means leave a bitter aftertaste, ill-directed accomplishments a sense of guilt. A good and satisfying feeling arises only with accomplishments resulting from unfeigning evolution of harmonious interactions. In the latter circumstances, they are as naturally emergent without anxious concern as the fruit follows the flower.

You should therefore focus your attention not on the rewards but on the sheer participation. Attachment to victory or trophy inevitably interferes with the genuineness of the endeavors. A stress of anxiety develops. The value of the driving remuneration itself becomes exaggerated. Even when successful, the individual becomes disappointed, when the actual remuneration turns out to be nowhere that envisioned.

The case of Ludwig van Beethoven illustrates the point. After working hard and long on the Ninth Symphony, he had anticipated a considerable financial return. But when he sat down with his associates at the celebration dinner after the world premiere and learned of his share of the receipts, he became furious and accused the manager of cheating him. What was to have been a happy occasion turned out a ruination of friendships.

The superior person therefore is never attached to rewards as objects of pursuit or personal due. They are merely taken in stride as possible incidentals to what he is doing. But these are not intentionally borne in mind as the impetus of his activities. He is also aware that life itself is continual flux. Winning and losing is ever in doubt. What is certain is that the process of living goes on and can be pleasing and joyful as such or not, depending on whether he is completely absorbed in its fullness without an ax to grind or sidetracked by some expected compensation in the future. His own living instants are not plastered over with a series of imagined promissory notes from Nature. His life is free and wholesome unto itself at every point in time.

Harmony cannot be achieved through pursuit. For that which is pursued is cleaved from him who is pursuing. Whenever there is pursuit, life is splintered. There can be no manifestation of harmony, so fundamental to serenity, contentment, and abiding meaningfulness. Two quotations from contrasting cultures are sufficient to illustrate the traditional wisdom on the nonpursuit and nonattachment to the fruits of one's effort.

From the Hindu East: In the *Bhagavad Gita,* the God Krishna instructed the warrior Arjuna, "You have the right to work, but for the work's sake only. You have no right to the fruits of your work. Desire for the fruits of your work must never be your motive in working." From the Catholic West: Bernard of Clairvaux said, "Love seeks no cause beyond itself and no fruit; it is its own fruit."

Nonattachment, however, does not necessarily mean nonenjoyment. On the contrary, to enjoy what Nature offers is merely being responsive. Nonattachment means not trying to latch on to what Nature has not yet offered, is not disposed to offer, or has already recalled. The *Isa Upanishad* counseled, "Enjoy, do not covet His property." The Christian mystic of the fourteenth century, Meister Eckhardt, admonished, "It is permissible to take life's blessing with both hands, provided thou dost know thyself prepared in the opposite event to leave them just as gladly." When asked how he would feel if the Pope would suddenly dissolve the Jesuit order, Ignatius of Loyola replied, "A quarter of an hour of prayer and I should think no more about it."

23 Ineffability We swim in an ocean of words—memos, letters, briefings, litigations . . . talk, talk, talk, talk. Be careful not to swallow too much of it, lest you drown in it. As the old Taoist expression goes, "The wise person does not speak. The talented one talks. The stupid argues."

Be especially wary of sophists, whether they wear the robes of scholars or consultants. They can take any side of a preconceived notion and make it sound convincingly true. There is the story of Teng Shih of the sixth century B.C. A wealthy man was drowned in the Wei River and his body was picked up by a boatman, who demanded a huge sum of money from the bereaved family for its release. The dead man's family went to Teng for advice. "Wait," the consultant said, "for no one else will pay for the body." So the family followed his advice. After a while, the man with the corpse became anxious and also went to Teng for advice. "Wait," the consultant said, "for no one else can furnish the body."

Draw from your own experience and see how the events of major personal importance are cloaked in inexplicability. Words fail you as you try to describe love, to explain the exhilaration of spring, to convey the depth of grief. Do not place excessive reliance on words and equations in arriving at decisions or choices of considerable complexity and significance associated with human behavior. They are as likely to lead you from the truth as toward it. Real enlightenment is ineffable and indescribable.

If this be so, the question arises as to how one goes about transmitting the essences of reality, if they are in fact inexpressible in words. The allusive negative approach is often more effective than the explicit positive method. In the latter method the item of interest is directly designated and explained. In the negative method the item itself is not defined or otherwise directly confronted; only those items that it is not are mentioned as not being it. Discussions beat around the bush. By not analyzing the item itself, the item is left undistorted in its reality. By restricting discourse to items other than it, the features of the item are gradually made clear by removing the various layers blocking it from view and by avoiding the screen of words. At a certain point it suddenly looms unmistakable before the mind's eye of the beholder and is implanted directly into the self.

Parables are classical models of the negative approach. So are answers like that of the American jazz cornetist, Louis Armstrong, when asked to define jazz. "If you get to ask," he replied, "you'll never get to know." Even executives are constantly resorting to the negative method in relating to their subordinates. When asked by an eager action officer as to the reason for disapproval of what he thought to have been a beautifully conceived proposal, the seasoned superior often explains with some statement like: "It just won't fly."

Since the verbalizable positive method continues to be the primary means of communication in the technological society, one needs be well versed in both positive and negative methods. Be discerning, however, as to the appropriateness of the respective methods for the different cases at hand. The distinction was brought out very well by Wu Ch'eng-en in the following passage from his novel *Monkey*.

After a long and dangerous journey to worship Buddha and bring the sacred scriptures back to China, the priest Tripitaka, Pigsy, Sandy, and Monkey finally reached their destination in India. When they received the scrolls from the officials in Buddha's treasury, however, they felt cheated and went complaining to Buddha himself. "Listen to this!" shouted Monkey. "After all the trouble we had getting here from China, and after you specially ordered that we were to be given the scriptures, Ānanda and Kāśyapa made a fraudulent delivery of goods. They gave us blank copies to take away; I ask you, what is the good of that to us?" "There is no need to shout," smiled the Buddha. "As a matter of fact, it is such blank scrolls as these that are the true scriptures. But I quite see that the people of China are too foolish to believe this, so there is nothing for us to do but to give them copies with some writing." So he called Ānanda and Kāśyapa and instructed them to choose a few scrolls with some writing and give them to Monkey to take back to China.

It behooves you then to be conversant with both, so that you are able to operate with the written scrolls of society and to live by the blank scrolls of Nature.

24 **Gentleness**

An ancient Indian legend tells of an argument among a group of sages as to who is the greatest of the Hindu gods. They sought the opinion of the most respected Bhrigu. He agreed to find out.

Bhrigu first visited the god Brahma, without paying appropriate obeisance. This angered Brahma, but he was finally pacified. Bhrigu then went to see the god Siva, without returning the god's greeting. This outraged Siva, who nearly killed Bhrigu for his impudence, had not the god's wife, Parvati, intervened in time.

Bhrigu finally approached the god Vishnu. Finding him asleep, Bhrigu woke him up with a hard kick on the chest. Instead of losing his temper, the god apologized for not welcoming him. He then thanked Bhrigu for the kick, which left a permanent mark of good fortune. Expressing hope that Bhrigu had not hurt his foot in so doing, Vishnu ended by massaging it.

Reporting back to the wise men, Bhrigu concluded that Vishnu was supreme. "He overpowers by the most powerful of weapons—that of gentleness and generosity."

25 **Magnanimity** Philanthropy as one usually reads about it in the newspapers, is not necessarily an expression of magnanimity. A more fitting index is the ratio of one's being that is given to others to that retained for oneself. When measured by this standard, the most magnanimous person frequently turns out to be of comparatively modest means and low status. But his selfless assurance reaches out to a relatively wide circle of people in all directions. It is not out of pity or pride that the magnanimous soul gives of himself, but of a genuineness that requires neither justification nor compensation.

Magnanimous individuals are personally secure as an individuals standing apart from others; yet they do not feel or live apart. They have achieved this state of buoyancy by fulfilling their own reasonable personal needs in a way as to reserve a bountiful overflow of time, energy, and resources for devotion to others.

They encounter competition with relative aplomb, largely as a result of a judicious selection of the field that is compatible with their talents and capacity. The pinnacles of prestige do not entrance them. Nor do they glory in them, if they happen their way. Their take-it-or-leave-it posture to prestige and power is due not to ignorance or incompetence. On the contrary, they are quite familiar with the techniques of the tournament and the machinations of the wily. But they have fathomed the quagmires in which the shameless become nouveaux riches and the loose-talking become high officials. They make life a trifle happier for the poor associates scrambling in the pits beyond their depths, by allowing them some extra remunerations for their efforts from time to time, even though they could have readily scooped them for themselves and rightly so by the rules of the game.

Perhaps the statesman of recent memory most admired for his magnanimity is Chou En-lai. Time and again the late premier of China, who had built up the Chinese Communist elite, willingly stepped aside to let junior officials advance ahead of him. In 1945 he relinquished his second-ranking position to let Liu Shao-chi take over for the sake of party harmony. When Liu was deposed for heresy, Chou resumed his post. Then in 1967 he again gave up his status to his protege, Lin Piao. The latter died in an abortive coup. Whereupon Chou resumed the premiership until he died in 1976.

There is an unrehearsed largeness about the magnanimous person. He does not need to be prodded by Thomas Carlyle's advice: "My brother, the brave man has to give his life away. Give it, I advise thee—thou dost not expect to *sell* thy life in an adequate manner? . . . Give it, like a royal heart: let the price be Nothing. Thou *hast* then, in a certain sense got all for it! The heroic—and is not every man, God be thanked, a potential hero?—has to do so, in all times and circumstances." Actually, Carlyle puts the matter too dramatically. For the magnanimous person, it all unfolds rather inattentively.

Such largeness of soul was exemplified by Shichiri. He was reciting his *sutras* one evening, when a robber entered the room, stuck a knife against his neck, and demanded his money. "In the box in the drawer," Shichiri said, continuing with his recitation. As the robber was leaving, Shichiri requested, "Leave me some money for the taxes. The collectors will be around tomorrow." So the robber left some and started to leave again. Whereupon Shichiri politely inquired, "Aren't you going to thank someone who made you a gift of money?" So the robber thanked him and left.

A week later the robber was arrested during another attempt. He confessed to many robberies, one of which was at Shichiri's. But Shichiri refused to press charges, insisting that he had given the fellow a gift. The robber was sent to prison for the other offenses. When he completed his sentence, he came back to Shichiri and asked, "Will you be my teacher?"

26 Simplicity We should be careful not to confuse the outward show of simplicity with the simplicity of the inner being. When the outward manifestations flow from the inner simplicity, then only can we say that the person is leading a simple life. Diogenes sitting in a barrel may or may not be living a simple life. Rasputin, despite his peasant garb, certainly was not. Nor was Martin Luther, despite his religious vows. The latter two were not simple at all in their aspirations.

Similarly, a junior executive living in a modest cottage, driving around in a small second-hand car, and not belonging to any club may not be a person of simplicity, despite outward appearances. It is relatively easy to be outwardly simple. But to be inwardly genuinely simple is much more difficult.

Inner simplicity calls for freedom from desires, dogmatic beliefs, and domination of all kinds—internally as well as externally. The inwardly simple person feels no compulsions to conform to orthodoxies and public opinions. His mind is not led this way or that; he is not enticed to become this or that.

Not scheming for special advantages, the simple person does not resort to petty guiles and deceits. He does not fall for the not uncommon advice to executives seeking new employment, such as that given by the president of a "corporate headhunter" company in late 1978. He recommended the withholding of certain information in dealing with executive recruiting agencies. The applicant should not say, for example, that he is registered with other agencies, even if he were, or give any references unless he is assured of a firm offer. Such an approach, he argued, presents "one's experience and capabilities in the best light possible." This kind of hide-and-seek reminds me of the remark of the wife of the Bishop of Worcester on being told of Darwin's theory: "Descended from the apes! My dear, let us hope that it is not true. But if it is, let us hope that it will not be generally known."

It is the state of inner simplicity that throws the doors of the self wide open to the joys of the infinite little happenings of Nature—so well captured by Basho's haiku:

> All around
> That meets the eye
> Are cool and fresh.

And so it is that the simple person never feels abandoned.

27 Graciousness The annealing of an act into a gracious one requires a certain all-absorbing attention on the recipient, a certain sincerity of forgetfulness of oneself, a certain fitness to the fineness of the moment, and a certain genuineness about it all.

Relatively few people in America nowadays have the inclination necessary to perform more than an isolated gracious act here and there. Graciousness may be rapidly becoming not only a lost art in practice but also a forgotten one in theory. In 1975 a search of the 15 million index cards in the Library of Congress did not turn up a single entry on the subject of graciousness. Practically no mention of graciousness was found in the hundreds of leading American texts on applied psychology, personnel administration, peace-of-mind, how-to-get-along-with-people, and allied topics. The trait is apparently regarded as unessential by most people for professional success and even good living.

One factor contributing substantially to this relative scarcity of graciousness among Americans is their emphasis on "saving time." They hurry through this to "save time" so that they can hurry through that. The fact that time is simply there and cannot be spent or saved does not dawn on them. They confuse the saving of time with the stuffing of time. So they stuff it to such an extent that they snuff out incompatible qualities, such as graciousness and deliberateness. In the 1977–1978 session of Congress, Congressmen introduced 22,313 public and private bills and resolutions. Of these, 804 were finally enacted into law. In addition, the Senate confirmed about 63,000 military and civilian nominations by the President.

After a relatively short period, the scurrying about becomes an essential component of the executive syndrome. It provides the exhilarating sense of aliveness. The important people begin to gauge their own stature by the jerkiness of their motions and the length of the line of supplicants awaiting their appearances. They are torchbearers of a tradition going far back in history. "Methinks," wrote Geoffrey Chaucer in *Canterbury Tales* about one of his scurrying contemporaries in the fourteenth century, "he seemed busier than he was."

Harold Nicolson had noted that in nearly all societies a certain kind of civility usually begins with a minority, which often is taken up later by a larger or smaller segment of the rest. Perhaps such a pocket of gracious civility does exist in your environs. Perhaps also, you are part of it. If so, your very presence is providing a leavening—ever so slight it may be—to American life. "The fact that a person resists the whole spirit of his age, stops it at the door and calls it to account, *must* exert an influence!" as Friedrich Nietzsche once said. "It is indifferent whether he wishes to exert an influence; the point is that he *can.*"

28 **Compassion** A useful criterion of goodness is an everyday empirical reality that everyone acknowledges, coupled with an unselfish service with respect to it that everyone feels instinctively inclined to render. Gautama Buddha formulated a set of these in a straightforward manner. "I teach only two things," he said, "the fact of suffering and the possibility of escape from suffering."

The minimizing of suffering does not constitute a theological system. It is not even stated as such among the Ten Commandments. But one need not know anything about ethics or scholarship to lead a good life based on the alleviation of suffering. Suffering is real; suffering is human; suffering is here. No man or beast is exempt; everyone has tasted its bitterness; all creatures continue to be so exposed. The most ignorant of peasants agrees that it is good to do something now and always—without esoteric disputations over Job, without threatening arguments over heaven and hell.

The instinctive response to the sight of suffering has been recounted innumerable times. Mohammed told of the adulteress who saw a dog by a well with its tongue hanging out about to die from thirst. She took off her boot, tied it to the end of her garment, drew up some water, and gave it to the dog to drink. For that deed she was forgiven by Allah.

Nevertheless, facile "justifications" of suffering keep cropping up. Typical is the following passage by Soame Jenyns in the eighteenth century: "I am persuaded that there is something in the abstract nature of pain conducive to pleasure, that the sufferings of individuals are absolutely necessary to universal happiness." He referred to the bartering of pain for pleasure by individuals and of death for prosperity of empires. "To what infinite toil of men, and other animals, is every flourishing city indebted for all the conveniences and enjoyments of life, and what vice and misery for these very equipments introduce? . . . The pleasure annexed to the preservation of ourselves are both preceded and followed by numerous sufferings; preceded by massacres and tortures of various animals preparatory to a feast, and followed by as many diseases lying in wait in every dish to pain forth vengeance on their destroyers."

In many respects, Jenyns' statement does describe what actually happens. Before expressing approval, however, we should speak to specific cases. An action may be considered good if it causes a modicum of suffering, which interdicts greater later suffering to the same recipient. But suffering inflicted upon others may not be so in order to relieve oneself. And certainly it is not so to gain additional felicities and pleasures. Increasing corporation's profits, temple's converts, nation's potence neither justifies nor glorifies the wanton misery so clearly visible throughout the lands.

Other authors point to the perpetuity of suffering in the wilds of Nature—the lion chewing up the antelope, the toad snaring the mayfly, the honeysuckle choking the rhododendron. One is struck with horror at witnessing the sparrow hawk's attack on the jay, so vividly described by J. T. Baker. As the hawk drew closer, the talons reached out and clutched again and again. Then finally it hooked into the tail of the screeching jay and "crawled forward till they reached his back, like a climber hauling himself up a steep rock-face with his finger tips. The jay's flight was broken. His wings moved feebly, spasmodically, like the oars of a boat whose rower has suddenly collapsed. Then they drooped listlessly in the air. The two birds sank together like a crippled biplane, tilted, then dived into the brambles. The jay struggled, heaving up in a delirium of fear, but he was underneath and could not overthrow the hawk. He seemed defenceless. He had begun to die at the first touch of the knifing talons. Soon he was dead, and the hawk stood breathless above him, curved like a claw."

Despite their seeming insensitivity to the suffering of fellow creatures, creatures in the wild have not increased suffering over the ages. Nor have they decreased it, biological necessity being what it is.

Man, however, represents a completely different situation. He is the only animal endowed with the capacity of greatly lessening the amount of suffering in the world. This he had done in many cases, such as diseases, floods, and famines. At the same time, man is the only animal endowed also with the capacity of greatly magnifying the amount of suffering in the world. This too he has done in many cases, such as wars, institutional oppression, and personal meanness.

The record shows that man has not decreased the pain and anguish to his fellow creatures to the minimum essential for personal survival and growth. All other animals have attained this equilibrium long, long ago. Based on this fundamental comparison, it seems fair to judge man to be the cruelist of all of God's creations.

Herein lies the crying appeal for compassion to the human race: If you are the highest of all earthly creatures—as indeed you say you are—and if you are the image of the all-good God—as indeed you say you are—then reduce your infliction of pain to at least the relative level of the dumb beasts.

29 **Tranquility** Tranquility begins with a sense of belonging to a broadly based continuum. "After you have exhausted what there is in business, politics, conviviality, and so—have found that none of these fully satisfy, or permanently wear—what remains?" asks Walt Whitman. And you observe with the poet that "Nature remains."

Nature is the all-embracing continuum. Everyone has been, is now, and will be an element in it, not as a discrete particle, but rather as an interpenetrant field. Tranquility prevails when this original state is intimately lived, when one no longer fights it by trying to assert his separate quantum. With this comes a degree of genial unconcern, which extends beyond love of life and fear of death. There is no special rejoicing on one's own part at his birth—how can one? Nor is there any special regretting on one's own part at his death—again, how can one? Life comes to one and life goes. One gracefully accepts life for what it has to unveil and gracefully acknowledges the final curtain for what it has to end. By not interposing interpretations between Nature and oneself, as the Taoist books would say, his "joys and sorrows are in direct touch with the four seasons."

Among the things that life has to offer are society and her man-made institutions. This man-made society is to be reconciled with the larger universe of Nature. If you permit your actions responsive to the prevailing institutions to suppress your relations with other elements of Nature, you may be driven neurotic. On the other hand, if you permit your actions responsive to the noninstitutional sectors of Nature to suppress your relations with the prevailing institutions, you may be driven destitute. The dual threat can be dissolved by penetrating the illusions of civilization, while acting out one's role within it. Instead of an expedient belonging to this and that institution as one is pushed around by competing and exploiting institutions, one relates to the steady Whole with its continuously appearing and disappearing eddies.

A distinction is to be drawn between the ethics operating in society and the harmony prevailing in Nature. Many societal apologists have rationalized the former in terms of the latter. They identify man as a social animal, like ants and bees. Group living is their natural state. A person is not to live alone but be an integral part of society and her institutions. It is the function of society to satisfy this natural instinct. What is often overlooked in this line of reasoning is the redefinition of the word "social" from the natural to the man-made context, implying that the two are qualitatively the same. This is not necessarily so.

It so happens that the man-made realm does include within its own framework some of the same features of the natural realm, if for no other reason than that society itself is part of Nature. In so doing, however, society preempts the position of primacy. Many of the institutional precepts and practices are desirable by any standard, such as feeding the hungry, clothing the naked, and healing the sick. But when they are implemented to the degree, in the manner, and through the channels as prescribed by a particular institution, they become primarily acts of obedience to that institution and an affirmation of its authority to impose other binding rules and laws on the community that may not be considered desirable by any other standard, such as fomenting hatred, burning disbelievers, and obliterating cities. Much of social activity thus turns out to be the erection of just such imprisoning walls.

We suggest that you maintain private gateways through the societal corral to the Beyond. A harmonious coalescence can then be achieved between yourself "in office" as a member of the man-made society and yourself "out of office" as a being of Nature. You can then say with Ch'eng Hao of the eleventh century that there is no difference between Nature and you.

RECTIFYING SELF

As a human being, you are unique among animals at self-beclouding. You live through imagination and figments prod you on. Before you can see your way to the right path, therefore, you must first be clear on these processes. This section treats of the responsible virtual presences that are not real but effective, of their proliferation in the urban settings, of enjoyable interludes while rectifying yourself, and of the avoidable dangers of intellectual snares, theological games, and high priests alienating you from your primal belonging.

30 **Virtual gods** Human beings live in a profusion of infinities. The infinity of reality is complexed into a higher order by the imagination. The one-dimensional infinity can be expanded into infinite dimensions. The positive can be imagined to be negative and vice versa. Reality can be displaced by a nonreality, a nonreality by another nonreality, ad infinitum.

The power of the imagination is exemplified by the invention of the square root of minus one. There can be no such entity in actuality, even by mathematical rules. It cannot be plus one, because plus one times plus one equals plus one—not minus one. Nor can it be minus one, because minus one times minus one equals plus one—not minus one. Yet this purely imaginary number can be introduced in calculations involving real events to produce very useful answers in the practical sense. This is a mathematical example of what has been called a virtual presence. A virtual presence is something that does not exist in the commonsensical way of looking at things but exerts real and practical effect on human beings as if it does.

Virtual presences constitute major ingredients of human thinking. "Free enterprise" is central in American politics; the "gene" in genetics; the "devil" in religions. Much of social success centers around the conjuring and enhancing of virtual presences. As Walter Bagehot has noted, "No orator ever made an impression by appealing to men as to their plainest physical wants, except when he could allege that those wants were caused by someone's tyranny. But thousands have made the greatest impression by appealing to some vague dream of glory, of empire, or nationality. The ruder sort of men—that is, men at one stage of rudeness—will sacrifice all they hope for, all they have, *themselves,* for what is called an idea—for some attraction which seems to transcend reality, which aspires to elevate by an interest higher, deeper, wider than that of ordinary life."

Spokesmen of the virtual presences are especially polished in the art of disputation. They can reach into any body of data and extract support for their own interest. Illustrative are the diversified explanations that are advanced to explain the tragic events that occur from time to time. The six-minute earthquake of 1755 in Portugal provides an example. On that All Saints Day, 15,000 worshipping men, women, children, priests, and nuns were crushed to death under the bells and rubbles of the churches. The Jesuits claimed it was an expression of God's wrath. The Jansenist Lurent Étienne Rondet argued that the disaster was God's reaction to the Jesuits and the Inquisition. The London Protestants ascribed it to heavenly disapproval of the Portuguese for their worship of the Virgin Mary.

The virtual presences themselves are constantly modified to give maximum force to one's own position. Logic is transformed into a kind of virtual logic to overcome an impasse in conventional logic. The eighteenth century Moto-ori Norinaga thus defended the traditional account of the creation of the islands of Japan from drops falling from the sacred spear of the gods, two of whom mated to give birth to the Japanese race. "The very inconsistency is the proof of the authenticity of the record," he declared, "for who would have gone out of his way to invent a story so ridiculous and incredible?"

There was a time long ago when the virtual presences were the modest creatures of temporary practical necessity; today, they have evolved into the awesome gods of Justice, Patriotism, Law, Success, Freedom, Love, Progress, and other divinities of the virtual pantheon. There was a time long ago when their very existence depended on the whims of man, their creator; today, man, their slave, is beholden to them.

As the virtual gods grow in influence, their high priests and courtiers tighten their control over the communicants in their divine name. A prototype of the more successful of these courtiers, for a while at least, was Girolamo Savonarola. He exercised a powerful hold on the people of Florence during the fifteenth century. It was not infrequent that after his sermon at the frugal wedding reception repast, the newlyweds would take a vow of chastity for varying lengths of time, some even for life. When some of the things Savonarola forced on the

Dominican monks of the San Marco monastery brought ridicule from the Italians, he preached from the pulpit: "I have made you all become as fools, is it not so? But it is not I who have done this. It is Christ."

Egged on by their increasing appetite for gain and glory, the courtiers transform the virtual gods of special purposes for which they were respectively created into virtual gods of conglomerates. The once separate jurisdictions now overlap. The gods are no longer to preside over little goddoms. They are to be lords of the universe. But there can be but one such lord. Thus began the Interminable War of the Virtual Gods.

The greatest solidarity of cooperation among real human beings has always been exhibited in the waging of real wars on behalf of virtual gods. A gripping inspiration pervades the scene, overwhelming all conflicting inspirations. The industrial sector pours out the arms; the healing doctors mend the wounded to fight some more; the chaplains reconcile the butcheries of the warriors with the high-sounding ideals of the virtual gods . . . all pushing the people to kill and die—countless in World War I, countless more in World War II, and still more countless in World War et sequitur. As the *levée en masse* decree of the French Convention of 1793 proclaimed the programs for all modern governments, "Young men will go to the front; married men will forge arms and transport foodstuff; women will make tents, clothes, will serve in the hospitals; children will tear rags into lint; old men will be carried to public places, there to stir up the courage of the warriors, hatred of kings, and unity in the Republic."

In peace as in war, human misery is made acceptable through skillful virtual transformations. In his Charles Eliot Norton lecture at Harvard University, E. E. Cummings spoke of a typical sample on a small scale. A magazine editor was advising a new contributor on the characteristics of a well-written article. "Well, imagine you're describing a record-breaking Chinese flood," he came to the essence, "millions of poor unfortunate men and women and little children and helpless babies drowning and drowned; millions more perishing of slow starvation, suffering inconceivable, untold agonies, and so forth—well, any reader of this article must feel definitely and distinctly better when she or he finishes the article, than when he or she began it."

The continuous clash of idolatrous competition, however, is taking its toll in spiritual bewilderment and social instability. Politicians are troubled over the exploitation of the masses. Businessmen are questioning the ethics of their tactics. Ministers are unsure of their legacies. Educators are confused by relevance. Students are disturbed by the insincerity of the entire enterprise. People are lost in the supersaturation of virtual gods; they flounder in desperation seeking the harmonious living that they feel they deserve after decades of hard work and earnest search. Yet when the virtual gods are pitted against each other, brotherhood among real people goes by the board. The real people suffer and the real courtiers profit.

The old virtual gods pass away with their exhausted minions in the conflagrations. Reincarnated virtual gods with new recruits arise from the ashes. The cycle begins anew.

31 **Modern Valhalla** The walling-off of man from Nature accelerated during the last thousand years. It began in an emphatic way with the Graeco-Romans. By fencing a delimited area out of the boundless fields, they formed the polis of Athens and Rome. They then looked inward and created the state with a set of common laws. Nature, in her fullness and lushness, was somewhere else. As Socrates announced, "I have nothing to do with the trees of the field. I have to do only with the man of the city."

Homer's Greece was not the Athens of Socrates. It was rich in forests and meadows, luxuriant in tall pines and oaks, deers and foxes, geese and grouse. Men and women wore the same woolen garments and nudity brought no offense. The gods were identified with the elements of Nature. Zeus was the king of lightning and thunder; Hera, his wife, had control over the mists and fogs; Aphrodite gave sexual charm to women. Homer's *Iliad* sang of the world of Nature—the bees and horses in the thick woods, the flowing rivers among the many-ridged mountains, the heroic men with great eloquence, and the gods rising from the waves. Everything was throbbing with the same life, as in the passage on Hector: "And even as when a stalled horse has fed his fill at the manger, breaketh his halter, and runneth stampeth over the plain—being wont to bathe in the fair-flowing river—and exulteth; on high doth his head and about his shoulders his mane floweth streaming, and as he glorieth in his splendor his knees numbly bear him to the haunts and pastures of mares; even so swiftly plied Hector his feet and knees, urging on his charioteers, when he had heard the voice of the god."

The sentiments of Homer were a far cry from those of Socrates, as the city-state became the focus of civilization. The anthropocentric character of the Greek culture was reinforced with the increasing density of urban populations. Within the enclave of the polis, society became structured and institutions became increasingly dependent on intellectual prowess in organization, law, and money. The citizens developed greater sophistication in discourse and disputation. They became uneasy with solitude, fearful of the future, and apprehensive over death. These constitute ideal conditions for the prospering of the real courtiers proclaiming the gospel of the virtual gods.

As long as the power and affluence of the polis continue on the upswing, fed by profits from expanding dominance over the outlying regions, pouring into it as the hub of an extended sphere of exploitation, the urban masses live zestfully on. But as soon as the rate of incoming wealth decreases, they become hard put to adjust to the declining slope of the cycles. A pall of pessimism hangs over the skyline like a debilitating smog. Again, the real courtiers of the virtual gods resort to the only approach to social problems they know of, which is the creation of novel and more fabulous virtual gods to rally the inhabitants.

Caught in the turbulence of rapid changes, the townsmen become apprehensive over their ability to maintain the pace. Yet inactivity hangs heavy on their hands. They feel adrift from the whirl. The bothersome boredom compels them to keep busy. Take up traveling, keep the radio blaring, do anything—only not be alone with nothing to do.

The compulsion to do something plays further into the hands of the courtiers of the virtual gods, waxing more importantly than ever in their modern Valhallas, spinning ever more entrancing rituals of worship. The wheel of societal entanglements rolls on and on.

32 **Family** Maintaining a wholesome and happy family life is getting increasingly difficult in the urban American setting. There are many influences working against the unity of the group and love among its members. The impact of tradition and religion on the household is lessening. Adultery among parents is more commonplace. The divorce rate is going up. Drug usage among the younger is more widespread. Government usurpation of family prerogatives and responsibilities is rising. The constitutional emphasis on the individual is being interpreted by many as "Every person for himself or herself." Parents are "deprogramming" children and children are suing parents.

The drive toward exaggerated egalitarianism is being imposed willy-nilly on children and adolescents to such an extent that it is raising havoc with their natural innocence and development. They are being deluged not only by inadvertent TV and other shows but also classroom exercises with thoughts and problems that befuddle and disturb even the most matured of adults. The responsible elementary school teachers, academic theorists, and mass-marketing promoters say that they are educating the children on "relevant social issues in order to better prepare them to participate in a democracy." But, in reality, they are choking the children's emotional capacity to assimilate. It is not surprising that atherosclerosis and ulcers have been increasingly reported among younger adults and adolescents beginning around the late 1950s and that suicide rates have soared for the prepuberty group during the 1970s. According to a World Health Organization report of 1979, 0.5 children out of 100,000 five-to-fourteen-year-olds committed suicide in Sweden in 1971; 13.5 did so in 1976.

The family structure is being endangered not only by the radical elements of the community but also by the conservative. The concern has been expressed by James Hitchcock in 1973 in these words: "the average man fails to notice how much the 'conservative' forces in society also help undermine family solidarity, especially by inculcating a consumer ethic which entices families onto a debilitating and distracting financial treadmill and by enticing them also to their separate pleasures, in comparison with which family activities appear boring and insignificant. He also fails to notice the utter moral neutrality of the 'conservative' capitalistic system, which thrives by keeping people discontented and by creating new 'needs' which it then fills and which is prepared to embrace every kind of innovation once it has been shown profitable."

One of the greatest threats to the unity and happiness of the educated American family is obsessive professional ambition on the part of the parents. The corroding competition between family and work for the father's time and devotion goes on relentlessly. A shaky equilibrium is reached. For births, deaths, major illnesses, a few emergencies, and special occasions, the family comes first. For the rest, the institution. The once loving spouse and fond parent has given way to institutional automation and absentee provider.

The patient wife understands. If the children are going to be brought up in proper style, the father must please the institution. She too is eager for his professional attainments. The institution remains oblivious of the family drama and consumes his sacrifices as a matter of routine. Once in a while the boss gives out with a "Thanks, Jim. Really appreciate it." And the father dashes on with greater fervor than ever.

In the meantime, the women's liberation movement is taking a curious turn. Instead of liberating themselves from the shackles of their former lives in the home, many women are now offering themselves up for the shackles of institutions. They too want the right of being ulcerated in the competitive strife. They, too, demand the power of ulcerating others. To them, this is much preferred to the boredom of holding the family together. The Demon and his high priests are waiting with open arms and drooling mouths to swallow this mass of red-blooded volunteers. Such delicate morsels!

Doubling the number of stress-givers in the arena squares the strain on any one competitor. People are being stressfully crowded so much in the pursuit of their own aspirations and pleasures that they have little time to spare for others. It is no wonder that the aged in America are begrudged; they take up so much time. Two-thirds of the Americans interviewed in a study conducted around 1960 were opposed to the idea of parents living with their children and indicated that they would not provide care for aged relatives. The more educated the person, the more he disliked the thought. The place of the aged in America is not a happy lot. "While we do not burn the villages of the aged, or fill the air with cries of joy over the departed," wrote Ben Seligman, "we do stuff our aged into institutions and boarding houses to let them await death slowly." In view of the fact that only five percent or so of Americans over sixty-five live in extended-care facilities or nursing homes, the picture may be an overstatement. Nevertheless, his point is well taken.

There is nothing particularly noble about tending to the old folks. After all, it is only natural to give medicine and soup to one's parents on their deathbed, just as they had given medicine and milk to him in his crib, and just as he hopes someone will lovingly give him medicine and soup on *his* deathbed when the time comes. It is just simple fairness and decency.

Leo Tolstoy's story comes to mind about a father asking his young son what he was trying to make out of the block of wood, which he had been whittling for some time. "I'm making a wooden bowl, father," said the child, "so that when you get very old, you too can have one to eat from in your own little corner away from our dinner table, just like grandpa is doing now." The unfilial father saw the light and grandfather became a beloved member of the family again.

33 Sweets Charles Lamb chided Robert Lloyd, who had said in a letter that the world "seems drained of all its sweets." In his return note of November 13, 1798, Lamb replied, "At first I had hoped you only meant to intimate the high price of sugar! But I am afraid you meant more. O Robert, I don't know what you call sweet. Honey and the honeycomb, roses and violets, yet in the earth. The sun and the moon yet reign in Heaven, and the lesser lights keep up their pretty twinklings. Meat and drinks, sweet sights and sweet smells, a country walk, spring and autumn, follies and repentance, quarrels and reconcilements, have all a sweetness by turns. Good humour and good nature, friends at home that love you, and friends abroad that miss you—you possess all those things, and more innumerable, and these are all sweet things. You may extract honey from everything . . ."

One chances across many an occasion for the relishing of sweets even in the midst of great difficulties. There is the old Buddhist parable of the traveler who was chased by a tiger to the edge of a cliff. He caught hold of a thick vine and swung over the side. As he looked down, he saw another tiger snarling upward at him from below. As he looked up again, he saw two mice gnawing away at the vine. And right in front of him slightly to the side was a luscious bunch of grapes. Clinging on to the vine with one hand, he reached over, picked the grapes one by one, and plopped them into his mouth. "How delicious!"

34 Interludes

A peculiar urge seems to be gripping many Americans. It is the chase after fun. About $200 billion are being spent annually on recreation and leisure. Ten million Americans travel abroad; five million buy campers; eight million ski; another two million surf.

They crowd the mundane galleries. They frequent the gaudy restaurants with mediocre cuisine. They flock to hear "big name" speakers mouth the patter of ghost writers. They are drawn to cheap allurements. They are swept by the ballyhoo of the "in" crowd—whether it be the one-man show of some recent "genius" or bizarre multi-media phantasmagoria. They end up patrons of poor taste.

A commentary on such dissipations was made by Lucius Beebe in 1958 in an editorial about the multimillionaire Texas rancher who died leaving an estate of $100 million, first editions of *True Police Romances,* 290,000 silver dollars, and forty-one Cadillacs. "If this were an isolated example of eccentricity and tastelessness in men of wealth, it would still be a matter for tears; but when you realize that it is, with slight variations on a witless theme, typical of the generation, it becomes a catastrophe of formidable proportions. . . . Forty-one Cadillacs! If the miserable man had owned forty-one Derby winners or maintained forty-one mistresses, he would have achieved some measure of worldly satisfaction in his wealth; some justification for having been around. As it is, no one need envy him. All he rated in the end was a Cadillac Hearse."

Many people about your age seek diversions of extramarital sex. A questionnaire survey during the 1970s by the American Life Extension Institute showed one out of five executives admitting to extramarital sex. During the first ten years of marriage the most frequent partner is a girl "in the neighborhood." Between ten and twenty years, it is a girl "in the office."

Intra-office sex is convenient and often more delectable than the homespun variety. The price, however, runs much higher than the gold earrings, favored promotions, and expensive dinners. The gossip mill voraciously devours the tidbits and spews them around with delicious exaggerations. The relationship interferes with work efficiency and professional demeanor. When one calls off the liaison, the disagreeable reminder keeps bumping into the other. A former president of Harvard University was reported to have discouraged the practice as he drew the line in explaining the terms of tenure at the venerable institution. "Fornication is not a sufficient cause for the removal of a professor with tenure," he decreed, "but fornication involving the spouse of another faculty member is."

Although it may seem necessary for most executives to continue in the rat race of making dollars, it would seem rather silly for them to join another rat race of spending dollars for dubious fun and risky gratifications at the same time. Do not fall into the common trap of equating standard of living with expenditure of money. In 1979 the *Wall Street Journal* reported that for every dollar spent by Americans on goods and services, the average Frenchman spent sixty-eight cents and the average Japanese spent fifty-six cents. The columnist concluded that the Americans enjoyed the highest standard of living in the world. But is a person eating a sixty-dollar dinner at the *Pavillon* in New York City necessarily enjoying a higher standard of living than another eating a four-dollar one at a campsite beside a mountain stream?

Furthermore, you no longer have the physical stamina in your middle age to keep going night after night, so be more selective about the kind of things on which to spend your spare time. You have experienced the range of human excellence in the arts and entertainments, so be discriminating between the exquisite and the pedestrian. Savor rather than sample. As the seventeenth century scholar Chang Chao puts it, "It is contrary to God's will to eat delicious food quickly, to pass beautiful scenery hurriedly, and to speak of deep sentiments superficially."

Look less and less to externally dependent activities for relaxation and joy. Look more and more to sources within your own control. By way of reminders, here are several.

1 Congenial dining.

American businessmen have already ruined many a midday and evening dinner by converting them into professional meetings. Government officials are extending the practice into the morning. Working breakfasts now constitute status symbols in Washington. Americans are rapidly losing the art of gracious dining.

Delicious food and wine do add to the pleasure. But they need not be expensive. Water is sweet enough a drink among friends—so it has often been truly said. What is necessary is good company. So make it a regular feature of your life to invite a cluster of congenial friends and bring a gaiety of spirit to the table. Remember that the Athenian general Alcibiades of the fifth century B.C. had even forbidden music from his dining room in order not to interfere with the conversation. Let spontaneity take over.

If the company is well chosen, charm and wit are ever present. There is never a trace of vain twaddle, an air of challenging debate, or a polemic of matching skills. When the discussion concerns a philosophical paradox, the guests are speculative in their learning. When it concerns the inflation of the dollar affecting the stability of the nation, they are sound in common sense. When it concerns some vignette of life, they are expansive in exchange. The differences of opinion spark welcomed enlightenment and the pleasantries bond lasting affection. It is during times like this that we realize that what we enjoy most in life is friendship and what we enjoy most in friendship is convivial conversation.

2 Enriching reading.

Many readers avidly immerse themselves in books of all kinds. This devouring is not especially enriching. As John Mason Brown puts it. "The idle people who skip from a love story about ancient Castile, to a fictionalized biography, a volume that seems to promise them a mature mind or a collection of short stories by an author they never heard of merely because a clerk in a bookstore has told them to do so, are wasting their time, though justifying the clerk's pay."

Approach writers of wit and wisdom in an unhurried fashion. Stay for a considerable time with one who has something worthwhile to say. Open your mind without an intellectual sieve of your own to his thoughts and commentaries from a number of angles, so that you can appreciate them in their different ramifications and thereby see the whole. Only in this fashion can you make friendly and conversant contact with him. Before meeting the German author Johann Wolfgang von Goethe in Erfurt in 1808, Napoleon himself had read his *The Sorrows of Werther* seven times.

3 Delightful musing.

The pleasure of musing was described by Alfred E. Newton in these words: "What a delight it is, at the end of a busy day, to throw one's self into an arm chair before a wood fire, and think. No, not think! muse is a better word. I am by no means sure that I've ever thought and I'm not certain that I wish to; looking about me, I see thinkers and it does not appear that they are any wiser or happier than I."

35 Laughter "Big shots" and "big savants" tend to take what they say altogether too seriously. They go about with deeply furrowed brows, as if to suggest that the mark of wisdom is a dour countenance. When they occasionally slip and crack a minor joke, they quickly choke it off with a wry smile to make sure that it does not get out of hand and erupt into undignified laughter. Motse of the fifth century B.C. taught that one should not sing in life nor mourn in death. This appears to be overdoing things. When one wants to sing, is it not natural to sing? When one wants to weep, is it not natural to weep?

The Olympian gods themselves were masters at laughter. There was the incident of Hephaestus trapping his wife Aphrodite in the arms of Ares in his net and calling upon the gods to bear witness. They hurried to the scene and, upon seeing the lovers entangled and imprisoned in situ, roared with laughter and shook the sky. When the young god of war confessed that the love of Aphrodite was well worth being caught that way, even if all of the gods looked on and the net were three times stronger, the gods roared out again.

The only available defense against certain incongruities of fate is laughter. Laughter dissipates the tension of the double bind and releases the elements back into Nature to reform themselves into more sensible combinations. Laughter is kinetic hope. The cloud of frustration is driven off by its burst.

36 **Intellectual snares** Highly educated people are forever digging and stepping into pitfalls of the intellect. The following are among the more fashionable.

Theoretical models are popular expressions of current scholarship. These stress similarities within larger aggregates, as contrasted to uniqueness among individuals. Theory itself is to see events not only simplified but also at a distance. Evil at a distance loses its poison; good at a distance loses its warmth. Everything is reduced to dead statistics and inanimate photographs. Isak Dinesen mentioned that "All sorrows can be borne if you put them in a story or tell a story about them."

The larger the number of theories governing one's life, the more difficult it is for the individual to perceive his true feelings and his true nature. Life is disillusioning to a person only because he chooses to live illusions and then is forced by painful realities to open his eyes. Life is discouraging only because he chooses to live ideals and then is forced by practical necessities to open his mind. Life is despairing only because he chooses to live creatively and then is forced by the Frankensteinian monsters to repudiate his past. The most insidious ramification about the whole business of theoretical guides to conduct is that, pending enlightenment of reality, adherents frequently act on matters of faith with far greater zeal and frenzy than on matters of fact. Susceptibility to theories brings with it a dangerous tendency of unreasonableness, because the reality of unreasonableness itself is readily hidden from sight by a theory of reasonableness.

Theoretical generalizations like "mankind" gain feeling-significance only if calibrated against real individuals. This is illusrated by the reaction of Horace Mann during the dedication of a recreational center for boys. He had told the audience that if all the money and effort that had been expended led to the salvation of just one boy, it would have been worth it. One of the patrons came up to him afterwards and demurred: "Mr. Mann. Weren't you exaggerating a trifle when you said that all our contributions would be worth while if they only saved *one* boy?" Mann shot right back: "Not if he happened to be *my* boy!"

One of the most slippery of traps for oneself as a leader is the rationalization of one's beliefs in emotional and spiritual matters. The individual begins with a moving personal experience and reacts appropriately. Because of some educated reverence of the mind, however, he or she feels compelled to formulate some rational justification. An approved body of doctrines is made available through his or her institution. When others are not in intuitive agreement, he or she resorts to these rationalized arguments to convert them over. As the objections become more varied and numerous, the collection of intellectual fabrications grows increasingly complex. Sooner or later the body of knowledge and speculations leads to self-contradictions. Having used the previous dogmas as a basis of confrontations, he or she cannot repudiate them at this point. So he or she devises even more ingenious and subtle explanations. But the greatest harm is yet to come. After a while, these rationalizations themselves demand consistent expression in action. Then and there the unwitting institutional trap is sprung. Acting in deepest sincerity under the spell, he or she becomes oppressive—arbitrarily to others and arbitrarily to oneself.

One of the cleverest traps for others is the projection of inferences through selected truths. This art is highly polished in politics. During early 1979, the American government was anxiously negotiating a SALT II nuclear arms treaty with the Soviet Union on the one hand and selling it to the American people on the other. As part of the latter campaign, a high government official said in his speech that "To reach these [SALT II] levels [of strategic nuclear arms], the Soviet Union will be required to reduce their overall number of strategic arms. Over 250 Soviet missiles or bombers—ten percent of their strategic forces—will have to be destroyed or dismantled." Upon hearing these words, the listeners got the impression that the Soviet strategic nuclear force of 2500 launchers would be ten percent weaker. But, as the *Washington Post* pointed out, the Soviet Union can merely get rid of its obsolete stock and more than make up for them by adding additional bombs to the launchers permitted by the treaty. The net effect under the treaty could well be a strengthening of the Soviet force by several thousand deliverable nuclear warheads.

Variations of the same theme are not uncommon in the petty bureaucratic manipulations of data by way of extracting information out of context to push one's own programs. There was the case uncovered by the General Accounting Office in the files of a federal research foundation in 1976. The staff summary of a peer review of a proposal read as follows, as submitted to the top executive board for approval: ". . . I am sympathetic to many of the objectives that lie behind this proposal." The actual statement in the critique had read: "While I am sympathetic to many of the objectives that lie behind this proposal, I find myself drawing back from certain essential aspects of it. My objections are partly philosophical and partly pragmatic. Because of these, I count it a serious weakness of the proposal that no discussion of some of these matters was included in the presentation."

These witting sleights of hand are first cousins to the unwitting partialized truths. Partialized truth is, of course, distorted truth, and distorted truth is no truth at all. Yet people are led to believe that partialized truth is still the truth. They continue to feel that with the accretion of each bit of partialized truth, they become freer persons.

The most highly respected among the purveyors of partialized truths today are the learned elite in their license of specialization. The agreeable habit of focusing their endeavors on a single aspect of an event or phenomenon and leaving the integrated whole for others to contend with engenders an equally comfortable sense of partialized social responsibility within the scholarly community. This is the self-circumscribed dedication to the innovative phase of a social process without a prior clarification and communication of the potential or inevitable consequences should it prove successful. *That*—so the new breed of social specialists insists—is for "others" to shoulder. But the "others" are in no position to follow through in their lay ignorance of the deeper implications behind the jargon and curlicues, for example, of scientific writings. The submissive masses are compelled to remain tethered in the welter of partialized truths and fait accomplis.

A case in point is biologists doing research on the in vitro cultivation of human forms. Human eggs are being fertilized in test tubes; the emerging embryos are being transplanted into human wombs; the maturing babies are being delivered. Investigations are continuing toward the ultimate elimination of the need for the human womb in the propagation of the species.

All this is being conducted without any genuine attention to the bioethics involved. Ignored also are the potential aggravation of the social problem of overpopulation, the actual disposition of deformed bodies and mental monsters produced in the trial-and-error experimentation, the empirical practices of test-tube abortions of post-trimester fetuses, the doctrinal matter of when killing a life constitutes murdering an individual, and so on and on.

The aggressive pursuit and implementation of such partialized truths raise two central questions of modern complex democracies: If a person is at liberty to choose but is ignorant of the consequences of his choice, how free is he? If a person is free to pursue his own pleasures while refusing to consider even the more obvious of potentially ineluctable damage to others, how free are the others?

37 Theological games Many people are not entirely satisfied in doing something just because they had been told to do it, or that it makes sense to do it, or that they get paid to do it. They seek some higher rationale to give meaning to the collection of their many little acts. The fulfillment of this subconscious craving is an important factor in the progress of civilization. Most of the social, political, and religious upheavals begin as small coteries offering the stress-laden community an opportunity to develop a new set of myths, dogmas, and rituals with the requisite enthusiasm. The movement can be early Christianity, the Mau Mau uprising in Kenya, or the Islamic overthrow of the Iranian Shah in 1979, for all of them were evangelical in their combination of earthly aims and spiritual passion. By appealing to some higher entity, the leader was able to rally the bickering segments of his followers around a unifying symbol.

For centuries in the West, the God of the established religious hierarchy served as the primary reference for most people. Social values, such as beauty, goodness, truth, and charity, are transcendent only in so far as they can be associated with some kind of divine purpose. As the people became more educated, however, demands arose for a more rationally based connection to God. The ensuing adaptations made God continuous with human beings in terms of the prevailing emphasis on rationality. Otherwise modern man is faced with an unbridgeable gap between him and the transcendent reference of his heritage.

Yet by pressing for the humanness of worship, modern man humanizes the transcendent God and secularizes religion. As soon as man realizes this kind of freedom and begins to consider himself a problem not for God but for himself, he becomes inflicted with an uneraseable uneasiness. This self-problematization perfuses the Western literature. It gives rise to diverse and untraditional interpretations of God.

To Dietrich Bonhoeffer, one can envision "Christianity without religion." He asks the question as to what would happen if people come to feel that they no longer have need of any religion, no sense of guilt, no wish for personal salvation, no requirement for "that hypothesis" of a Christian God. A new Christianity is recommended based on something other than the promise of religion and the sense of insufficiency.

To Rudolf Bultzmann, the mythological element of the New Testament is antiquated and unintelligible to modern man. This refers to attempts to make the Gospel something *more* than bare history, including references to preexistence, miracles, ascension, and incarnation. He proposes a demythologizing program.

This line of thinking inspired the Bishop of Woolwich, John A. T. Robinson, in 1962 to challenge the Christian myth of "God out there," intoning the theme: "the death of God."

Until deliberations of this sort on the transcendent and outward manifestations of divine worship make some significant differences in one's life, however, they remain merely theological games and ceremonial diversions. Consider the case of Mahmud (997–1030), the Sultan of Ghazni in eastern Afghanistan. Before attacking the town of Somnatch in northern India, he knelt in prayer and asked for God's blessing. When he conquered the town, he killed all of the 50,000 inhabitants and carted the wealth off to his capital.

Do not delude yourself by high-flown generalizations and rationalizations. Assess your own realities in terms of tangible measures. The following types are relevant: Regarding friendship, will you betray your closest friend to avoid a contempt-of-Congress citation? Regarding ethics, will you spread rumors about the alleged weaknesses of your associate if this will assure your promotion into the executive vice-presidency, for which you and he are the only surviving candidates?

Words and show are often nothing more than forms of charlatanism. Truth lies in the act.

38 **The Grand Courtier**

The power of the courtiers of the virtual gods was dramatically portrayed by Fëdor Dostoevsky's Grand Inquisitor in *The Brothers Karamazov*.

Fifteen centuries after the Resurrection, Jesus Christ again appeared on earth out of compassion for the suffering people. He quietly walked about the public square, where only the night before an elaborate *auto da fé* had been staged. Everybody recognized him, as He blessed the populace and healed the sick.

Just as Jesus raised the little girl in the coffin back to life, the Grand Inquisitor passed by. He signaled to the guards. "So great was his power and so conditioned and frightened of him were the people that the crowd immediately parted before his guards and amid the sudden silence, the silence of the grave, they seized Him and led Him away."

Christ was then locked up in the dungeon of the building of the

Holy Office. Later that night the Grand Inquisitor visited Him and reminded Him of His statement that "I would make you free."

"Thou didst just see these free men," the Grand Inquisitor continued. "Ay, all this business has cost us dearly. But we have achieved it in Thy name. We have struggled for fifteen centuries to subdue them. Now it is all done. We have succeeded." He reiterated that it was not Christ but the Grand Inquisitor and his cadre who had brought this about. He recounted how arduous a task it was to bring the people to their present threshold of happiness and to their grateful belief that they are utterly free. They have been given bread and compelled to labor for it. Their spare time was filled with songs and innocent dances. Their lives with wives and mistresses were regulated and their sins were forgiven with proper dispensations. For all that "they will submit to us with blitheness and joy. The most excruciating secrets of their conscience—everything, everything!—they will open up to us. We will decide everything for them. And they will joyfully accept our every decision, since it will ease their great anxieties and their anguish of personal decision."

Finally, the Grand Inquisitor pronounced the sentence for Christ trespassing on the Grand Inquisitor's empire and disrupting law and order. He will have his mob build a great bonfire, rake up the embers, and set Christ on it. "For if there is anyone most deserving one of our blazing fires, it is certainly Thou. Tomorrow morning, I shall burn Thee!"

The Captive said nothing but suddenly kissed the Grand Inquisitor on his bloodless nonagenarian lips. The old man shuddered, opened the cell door, and commanded, "Go. And return no more. Never! Never!"

And He departed.

39 Primal belonging The gradual alienation of the selves of human beings from the self of Nature began long ago. The ancient Egyptians and Mesopotamians used a high proportion of mythmaking in dealing with man's suffering, death, and other perennial problems. Their myths encouraged a continuing direct participation in Nature, which included all things and all creatures. The Hebrews, however, reduced the mystical element to a minimum in their more precisely stated religion. In so doing, they segregated God from Nature. To the Egyptians the sun represented all that they could know about God; to the Mesopotamians, the sun was the God of Justice. But to the Hebrew Psalmist the sun was merely an instrument of God. God has transcended Nature.

The practice of intellectual abstractions further eroded the sense of a harmonious totality of man and Nature. Spurred by the critical deliberations of the Greeks, subsequent thinkers isolated rational objectivity from intuitive subjectivity. This was followed by a flood of other distinctions: laws from morality, religious dogmas from personal ethics, public good from private welfare. The disintegration of the intimacy between the individual and Nature accelerated when man-made institutions became formally established as the supreme practical authorities in the conduct of human affairs, thereby displacing the theological God Himself as the *de facto* God on earth. The climax was reached in the twentieth century, when the institution displaced the individual as the unit of social concern and the individual viewed himself as an element of the institution. The insulation of man from Nature became practical as well as theoretical.

An emptiness ensues with the exclusion of Nature from the centrality of our lives. A vacuum that cannot be filled by the artifacts of civilization. Nor by the prolific inventions of science. Not even by the man-fancied God.

More than ever modern man feels an acute loss of something, of which Iqbal had written in the nineteenth century:

> We have a world lost in the depths of our hearts,
> A world which is waiting for its resurrection.

The Persian poet spoke of this eternal world "with renewing flames and renewing leaves, fruits, and principles." He longed for a rediscovery of a primal belonging that binds all people together. His vague Old Consciousness is akin to the *kokoro* of the Japanese. The latter may be regarded as loosely equivalent to God or Godhead. According to Daisetz T. Suzuki, the *kokoro* "also wants to know himself; he did not or could not remain himself eternally absorbed in meditation. Somehow he came out of his isness and uttered a *mantrum,* 'Let there be light!' and lo the whole world leaped out into existence. From where? Nowhere! Out of nothing. Out of the Godhead! And the world is God and God is the world, and God exclaims, 'It is good!' "

The light is still there. You need only raise the shades and let it in. Then as you rediscover the Godhead, the Godhead rediscovers you.

BELONGING WITH NATURE

There is a tendency to think in terms of "man and his environment"—as if the two are separable elements of Nature. They are not, of course, in the complete sense. Herein begins man's egocentric alienation from Nature. You can regain the feeling of being one with Nature by paying special attention to several facets of this relationship. Your self is identified by its impacts on others. Your te is united with the Tao. Your life is infused with a broadly and deeply anchored meaning to the degree of its congeniality with your fellow creatures. This section prompts us not to forget these fundamentals.

40 **Impacts on others** An electron is identified by the track it makes in the cloud chamber, the scintillation on a screen, the electric current in a wire, and other external effects. Similarly, persons are identified by their impacts on others. A hand is beautiful, because it produces beautiful things—a lovely painting, a delicate needlework. An individual is good, because he or she performs good deeds—a starving man fed, a wounded bird cared for. An executive is effective, because he or she gets useful things done—a program realized, a company operating at a loss turned around.

The quality of one's human sensibilities, then, is not gauged by his emotions or exertions, but by the responses of others to his actions. "You see, really and truly, apart from the things anyone can pick up (the dressing and the proper way of speaking and so on), the difference between a lady and a flower girl is not how she behaves, but how she's treated," explained Eliza Doolittle in George Bernard Shaw's *Pygmalion.* "I shall always be a flower girl to Professor Higgins, because he always treats me as a flower girl, and always will; but I know I can be a lady to you, because you always treat me as a lady, and always will."

As an executive you may wish to consider which of two orientations regarding employee welfare is to be a more fitting projection of your true self. One was expressed by the chief executive of General Motors during the 1920s, who said that "industry has every reason to be alarmed at the social, economic and financial implications" of the Social Security bill and by 93 percent of the respondents in a poll of top industrial executives in 1978, who indicated that they were unwilling to pay for the projected increases in Social Security. The other was expressed in the new employee benefit program announced at the same time by the nation's largest apparel company, Levi Strauss: each of its 35,000 employees was to receive one share of stock for each year of service.

The loss of this primary point of reflected reference is the beginning of the loss of one's self. It is for this reason that the prevalent preoccupation of trying to get others interested in oneself and one's own work is certain to aggravate one's self-consciousness and ensure the lasting absence of peace of mind.

The pull of self-centeredness is so strong that it shows up even as one is trying to help others. One wants to make sure that the beneficiary knows who the benefactor is. This, too, can boomerang in unanticipated ways.

The story is told of the great Italian violinist and composer Nicolo Paganini. While he was strolling along the streets one day, he heard an organ grinder playing one of his pieces in such a terrible fashion that he got irritated. He walked up and grabbed the organ from the astonished fellow. Paganini then manipulated the gears, applied the brakes, and otherwise played the piece as it should have been played. "Perhaps, you may want to know who is teaching you how to play this piece," Paganini tried to impress the organ grinder, as he handed back the organ. "*I* am Paganini, its composer!" The next day, Paganini passed the same organ grinder, only to hear him grinding away in the same old way. But on this occasion, there was a large sign over his instrument: *Pupil of Paganini.*

41 **The Tao and the te** According to Taoist philosophy, Tao is the indescribable and unnameable progenitor of all things. The nameless Nonbeing at the Great Beginning gave rise to the One, which is without form. When things obtained from the One that which made them what they are, they came into existence. The Whole as the Way is the Tao and its particularized presence as virtue in the person is the te. Tao is the uncarved Nameless; te is the carved named.

The good life consists of manifesting the te in its unfeigned naturalness. Since Tao and te lie beyond distinctions, the simple life does not involve finger pointing at this or that with frowning faces. When effort is directed toward this or that heroic endeavor, whether it be humanhearted or evil-minded by conventional standards, the simplicity of nondistinction is lost. The person is then being guided by man-made differentiations and is no longer treading the path of the Tao. That person is sidetracked by fragmenting desires and knowledge, is no longer at peace with the universe as Tao nor with himself or herself as te.

An executive walking in the te of the Tao does what comes naturally. He accomplishes much without interfering. He follows the non-dictatorial road to leadership. To rule indiscriminately through rigid laws and orthodox institutions is acting through unnatural impositions. It is attempting to circumvent and restrain the te of individuals, like trying to standardize the height of birds by shortening the legs of the crane and lengthening those of the duck.

By flowing like water according to the nature of things, the te of the person remains one with the Tao. By remaining one with the Tao, he or she transcends the finite contraries and identifies with the infinite. By identifying with the infinite, his or her harmony is no longer relative but boundless in the undifferentiated Tao.

42 **Subsuming and resonating** Just as it is impossible to demonstrate the rigor of a mathematical system from within, so must one go beyond one's own operation to give it meaning and direction. This is accomplished through the principle: subsume yourself and resonate.

In applying the technique of subsuming and resonating, one needs to be clear as to the level of his or her own operational concern and the level and nature of the context in which these operations are imbedded. One then imparts social significance to the operations by subsuming it in the larger context and looking at them from the viewpoint of the larger context as well. Yet since one remains operationally responsible for one's own contributing entity, one must continue to maintain its autonomous identity and vitality. The synergistic benefits are then sustained by constantly resonating one's unit against the context.

Within the immediate context of one's own job, what one does is subsumed into and resonated with the character and purpose of the parent institution. An executive in a wholesale bank, such as the Morgan Guaranty Trust Company of New York, follows, in the phrase of its Chairman Walter H. Page, "a rather special management style." The individual transactions are generally very large, with the rates on its assets not especially costly. Paramount attention is given to protecting the funding by maintaining "a relatively high capital base, so that there should never be a question of the stability and credit standing of the bank." The Morgan Guaranty executive does not try to imitate what the official at the Bank of America does, simply because the latter happens to be the largest bank in America.

The principle of subsuming and resonating is applicable to everything one does. Its use in gauging the state of scientific research may serve as an illustration. The progress of science has now reached the point when the subsuming of the scientific community as an integrant of humanity has become a practical and urgent question for all concerned. If as a scientist, one subsumes oneself as part of humanity, then one's choice of areas of research is greatly influenced by what one as a human being sees as not endangering one's fellow human beings. Furthermore, one welcomes the right of others in having some say in what one is doing, for they, too, are going to be the beneficiaries and/or victims of the consequences. On the other hand, if one does not subsume oneself as part of humanity, then one feels free to indulge in whatever kind of research one's fancy takes. The public at large and its representatives are then regarded as having no business butting their noses into one's own scientific affairs.

By and large most research directors of large institutions have learned the principle of subsuming and resonating, at least pro forma, from their continuous interfacings with society. A typical interaction of this character is their justification of research programs before budgetary officials. A gifted research administrator appreciates the fact that the decisive factor determining the allotment of money to his or her particular program is not its need nor even its scientific contributions per se, but the relative need of the program as compared to others in the overall subsuming context, as judged by the values of the subsuming context alone. Being sensitive to the feelings of the officials within the subsuming context, the research director then presents the supporting brief in such a fashion that there is an explicit answer to the budgetary issue in his or her favor.

In contrast to experienced research executives, scientists as a group have not yet reached this degree of social awareness. The dichotomy is being spotlighted in the current controversy over whether research on genetic engineering is to be controlled or even outlawed. Laboratory experience during the 1970s demonstrated that new viruses and bacteria can be developed by splicing genes together. Various heretofore nonexistent viruses and bacteria have been actually produced. This achievement suggests that, if the research on genetic engineering is allowed to continue as it has in the past, new and uncontrollably virulent-disease-causing agents might wittingly or unwittingly be produced.

Some biologists are calling for a halt to the research. Most workers in the field, however, are insisting on their continued untrammeled freedom of inquiry. A third group is attempting to mediate by offering a set of guidelines for careful experimentation. Guidelines have been issued and already broken in practice. The controversy appears as intractably heated as ever.

In the meantime, the anxiety-laden bystanders are listening to the debate with dismay. If people are convinced that scientists do genuinely embrace the principle of subsuming into humanity and resonating with it, then they will most likely endorse the granting of intellectual freedom without worry that this will lead to their own ruin. But if people suspect that scientists never did and never will so genuinely subsume themselves, they will assuredly overreact to rumblings of Frankensteinian threats and resort to thought-control. The first step in this direction happened in 1977. The Secretary of Health, Education and Welfare asked Congress to enact a genetic engineering research licensing law. This is the nation's first proposed ban on basic biological research. No unlicensed person is to be allowed to do investigations in the field.

Unlike those rugged individualists who refuse to subsume themselves in a higher entity, others go overboard in the opposite direction. They subsume themselves so completely that they fail to resonate as a distinctive element. They forget that unless they maintain their own identity and render some distinctive contribution as individuals, they are not really subsumed but only dissolved. They are as creatively noncontributing as slaves on the plantations of former centuries and sycophants in the front offices of today. Hindus who try to live only in the Brahman and Christians who try to live only for the eternal hereafter are alike incomplete. Only those Hindus who resonate the Atman of the self against the Brahman of the universe and Christians who resonate the this-worldly instants against the other-worldly timelessness are whole.

Only those executives who resonate their actions within the institutions against the rhythms in the Beyond are consummate.

43 **The environment and kinship** Some subtle but significant qualitative change in orientation is taking place in the environmental movement in this country with the establishment of the Environmental Protection Agency. The movement to protect the natural environment originally began with small groups of "nature lovers," like the Sierra Club and the National Audubon Society. The members enjoyed Nature in her unspoiled state. The cry to keep the air pure and the waters unpolluted was uttered on behalf of the smog-stunted trees and the poisoned fish and birds. As the scientists joined the movement and showed the carcinogenic properties of some of the polluting chemicals, the emphasis shifted from empathy with God's creatures to concern over man's health. Safety thresholds for human exposures became the primary criterion of pollution.

Debate over specific government regulations then took the form of what is the optimal trade-off between relative risk of a given pollution to human health and the economic impact of preventive measures. The consent agreement tentatively accepted by the Tennessee Valley Authority and the Environmental Protection Agency in December 1978, for example, was criticized by the Director of the Council on Wage and Price Stability as "an unnecessary cost burden."

Many in the economic sector are not asking themselves whether a given profitable action that pollutes the environment will injure plants and animals, but whether it can withstand the political attacks of the environmentalists, who are now no longer primarily motivated by their former love of Nature, but by the present fear for themselves. Since most members of the latter group have become as self-centered as the business promoters, the whole affair is taking on the tone of a conflict of self-interests.

The paradoxical upshot of the environmental movement and the practical response is the further estrangement of man from his environment. No longer are man and his environment one in Nature. Instead, man has become a "we" and the environment a "they." "They" are to be maintained at a certain standard so that "we" can live better. "We" in turn have become split into two opposing camps—those who want to live more economically affluent in the short haul and those who want to live more biologically healthy in the long run. The rest of Nature has been relegated from the status of kin to that of milieu.

Regain the spirit of kinship in the lusty growth of Nature on her own. Live it. Wade in the clear mountain brook. Breathe the scent of the honeysuckle. Stroll through the drifts of daffodils. See how pleasingly quiet is the land of the wild turkey and how unspoiled is the world of the woodchuck. Immerse yourself in Time, as it comes alive as past in the petals on the ground, as present in the blossom, as future in the bud.

Absorb the sensations of Loren Eiseley as he steeped himself in Time's antiquity in his own revelry among the old trees. "The brown needles and the fallen cones, the stiff, endless green forests were a mark that placed me in the Age of Dinosaurs," he wrote in *The Firmament of Time*. "I move in silence now, waiting a sign. I saw it finally—a green lizard on a stone. We were far back, far back. He bobbed his head uncertainly at me, and I reined in with nostalogic intent, for a moment, to call him Father; but I saw soon enough that I was a ghost who troubled him and that he would wish me, though he had not the voice to speak, to ride on. A man who comes down the road of time should not expect to converse—even with his own kin. I made a brief, uncertain sign of recognition, to which he did not respond, and passed. Things grew more lonely."

And so complete your own self through its relations with fellow creatures. "Once again, I set down the core of what I continue to believe," Henry Beston described the feeling during his solitary living on the Great Beach of Cape Cod. "Nature is a part of our humanity, and without some awareness and experience of that divine mystery man ceases to be man. When the Pleiades and the wind in the grass are no longer a part of the human spirit, a part of very flesh and bone, man becomes, as it were, a kind of cosmic outlaw, having neither the completeness and integrity of the animal nor the birthright of a true humanity."

44 **Solitude** Right solitude is not an escape from the hurly-burly world. Neither is it the meditation over one's actions of the day and reflection as to what should have been done differently. These practices are highly desirable on their own. But the solitude under discussion is one of free access in the naturalness of open awareness.

While saints and sages of all cultures have advocated variants of this kind of solitude, the Japanese have incorporated it into their everyday living, much more so than most other peoples. They maintain a quiet room for the purpose. The structure is about twelve feet square, thatched with straw, and sparsely furnished—perhaps with a vase, a small table with incense, and a cushion on the matted floor. The unobtrusive hut blends into the natural surroundings. Sitting within the hut, the person becomes one of its integrated elements, fused with the birds singing outside, the waters murmuring in the stream nearby, the trees swaying overhead. All are part of the same conversation.

Ideal settings of this kind are unfortunately denied most inhabitants of the modern Western metropolis. But they are not essential. All that is needed is a half-dreamy yielding. A comparable state of being was extolled by Marcel Proust in his piece about an artist in contemplation over a double-cherry tree. The artist attempts to shut off the distractions of the outer world as he stops before the tree and strives to regain the feeling that had just come to him. He tries to hang on to it, as translated by Sylvia T. Warner, "as he was walking through the public gardens it caught his eye, along on its grass-plot, so covered with white blossoms that it seemed as though countless little pellets of snow were still clinging, as after a thaw, to the tips of its branches. He stands in front of it, but what he is in search of is certainly something over and above the tree, since he no longer feels what he had felt—when, all of a sudden, he feels it afresh; but he cannot fathom it, and is at a loss." It seems that the poet is gazing into both the cherry tree and his mind at the same time. What he sees also appears to be blotted out from time to time "by something within him, so that he has to wait for a moment, just as he has to wait a moment when a passer-by blots out the double-cherry." It is in this way that the poet maintains his "communication with the beauty of the whole world" and finds happiness in "those rarified moments which seem to him authentic existence."

You will find that all disturbances of financial anxiety, religious disappointment, vengeful anger, competitive greed, selfish ratcheting, expedient betrayal, nimble-mouthed jabbing, and double-faced power disappear during these periods of authentic solitude. Nothing evil, degrading, and disingenuous intrudes. The reason is simple.

Discord arises only when special effort, particularly with an egocentric ax to grind, is exerted, thereby disturbing the natural state of harmony. When the whole is in discord, so is the part; when the part is in discord, so is the whole. When left alone, the natural state of Nature is harmony throughout; that of man is harmony within.

Solitude is an effortless and unfeigned congruency between Nature and self. One cannot help but emerge more meaningfully complete and rejuvenated.

BEHAVING AT WORK

This section covers a host of behavioral manifestations that reflect the style of the philosopher-executive in the workplace. They fall into four groups, namely, (1) maintaining freedom from the external pressures of competing peers and incarcerating work and from the internal propensities toward neurotic ambitions and cynicism, (2) relating to co-workers as kinsmen in Nature, (3) preparing the way for the next generation through a sharing of oneself, and (4) caring for people as an essential factor in executive plans and actions.

45 **Peers** Out of practical considerations, one needs to pay attention to the standards set by professional peers. It may be well to bear in mind at the same time that in many respects, "peers" is nothing more than an euphemism for competitors, infected with the humbug of keeping up with the Joneses. Each one vies against fictitiously inflated Joneses, and the real Joneses vie against fictitiously inflated him. Each successive superfluity imprisons them all into deeper financial and psychic debt, as the profiteers of simulated affluence seduce them onto the blundering cascades of vanity.

The folly is widespread and deeply ingrained in human character, as depicted by Ruth Benedict's report on competitive gift-giving among members of the Kwakiutl tribe. During the ceremonial feast, a tribesman presents a gift, say, fifty blankets, to another, who then reciprocates with a larger number of blankets. The former, in turn, responds with a still larger number. The escalation goes on until one of them loses face by not going the other one better. The drive to keep up is so irresistible that it is not rare for tribesmen to plunge themselves into bankruptcy and even suicide.

The same syndrome is seen frequently at the corporate level. Instead of being themselves, corporations, too, try to keep up with each other. This tendency among conglomerates had been criticized in 1967 by John R. Beckett, the president of a leading corporate acquisitor, Transamerica Corporation. "There's a great danger of people . . . trying to do what we're doing, and getting themselves completely overextended," he observed. "They're using too much of debt securities . . . paying too high a price to acquire something, and pyramiding. They could eventually get into very serious difficulties."

Let your peers pattern their respective lives to the images projected by The Demon. But shape your own life yourself. Should your behavior resemble theirs for a period of time within a circumscribed area, this would not have resulted from an a priori adoption of the peers' norms on your part. Rather, it would have emerged from the natural interaction of your own self with the total setting—a quasi-equilibrium in the value-reality-power coordinates.

There is no more reliable an index of your personal freedom than the reciprocal of your automatic responsiveness to peers.

46 **Neurotic ambitions** For some time you have been observing the lionized leaders of modern society. You have seen how these contemporaries of yours clench their teeth and fists in uncompromising dedication and undeviating resolve; how they throw magnanimity, compassion, and reasonableness to the winds; how they demand of themselves, of family, of all; how they let friendships not stand in the way of advancement; how they rather suffer the most hideous tragedy by love, love, love, love—or hate, hate, hate, hate—than stand aside uncommitted. They constitute the backbone of the tremendous achievements of institutions. They drag the molasses-masses along by the sheer force of tenacity.

Then there is the larger numbers of emulators, partly envying and partly failing. They become increasingly anxious with time over their own meager attainments, job insecurity, decreasing stamina, and death. They belong to that lineage of the maladjusted, doomed never to find personal peace. For the *Lieh Tzu* had warned over 2000 years ago that the desire for long life, reputation, rank, and wealth lead to the fear of ghosts, men, power, and punishments. They are fugitives from themselves; their lives are determined by externals. Wherefore, the old book advises: "But those who follow their destiny do not desire long life. Those who are not fond of honor do not desire reputation. Those who do not want power desire no rank. And those who are not avaricious have no desire for riches. Of this sort of men it may be said that they live in accordance with their nature."

Those who want are the slaves of those who have. Those who want most avidly are enslaved most readily. Only those who want not are free.

47 **Beggars all** Witness the people throughout the world kneeling before their God and chanting the most flagrantly selfish supplications, the politicians double-talking to the unwashed all over the country for votes, the scholars lecturing eloquently 10,000 miles away from home for the audience's applause, the Nobel laureates polishing their research proposals to the Ford Foundation, the salesmen hawking their wares, the panhandlers extending their palm for some coffee. All are beggars.

A general and high official of the eighth century, Yuan Chieh, recorded how his associates were embarassed and perplexed by his befriending a beggar off the street. Yuan explained that being a gentleman, he sought the company of gentlemen. "This beggar, I have discovered, is quite a cultivated gentleman. In fact, I am honored by his friendship." The explanation only left them more puzzled than before. So Yuan related how the beggar had described that he wanted to merge with the urban people and be one of them. "People don't like you if you pretend that you are peculiar or different. I beg because I am poor. There is no shame in it."

"We all beg," Yuan went on, as translated by Lin Yutang. "People all around us beg every day, and beg more shamelessly. Some beg for official posts, some for marriage to a family of some social standing. Have you ever seen their faces when they beg? Some beg the servants of the influential families to help them; some beg the door-keeper or the maids in order to get in, with sweat on their brows. The poor beg the rich and the rich beg the poor; the powerful beg the common man and the common man beg the powerful, . . . Prisoners beg to have their sentences commuted and sick men beg to be permitted to live a little longer. . . . How many men beg their wives at home? How many beg at the temples? How many beg their own servants at a certain crisis to do them a little favor?"

One station in life differs from the next in this respect only in that it provides a more or less accepted and/or remunerative set of conditions in which to beg. What difference does it make whether one person begs with more elegant trappings than another? Is the former, on that account, entitled to be proud and the latter compelled to be ashamed?

To Yuan's associates, there is a difference. To Yuan, there is none.

48 **Reasonableness** There is no greater human compliment that one executive can pay another than to say that he or she is a reasonable person to deal with. There is no better way of getting along with people than being reasonable. If people are guided in their social relations more by reasonableness than by the loose talk about justice, duty, responsibilities, and other institutional cliches, the world would be a much better place to live.

Furthermore, the straight line is not always the most effective path to corporate goals. It is true that the straight line is the shortest distance between two points. But functional efficiency often calls for the incorporation of the curve. As an anonymous Chinese writer reminded us some centuries ago, the arrow is straight, but the bow is curved; the mast is straight, but the sails are curved. It is more constructive as a rule to convey a circuitous hint to the boss rather than a blunt criticism.

The reasonable person does not try to "dominate" events or "control" situations. The reasonable person is aware that no one person and no one element can "control" the situation, of which it is only a part. To attempt to forcibly control means being out of tune with reality and to become vexed, anxious, and finally overwhelmed when the situation does not respond as expected. The reasonable person "masters" the situation by not losing his or her wits to it. He or she does not hack away at his or her own spirits like a woodsman chopping trees in the forest. The reasonable person is never disputatious. He or she is neither so brusque as to interrupt others nor so thin-skinned as to be offended when interrupted. He or she remains calm, well-poised, and ever ready to make his significant inputs when the situation invites his or her contributions. Above all, the reasonable person does not cause others to lose face. Averell Harriman was highly respected as an international negotiator because he was always able to come up with face-saving resolutions of complex disagreements. By so doing, the reasonable executive exercises the greatest economy of effort. His or her own life is enhanced. As Li Mi-an of the sixteenth century summarizes the case, "flowers in half-bloom are the prettiest . . . horses with reins at half-slack trot best."

One practical indication of your own reasonableness as a manager is the manner of your dismissals. Do you inform the individual as to the real reason so that he or she may correct his or her shortcomings in a new start elsewhere? Do you assist him or her in getting reestablished, especially when the reasons are perfectly human failings? Do you provide ample lead time and separation pay? And do you heed the old Chinese proverb: When friends part there's no need for harsh words?

The former president of Avis Corporation, Robert Townsend, related how he went about discharging one of his officials. As mentioned in his book, *Up the Organization,* he became suspicious that the personnel vice-president was having an affair with one of the executive secretaries. When all three secretaries in the front-office suite got a raise, he decided to do something about it. First to get the proof. "Suppose it were me," Townsend thought to himself. "Suppose my boss called me in and told me I was fired and why. If I were innocent, I'd go off like a roman candle. If I were guilty, I'd sheepishly ask, 'Whom did you get the story from?' " So he called the person in and told him he was dismissed and why. Townsend related what happened: "He lowered his eyes and asked, 'Who told you that story?' He was a good man. I helped him start again a little way from temptation in another company."

The ultimate test of reasonableness arises in one's dealings with his enemies. The legend of the Hindu god Vishnu is enlightening in this regard. The great serpent Kaliya had set out to destroy the world. When Vishnu defeated the great serpent, the latter justified his insurrection in these words: "Since you have created me with strength and poison, I have behaved accordingly. If I had not acted the way I did I would have violated the laws you laid down from every creature according to its kind. I should have challenged the order of the universe." After listening to his line of argument, Vishnu decided that under the circumstances annihilation of the demons would have been unreasonably severe a penalty. So he simply decreed a boundary between them and the human race.

49 **Limit of elasticity** At any given point in time, there is a certain play available for the exercise of personal ambition and institutional changes without destructive turbulence. Many executives in their anxious climb to power pay insufficient attention to the limit of elasticity. As a result, their lives are continually disrupted not only by unnecessary strife but unproductive upheavals.

There is the case of the eager young executive who assumed the presidency of one of the largest soap and detergent companies in the world in 1950. He was intent upon making an immediate and major impact upon the coporation and the community. But the resulting uproar soon proved too choking for the board of directors to digest. His career with the company came to a premature end.

The more astute managers retain a sensitive barometer as to what the climate can accept and modulate their inputs accordingly. The handling of government relations provides an example. Acting as the Washington representative in the 1970s of New York's Manufacturers Hanover Trust, John R. Price, Jr. maintained a careful balance between keeping the relevant federal bodies informed formally and systematically and detaching his own agency from day-to-day minutiae. His full-time staff of two persons was not even based in Washington. He had learned that a "heavy Washington presence runs the risk of legislative overkill. Legislators and their staff tire of being badgered by interest groups taking predictable, ideological positions on issues. So when we do show up on the Hill to present our position on some measure, they know we're concerned and they'll listen."

Sol Chaikin, the president of the International Ladies Garment Workers' Union, always recognized the limitations of the industrial context in which his workers operate. It is a labor-intensive business, employing the working poor and underprivileged. They cannot hope to share the gains of increasing productivity in the capital-intensive sectors. They cannot expect to earn the $9 an hour, plus substantial fringe benefits, of the autoworkers in the Big Three companies in 1979. To force such demands upon the smaller clothing producers would be driving them into bankruptcy with the concomitant loss of jobs. The enlightened leader therefore searches for other means of obtaining the basic levels of pensions and protections. The laws of the land might prove more rewarding than collective bargaining with frail industries.

Seasoned executives are not only aware of the quantitative limitations to the changes that can be effectively and safely introduced within any span of time but also the qualitative ones as well. There is a boundary even in the doing of "good," beyond which a prudent executive will not go. A commonly bandied-about subject of this kind is the so-called "corporate social responsibility." As Henry Ford II, the Chairman of Ford Motor Company, pointed out in 1978, "a corporation is not an all-purpose mechanism. It is a specialized instrument designed to serve the economic needs of society and is not equipped to serve social needs unrelated to its business operations." There is no question but that, as John D. de Butts, Chairman of A.T.&T., puts it, "business health and responsible social behavior go together." The crux is: "How much can we effectively do? . . . What projects are best left to government or voluntary efforts? That such questions are inevitable and unending is not in the least surprising." Over and beyond a certain judicious contribution, the major issue is no longer one of "corporate social responsibility" but that of the desirability of the corporation being transformed into, in Noam Chomsky's phrase, "benevolent despots."

Too much of anything becomes too bad. To paraphrase Paracelsus, it is the dose that makes the poison. "Reversal is the nature of the Tao"—so said Lao Tzu.

50 **Work commitment** There is a widely held belief among educated people that one's profession and work should constitute the principal source of self-expression and realization. Such worship of work is conducive to maximum social progress. It makes institutional exploitation of human beings to the limit of their endurance that much easier. This, of course, pleases The Demon no end.

Basically, employment is nothing more than a contract between two parties. For a fair amount of one's energy, time, and competence, the institution returns a certain payment in terms of money, commendations, and enjoyment. Nowhere in the implied as well as written job sheet is there any reference to enslavement by the payer. Nor is there any mention to self-fulfillment for the payee. Since so many of one's waking hours are spent at work, however, it is only sensible to make it as pleasant and as productive as feasible for one's associates and oneself. But this is a far cry from constituting the work setting as the chief source of satisfaction and creativity in living. The fact is that the more a person frees himself from the bondage of work, the less is that person disturbed by the vicissitudes of the boss, the arbitrariness of the institution, the disagreeableness of the assigned tasks, and the inevitable failures that occur from time to time.

By placing work in the proper scheme of things, it becomes merely one of the many activities that must be undertaken in the process of living. Breathing is certainly more essential than work, yet one does not speak about "commitment to breathing" like one speaks about "commitment to work." One just breathes as usual—that is all there is to it. If one must walk to the grocery store to pick up some food, one just walks and gets there—that is all there is to it. If, as a commander of a regiment, one has to fight, one just fights—that is all there is to it. So if one has to work to earn a living, one just works—that is all there is to it.

There is an obvious essentiality to do a certain minimum of quantity and quality of work, just as there is to do a certain minimum of walking to the grocery store. But this does not preclude you from exercising some kind of detachment about your work, just as you do about your walking to the grocery store. Or from not becoming bored with work, just as you are not bored with walking to the grocery store. This detachment would contribute much to your relative equanimity when the big boss decides to assign a new mission to someone else, to transfer one of your functions elsewhere, or to terminate one of your larger projects—as happens not infrequently.

Furthermore, just as you do not huff and puff in walking to the grocery store, so do not stretch your capacities to the limit at work. Except in an emergency, accept a position or plan an objective that can be credibly met with only a portion of your abilities and energies. Moderate your enthusiasms for institutional challenges and limit your scope to the plausible. Remind yourself repeatedly that no matter how superior a person you may be, you can never satisfy all the ever-expanding demands placed upon you by The Demon and his agents. Show the good sense, therefore, to leave some of the world's tasks to your fellow human beings and future generations.

Once you keep well within the comfortable side of the stress limit, your poise acquires an assuaging stability. There is no need for a mask of excellence to conceal your natural makeup. There is no apprehension over potential crises, for you can always put on a sudden surge of concentration and energy out of your large accumulated reserve. You are well on the way to the nine virtues, recorded by Kao Yao in the *Book of History:* the combination of affability with dignity, mildness with firmness, frankness with respect, executive ability with reverent caution, docility with valor, tolerance with discrimination, straightforwardness with gentleness, boldness with sincerity, and courage with righteousness.

There are psychiatrists who would say that the absence of desire for great achievements is the consequence of the influence of parents who had a strong subconscious determination of not letting their children grow up. Then there are the driving people who would castigate such, to them, lukewarm dedication. Let them decry, for their criteria of common sense are different. Do not let your own life be governed by these externals. The good life, after all, is never a state of strain. Perfection comes annealed.

The common argument is raised: "What if *everybody* adopts this outlook on work? Would that not be bad for people?" In the highly unlikely event that this hypothetical situation did come about, there would be a decline in the absolute rate of material progress. Obviously, ten executives operating at a moderate pace will not drive the production as high as ten executives under relentless pressure. But let us examine the underlying assumption implicit in the iffy question. This is that continuing and even accelerating economic growth is a basic good for the nation and the individual.

The fact remains that increased production capacity in either goods or knowledge is not the limiting factor in alleviating suffering in the world at large. No further progress in the design and output capacity of automobiles, ships, and planes is required to distribute adequate food to all the hungry mouths on earth. No further progress in medicine is required to bring major relief to sick bodies in the ghettoes. No further progress in theology is required to bring peace of mind to anguished souls in the suburbs.

But further progress in space sciences is needed to add a hyper-dimension to holocaust in future wars. Further progress in manipulative psychology is needed to bring a superautomatic responsiveness of the masses in future tyrannies. Further progress in objective learning is needed to bring an overriding insensitivity to spiritual and aesthetic values in future materialism.

There should be little cause for guilt feelings on your part, therefore, because of your leavening sanity. There will be that many fewer ulcer and cardiac patients in the hospitals, less pollution of the air, decreased fatalities on the highway, reduced social conflicts throughout the world, and more oil and other capital assets left for your great grandchildren.

Furthermore, since gentle and gracious, good and tranquil people will continue to provide a fair day's work for a fair day's pay, steady progress will go on. Instead of the material progress being reduced below the essential threshold, it would more likely be brought into a rate, which is more compatible with a harmonious introduction of new products and practices, well-tested and deliberately analyzed ahead of time with respect to human consequences. The world itself will flow on more equably than before.

51 **Avocation** Many individuals find absorbing freedom from the troubles of the workplace in a hobby of some kind. The most popular hobbies in America belong to the collection variety. There are three million stamp-collectors in this country. The second largest group consists of 400,000 collectors of handmade glass. Others concentrate on coins, matchbox covers, chinas, theater programs, antique furniture, or other items. The wide appeal may be due in part to the acquisitive habit, overflowing from the work environment. Some retired people find an extra attraction in the commercial aspect of their hobbies. Leather working, pottery, gem cutting and polishing, needleworking, copper enamelware, quilting, restoring old homes, and the like often bring a few extra dollars to augment the low pensions.

For the person blessed with more than average insight and talent who is seeking a broader-based serenity, another class of avocation is worth considering. A carefully chosen avocation of this type would strengthen one's free and intimate association with Nature and sustain one's sense of primal belonging. Examples are landscape painting, wood carving of bird and animal groupings, researching myths and folklores, writing fables, and composing poetry. As a minimum, the optimal avocation would meet three conditions. The first is the presence of an open and reciprocal sensing of Nature, which increases one's empathy in her ways. The second is the nondefiling of the environment of Nature. The third is the absence of commercial motivation.

A person with an appropriate avocation of this kind suffers much less from his or her main supports upon retirement from active work when the time comes. Retirement actually gives this person the opportunity of devoting more hours on the interest which had long since been the more enduring source of inner gratification. Through this means, he or she and Nature have been maintaining a private dialogue over the years in an activity that was always beyond the direction of The Demon and His agents. Furthermore, no matter how badly things turn out in the office, they can never depress his or her morale below the baseline of his or her avocation. There is thus maintained a continuing psychic springboard on which he or she can bounce back.

In some respects, this pattern of living resembles that of the high officials of Imperial China. They spent the afternoons away from the office devoting themselves to painting, calligraphy, poetry composition, and amateur archeology, searching for highly prized bronzes, stones, and stela with ancient inscriptions. Participation in these avocations afforded them a sense of continuity with their ancestors of the infinite past as well as their descendants to come in the infinite future in a universe beyond themselves. They succeeded in an accommodation between the person and the institution, whereby Nature was intimately included. As Joseph R. Levenson had put it in *Modern China and Its Confucian Past,* "In earlier times, as the old saw has it, a man might be 'a Confucianist in office and a Taoist out'—indulge with part of his being a Confucian passion for the ordering of social life, and the other part seek, or affect to seek, the Taoist harmony of man immersed in nature, as distinct from the Confucian harmony of men among masses of men. Together, Confucianism and Taoism made the whole man, the one implying a testimonial to civilization and the values and goals of social life, the other release from society and social concerns. The common thread of harmony tied them together."

It is as natural for a person to have an avocation, as Chang Chao said in the seventeenth century, as it is for flowers to have butterflies, hills to have springs, and rocks to have moss.

52 Reservoir of patience "How much interior patience and humility a servant of God may have cannot be known as long as he is contented," wrote Francis of Assisi. "But when the time comes that those who ought to please him go against him, as much patience and humility as he then shows, so much has he and no more."

When the Polish pianist and premier Jan Paderewski was effusively complimented by a lady for his patience, he replied, "I have no more patience, Madam, than anyone else. I merely *use* mine."

53 Occupational stress In your role as an executive, do not mislead yourself by your own institution's proclamations about its concerns for the well-being of the employees. In most of the espoused programs of institutions in general, getting the institutional goals met comes first. Getting it met more efficiently comes next. Diminishing personal pain and anguish comes third, as part of the calculations on productive labor. Even when institutions appear to be committed to reducing work stresses, the primary motivations are usually other than compassion for the human person involved. It is only that institutional objectives can be achieved more efficiently over the long run if certain apparently humanitarian actions are taken. The point is well made in the short story by the Turkish writer Hanjarlioglu.

All through the hot night, Rejeb could not sleep. He sat up in bed, looking at the weather-beaten back, the sunburnt neck, and the sorrowful face of his wife, breathing heavily with an occasional groan. He seemed to be oppressed with an indescribable feeling of some kind. So he got up and walked around the village. The beets had been planted; the animals had been taken care of; the people had been friendly. He could not find a reason for his uneasiness as he dozed off on the damp ground. When he awoke, he noticed that his wife had already watered the cattle for the day and prepared fresh dough. After breakfast by himself he had nothing to do but visit the coffeehouses and play cards. But still he could not rid himself of the disturbing feeling, as he decided to check the fields.

The sun was fiercely hot when he reached his wife, digging away at the parched earth. When he inquired about the progress, the lady reported that there were still three acres to be planted. "What?"

shouted Rejeb. "Three acres to go? What the hell have you been doing all last week?" But the woman was too frightened to answer. She trembled like a leaf and panted like a dying beast. Her eyes were inflamed from the glaring sun and reflected the misery of mankind.

Suddenly, Rejeb felt crushed. He realized the cause of his heavy heart. It was the terrible hardship of his wife. He dropped his eyes from remorse, slowly turned around, and decided to do something about it. The next evening, Rejeb came back from the store with two lanterns. He looked at his wife and said, "It is too hot for you to work under the scorching sun. Too much strain. Take these lanterns. From now on, you can work during the cool nights instead."

54 **The little thoughtfulnesses** Most of the cheer throughout this world flow from little gestures and sincerities. The composer and musical director Meredith Willson furnished us a model of a warmhearted person spreading sunshine all around. Max Terr was forever searching for things that just fit their intended purpose, not necessarily expensive but just right. He would always remember his friends in the process and passed on what useful tidbits he himself finally succeeded in finding. There were the perfect pencil for a composer, the ideal lamp for a musician, and the tasty cookies, referred to by his friends as "Maxie's cookies." After Terr's death, Willson reminisced how "not a day passes that isn't a pleasanter day because of the things he left behind him. I have his particular kind of pencil in every pocket of every suit, on the desk, on the night table and on the piano. Couldn't live without them. I have the light with the flexible stand Maxie insisted I buy, so I no longer strain my eyes. . . . In every room of our apartment there are memories of Max Terr."

There are thousands of opportunities within your own jurisdiction to disperse little packets of joy. A word of encouragement to a youngster, a pat on the back of a deserving subordinate, a memorandum to an associate acknowledging his or her contributions to your projects. When you give a raise to one of your assistants, invite that person into your office for a cup of coffee, telling the good reasons for the recognition, how you appreciate the fine efforts, especially when he or she went out of the way to extricate a fellow employee in difficulty without saying anything about it to anyone. An extra luster of meaning is thereby added to the fact of a fatter paycheck.

When someone makes a worthwhile suggestion in a meeting, grace your reply with a personal compliment, such as: "Your proposal is certainly worth considering. It reminds me of that wonderful idea of yours two years ago, which resulted in the complete redesign of our production line in the South Plant." Let your wit show the same kind of sparkle emitted by Charles MacArthur, when he first met Helen Hayes and offered her a bag of peanuts with the spontaneous remark that he regretted they were not emeralds.

When you visit the field installations, be sure to allow time for personal contacts with as many individuals as feasible. Introduce yourself to the apprentice machinist, smile, repeat the name, ask about his or her family and work. All it takes is a few extra minutes and you will have left another person slightly happier in your wake.

The matter of names is important. During the 1953 uprising in the Soviet prison at Norilsk, one of the inmates protested to the Moscow official dispatched to the scene. On behalf of his fellow prisoners, he demanded a minimum level of humane treatment, such as no more ten hours of forced labor without a noonday meal. Above all, no more being called by numbers, like cattle. "We have names!" he shouted. Francesco Sforza, the Duke of Milan in the fifteenth century, endeared himself to his soldiers by remembering the names of their horses.

Be especially thoughtful in your dealings with workers in distress. When a subordinate comes into your office with a grievance of some kind, be sure that you listen patiently and attentively, so that he or she is able to get it completely out of his or her system. Encourage him or her to go over the entire situation again, so that you can understand the total problem in its complete perspective. After that, ask a few questions in a calm and empathetic manner to clarify some of the points that remain confused in your mind and probably in his or hers as well. By this time he or she would have worked off much of the visceral anger and be ready to resolve the grievance with a much less emotional perception, and you yourself would have dissipated your initial irritation at his or her questioning the fairness of your procedures.

55 Nonadversary spirit Adversarial practices do speed accomplishments in many areas. They stimulate a continuing revitalization of otherwise stagnating institutions. This, in turn, results in broader benefits over and beyond those possible through more passive attitudes. The unrelenting demand to claim one's due has led to much of social justice and welfare in the last century.

At the same time, when adversary proceedings are allowed to get out of hand, they give the clever person, the unkind person, the aggressive person, and in particular the person who can hire all of them a savagely unfair advantage. The inarticulate, the considerate, the retiring, the poor soul who cannot engage even a tongue-tied spokesman is always outmaneuvered and outgunned. Before too long, the latter realizes in his or her defeats that "adversary" is the name of the game. In many cases, the only avenue apparent to the desperate is crime and violence. It is thus that a people become litigious.

These are fine-sounding generalities. Their real meaning in your own life, however, become manifested only when reduced to practice. Ask yourself: Will you strain your friendship over some professional disagreement? Will you voluntarily let your close friend and associate, who is having difficulty meeting a sales quota, have one of your $100,000-a-year accounts and arrange for the transfer without his or her ever knowing about it? Will you exaggerate the performance of your product ten percent above its capacity in order to close a $1,000,000 contract?

One can even see an adversarial and nonadversarial difference in the meting of punishment. The difference lies in the imputing of blame. As an upholder of the law, you may justly punish adolescent looters. But do not blame them. To blame them is one-sided. They, too, have *their* side. This is exemplified in the following incident during the 1967 urban riots in the United States, as reported in *Time* magazine. "One booty-laden youth said defiantly, 'That don't look like stealing to me. That's just picking up what you need and going.' Gesturing at a fashionable hilltop where many well-to-do Negroes live, he said, 'Them living up in View Park don't need it. But we down here, we do need it.' "

"Everything has two handles: one by which it may be borne, another by which it cannot," said Epictetus. "If your brother acts unjustly, do not lay hold on the affair by the handle of his injustice, for by that it cannot be borne; but rather by the opposite, that he is your brother, that he was brought up with you, and thus will lay hold on it as it is to be borne."

56 **Paving of the way for others** When the time comes, be selflessly conscientious in paving the way for your successors, so that they will enjoy a better chance for more impressive success than you. A commendable standard is Hermann Hesse's Rainmaker in *Magister Ludi.*

After an abnormally long drought, the Rainmaker called his son Turu and told him that things had not been going well. The devils seemed to be against him. It looked as if the Rainmaker will have to forfeit his own life in order to improve the situation. He therefore counseled his son that when the time comes, Turu is to promptly assume the role of Rainmaker. His first task is to order cremation of the body and dispersal of the ashes over the field. "The evil spell will then be broken," he predicted. "Be sure that no one seizes the tribe's corn stores. The punishment for this must be death. Things will get better next year and the people will say that it is good that we have a new young Rainmaker."

As the drought continued and despair hung over the community, occasional threats and curses were cast at the Rainmaker and demands made for the sacrifice of the tribal mother. The old Rainmaker decided that the time was ready to take the final step. With the permission of the tribal mother, he called a meeting of the people. As Turu dressed in ceremonial robes stood next to him, the Rainmaker declared: "I have been your Rainmaker for many years and I have discharged my duty to the best of my ability. The devils have set themselves against me and I shall be successful no longer. I have therefore offered myself up as sacrifice. The devils will then be satisfied. My son Turu will be your new Rainmaker. Now slay me, and when I am dead obey the advice of my son! Live well!"

The old Rainmaker then suggested that Maro be the person to kill him. Maro had been agitating against the Rainmaker and for the death of the tribal mother. But as he stood with his ax before the Rainmaker, the latter stared at him. He cowered and was unable to strike. He threw the ax down and disappeared shamefully into the crowd. The tribal mother then beckoned to a village elder, who had known the Rainmaker since childhood. The elder gave a curt and friendly nod to the Rainmaker, who willingly closed his eyes and lowered his head. The old man swung the ax and the old Rainmaker was dead.

Turu, the new Rainmaker, took over without a word. He motioned for the pyre. The people obeyed and Turu performed his first official act of firemaking with the two consecrated sticks.

The people have been served with new hope. The evil element in their midst has been neutralized. The successor has been given a good start. They respected the old man for his selflessness. They loved him for his love even to the sacrifice of his own life. They said farewell with traditional propriety. Everybody felt right about the transition. The old Rainmaker departed a philosopher-executive of the highest order.

57 **Institutional accommodation** Your proteges on the threshold of their professional life are faced with the basic social fact and personal challenge of the times: The institutions are in command, and your proteges need to accommodate accordingly without sacrificing their selfs in the process.

As members within the institutional milieu, they experience things that have not been stressed in their college classes. The words about goods and services in the charter of a corporation do not intimate the impersonal treatment of human beings. The words about scholarship in the catalogue of a university do not intimate the deep anxieties among the faculty. The words about charity in the sermons of a church do not intimate the sanctimonious intolerance rained upon those of opposite faiths.

Once your proteges begin to cast aside the sentimental credulity of their earlier days, they stand a chance of seeing through the verbal cosmetics of eloquent and persuasive speakers. Like Ralph Waldo Emerson, they anticipate the arguments. "I hear a preacher announce for his text and topic the expediency of one of the institutions of his church. Do I not know before hand that not possibly can he say a new and spontaneous word? Do I not know that, with all this ostentation of examining the grounds of the institution, he will do no such thing? Do I not know that he is pledged to himself not to look but on one side—the permitted side, not as a man, but as a parish minister? He is a retained attorney, and these airs of the bench are the emptiest affection."

At the same time, they begin to separate the institution from the people as individuals within it. The leaders are temporary mouthpieces. Many of them tend to ally the institution to their own personal goals and to use it for personal gains that are not condoned by the community were these gains sought in their own name. In this regard institutions sometimes offer excellent shields for ruthless ambition, and the ruthlessly ambitious pay loyal homage in return. There is also a considerable number of basically human-hearted chief executives at the helm. They, too, use the institution for the extension of their own philosophies of life.

But the institution has a life of its own. It evolves and prospers by sloughing off the relatively sluggish tissues and retaining the more vigorous, which burgeon forth in new growth. The institution stays on as the leaders and members come and go. Over and over, the members have learned the hard way that the replacement of a set of personalities or even the institutional identity itself frequently leads to no improvement at all from the standpoint of the lot of the individual as person.

The passing of Henry VIII in 1547 was looked forward to with considerable relief by the people, as the Duke of Somerset took over to rule in sweet reasonableness. Two-thirds of the palace guard were replaced, and the new regime began with a hopeful trend away from Henry's brutality. But disarray soon followed. Bureaucratic corruption, civil disobedience, and religious conflicts ran rampant. By 1549 many people yearned for the cruel sagacity of the old king in place of the liberal incompetence of the Lord Protector.

Impress on your proteges, therefore, not to look too hopefully on new leaders, laws, or reorganizations. Nor to be inveigled into power plays in the wishful thinking that *their* candidates will put the world aright, that the downtrodden will be uplifted, and that the assistance rendered will be rewarded. They will probably be let down. Nor yet to be seduced by the wrong kind of advice, as had been offered Kent Rowley, the late president of the Canadian Textile and Chemical Union. When he was a young man during the 1930s, a labor leader took him aside and said, "Rowley, you're a bright young lad and you can go very far. But to do so, you are going to have to make certain compromises." Rowley later referred to the recommended process as: "I used to be this, now I'm that, gimme some money." He chose to ignore the advice, to remain true to himself, and never to sell out anyone.

The unbounded optimism of the young, however, will lead them on, and they will find themselves badly rebuffed over and again. On those occasions, counsel them against making matters worse by trying to get even with the institution. These attempts are invariably futile, because institutions do not feel. They do not exult when a person joins them; they do not weep when he or she leaves. A person may harm one or more of the members of the institution. He or she may even hurt them so much that they might be banished from the herd.

But here again, the institution not only is not hurt, but is actually benefitted. By helping to rid it of the weaker members, the young person is engaging in the very activity responsible for some of the institution's most luxuriant growth—fierce competition. As a bonus to The Demon, another young and vigorous communicant has enchained himself or herself within His temple.

58 **Effectiveness** The eager inexperienced person is under considerable temptation to undertake a large number of simultaneous projects in hopes of quick results and accomplishments. The tendency to clank about with a hundred irons in the fire needs be brought under control if that person is to develop the knack of getting things done.

Begin your proteges on the simple rule of being clear as to what is expected of them for the job at hand. Overstepping or underimplementing the specific charge catches up sooner or later, and the entire effort might go for naught. Courts have cancelled the awards of arbitrators for doing just this. In the *Application of the States Marine Corporation of Delaware* in 1954, the District Court for the Southern District of New York declared that: "It is not the function of the court to agree or disagree with the reasoning of the arbitrators . . . [but] if the arbitrators determined matters not within the terms of the arbitration agreement, or failed to determine matters within the terms of such agreement, they exceeded or imperfectly executed their jurisdiction and their award should be vacated."

The ancient Persians had something to teach all of us on the prudence of looking at the same proposition under different circumstances before arriving at a final decision. According to Herodotus, "They are accustomed to deliberate on matters of the highest moment when warm with wine; but whatever they in this situation may determine is again proposed to them on the morrow, in their cooler moments, by the person in whose house they had before assembled. If at that time also it meets their approbation, it is executed; otherwise it is rejected. Whatever also they discuss when sober, is always a second time examined after they have been drinking."

Drill your proteges on the second nature of doing things right on the first try. "If you don't have the time to do it right the first time," the familiar shop saying goes, "when will you find the time to do it right the second time?"

One of the most important elements in getting a job done right the first time is an insight into the situation. To be adept at this, the young person needs to sharpen his intuitive grasp of the totality. In addition to the painstaking calculations required on the physical parameters of the problem, the indescribable art of sensing the crux of the issues through direct apprehension is required. This enlightenment cannot be arrived at by serial testing of options. There are too many possibilities for the time available. While rationality is necessary for accurate follow-through, intuition is essential for initial penetration and final decision.

A large job is to be broken down into bite-size tasks, each identified with a dated and logical milestone. The specific milestone may be a progress briefing to the boss, a phase report, an experimental prototype, a reduction of possible options to the serious few, or the first purchase installment from a client. In the attainment of these targets, the inexperienced are often sidetracked into chasing after interesting tangential information and ever-diverging knowledge without focusing them onto the concrete and necessary questions at issue. They let the desirable dictate the proceedings rather than the essential.

Dissuade your proteges from letting the cliche about keeping everybody informed get the better of their judgment. In particular, warn them against broadcasting premature disclosures about discussions surrounding tentative decisions, showing a fool an incomplete report, or composing long memoranda that shuttle in and out of everybody's mail basket. The last only waste people's time and irritate the more busy. Their nebulae of attentions are to be tightly clustered: an objective, an unfolding, a recommendation, an effect.

Implant in them the capacity of keeping their mind from wandering off the task at hand to the expected rewards—almost tasting the glory that is to be theirs. It is only natural to be thinking about bonuses, honors, and promotions. Many junior executives, however, spend much of their energies anxiously eyeing every possible vacancy to which they can aspire, fiercely competing for advancements, and trying to elbow everybody else out of the way. They are so enmeshed with office politics as the prime road to success that they divert considerable energies from the work itself.

Enjoin your proteges to sympathize with their ulcerating associates festered with this greed and let them be. Your proteges should not find it necessary to adopt similar maneuverings to protect their own chances. "Don't wrestle with pigs," the old adage goes. "You get dirty and they enjoy it." It is more dignified to stick to one's own job until it is done and done well. Let the fruits fall as they will. If the first batch does not fall right, there will be others.

The kind of effectiveness most appreciated by all is the steady and constructive contributions during a crisis. A good example involved the ballet master of the New York City Ballet. Three and a half hours before the premier of the *The Nutcracker* in 1954, the costumes had not yet arrived at the theater. George Balanchine and his associate, Jerome Robbins, dashed over to the costume workshop to see what was holding things up. Balanchine's biographer, Bernard Taper, tells what then happened. "When they got there, Balanchine, discerning that everybody in the shop was working feverishly to get the job finished, spoke not a word of exhortation or reproof. He simply sat down along the seamstresses, took up an unfinished costume, threaded a needle, and began deftly stitching a ruffle. Robbins found himself following Balanchine's example. 'After a while, I looked over at him,' Robbins recalls. 'Here it was only about three hours before curtain and there sat Balanchine sewing away as if he didn't have a care in the world. I said to him, "How can you be so calm?" He just smiled and went on sewing.' "

Throughout one's exertions, proper pacing is all important. The goals and attendant schedules are to be set up, which can be sustained without continuous pressures at peak capacity, speeding up as necessary, coasting as appropriate, and taking the usual quotas of interruptions and unanticipated roadblocks in stride. Imbue your proteges with the understanding, as reflected in action, that everything has its own incubation time. Their diligence and patience are to be adjusted to match. Relate to them the story told King Bahrām Gūr of the fifth century by one of his seven wives.

One day a prince visited a city in China and observed that all the male inhabitants wore black. When he inquired of his friend as to the reason, he was escorted to a tower in ruins and hoisted up into it in a basket. When he reached the top, he found himself in a fairy land. He was welcomed by the beautiful queen and royally entertained. He fell violently in love with her, but she asked him to postpone their pleasure till a later time. But he could not control his passion. Whereupon everything suddenly vanished and he found himself at the bottom of the tower. His friend then told him that all of the men in town had gone through the same experience and now wear black in mourning.

59 **Reticence** As far as steady advancement for your proteges is concerned, nothing is more helpful than the practice of the three reticences.

1 Not being overeager.

A subordinate should not move forward with a major plan without having calculated the potential gains and probable costs, as well as the probable chances of attainment. There is to be no misunderstanding as to the consequences if it fails. The qualitative ramifications, such as institutional customs, public opinions, political oppositions, individuals hurt and in what ways, indirect and long-term consequences, equity and ethics beyond the law are to be carefully reviewed. The proposition is to be sounded out with those who might be affected and tested out with experienced individuals. Finally the planner is to ask himself or herself: Does it feel right?

2 Not being overobliging.

One of the most valuable arts for anyone is how to say "no" and say it graciously. It is the only dependable warranty against being overloaded, used, or compromised.

3 Not being overtalkative.

When everything is said and done, a person never gets into trouble from not talking too much, even if it involves adding to the truth. As Michel Eyquem de Montaigne voiced his own preferences in this respect, "I speak truth, not so much as I would but as much as I dare." A person stands on safest grounds if he says only what is needed and helpful and not saying what is not—except on festive and recreational occasions, when joviality is the order of the day. A person gets farther if he or she treads softer and reveals less. A person puts others more at ease if he or she speaks quietly. He or she is gentler if he or she offers only one decisive argument against an associate's recommendation, instead of smothering him or her with the ten in mind. He or she looms less threatening if he or she remains anonymous.

There is an old African Nupe folk tale worth repeating at this point. While traveling through the bush, a hunter came across a skull. Whereupon he asked the skull, "Pray tell, what brought you here?" "Talking brought me here," the skull replied. After the conversation ended, the hunter ran off to the king. "I discovered a talking skull in the bush," he reported. "It inquired how your father and mother are." Not having heard of a talking skull before, the king summoned the Alkali, the Saba, and the Deji. But none of the wise men had heard of it either. So a guard was dispatched with the hunter to check on the story. When they came to the place, the hunter asked the skull to speak. But no response came forth. Again and again the hunter pleaded. But still no response. The guard then gave the hunter one last chance to prove his claim. When nothing happened, the guard chopped off the hunter's head, in accordance with the king's instruction. After the guard left, the skull turned to the hunter's head and asked, "Pray tell, what brought you here?" "Talking brought me here," the head replied.

60 **Intimate knowledge** Make sure that your proteges learn early to differentiate the symbolic knowledge of the talker from the intimate knowledge of the doer.

Typical of the person with only symbolic knowledge about humor but devoid of intimate knowledge is one who can tell all about the origin of jokes, the distinction between a pun and a conundrum, the names of all the leading comedians on Broadway, and even what the jester in the court of Peter the Great did, but he cannot crack a joke himself. This kind of understanding and comprehending is what the world of letters often esteems. But it is not what the world of action values. What the latter demands is the fellow who gets things done rather than the fellow who explains why it is not done.

Knowing something in the complete sense means doing it. The person who is not filial in his behavior does not know what filial piety means. For the person walking the path of wholeness, thinking is not divorced from doing. The thinking of the smell of a rose is not separated from the concomitant smelling of a rose. The moment he smells the rose, he thinks about the smell. Without actually smelling the flower, the can only think about what he thinks is the smell of a rose. The real smell escapes him.

The matured person does not shed tears of pity therefore if he or she cannot or will not do anything about a deplorable situation. Behavior and action, rather than attitude and thought, constitute the primary measures. Rather than rage against the evils of the world, he or she does some good himself. Rather than decry the declining fellowship in the community, he or she joins someone in a beer. To him or her, to be is to act. To know is to do. To know goodness is to do good. The rest is talk.

61 **Fellow workers** Cultivate in your proteges a genuine acceptance of people as they are.

About a third are fine and capable people, lots of fun to be around at work and parties, not too intelligent but intelligent enough for most projects, not too efficient but efficient enough for most situations, not too dependable but dependable enough for most crises. Another third comprises the mass-men, mediocre to average in talent but willing, obliging, rarely rocking the boat.

Many are typical suburbanites. They go along with whatever the prevailing fashion dictates. They feel more secure with the status quo and dread too abrupt a change. They dutifully show up at eight every morning at the office and "yesses" the boss all day long, taking home a briefcase of work a couple of days a week. They depend heavily on others, and when the latter do not come to their succor during times of crises, they are thrown into a morass of doubt. They like to be great successes, but are actually fearful for their current jobs, because they are not putting as much of themselves as they feel they ought to. They are doubly apprehensive that for the same reason they will not get that raise on which they had been banking in order to make the down payment on the new motorboat the coming spring or some such luxury.

A goodly number of the more educated associates are dyed with the notion that only certain kinds of work can be satisfying. Those who had been impressed with creativity as the noblest of professional outlets are often transfixed in the opinion that the only place where meaningful scholarship and major intellectual achievements can be realized is an academic setting. As a result the ones who find themselves in an industrial environment or a government bureaucracy frequently have difficulties in outgrowing the subconscious self-accusation of selling their souls for money or of failing to make the intellectual grade. An undercurrent of dissatisfaction with their lot permeates their life.

A special kind of Sisyphean discomfort is visible among many of the scientists, whose unconscious conflicts had already been implanted during their undergraduate years. Their early growth was lopsided, as they withdrew from social and psychosexual activities. Laboratory classes took more time. The budding scientists had put most of their aspirational eggs into one emotional basket. In the words of Lawrence S. Kubie, "the sense of security and the self-esteem of the young intellectual come to stand on one leg; so that when research is begun he invests in it a lifetime of pent-up cravings. After such a development, it is inevitable that scientific research will be supercharged with many irrelevant and unfulfilled emotional needs; so that the lifework of the young scientist tends to express both the conscious levels of his intellectual aspirations and his unfulfilled instinctual needs and unconscious conflicts." Even successes do not solve the deeper problems.

Scientists and intellectuals are not the only bleaters in disappointments. Among the loudest are those in their late thirties who had not done well in their early thirties and are now beginning to sense the handwriting on the wall that they are not going any farther than they are. They are unhappy in their job. To salve their pride, they blame the boss, the setup, the associates, the whole complex.

These perennially alienated intellectuals have been described by Clarence A. Brinton in *The Fate of Man* as "discontented with themselves as well as with the universe and their fellows, are prey to an existentialist whistling in the dark, and above all uncertain as to whether they really know, can really plan, let alone achieve, a better way of life here on earth. In fine simple terms: they lack what may be an essential of human existence, a confident sense that they understand their place in the universe; they lack a firm metaphysics, a firm teleology, a firm cosmology; perhaps we might as well say they lack a firm, consoling, yet duly stimulating *religion.*" This description, he admitted, is exaggerated. But it places the dilemma in focus. In addition, "they may be bewildered, but they are also indignant and very, very articulate."

The most dangerous and frequently cleverest is the young person after big-time success with the face of a fox and the moves of a marten. He or she is a well-timed part-time blamer, shifting responsibilities for his or her own mistakes onto others in a subtly wily preemptive fashion. He or she is a full-time bidirectional decrier, decrying the higher echelons for idiotic planning, mealy-mouthed support, and bungling interference; and decrying the lower echelons for incompetent implementation of his or her well-conceived programs, continual crybabying for excessive resources, and getting too big for their britches. He or she feels no compunction about cheating his or her associates out of due credit to advance his or her own fortunes. When the competition gets too close for comfort, he or she withholds a few pieces of crucial data from the others in order to make a resounding impression when he or she comes to the rescue before the big boss.

Subconsciously, such an individual has already imagined himself or herself beyond the stature of his or her immediate boss and has regarded the boss's boss as his or her real superior. One of the telltale marks is the seeking out of the boss's boss at all official and social gatherings and making sure that his or her talents are displayed at their best. Undoubtedly some of this kind do advance rapidly, for they represent some of the most nimble-footed and cunning-minded of the generation. And nimble-footedness and cunning-mindedness are among the most valued of institutional virtues.

Ready your proteges to observe these and other understandable frailties with measured personal modesty. Coach them to remember that what befalls others may very well befall them. How others react to a given stress may very well be exactly how they themselves would react under comparable circumstances. The sobering thought should make them much less harsh in the judgment of their fellows.

An example you may use is Vladimir Mayakovsky, who was saddened by the suicide of his poet-friend, Sergei Esenin, in 1925. When he read the suicide poem with the devastating lines:

> In this life to die is nothing new
> But to live, of course, is nothing newer . . .

he composed a counter-poem to neutralize their effect as a social duty. He was determined "to replace the facile beauty of death by another beauty, since toiling mankind needs all its strength to sustain the Revolution it has begun; regardless of the obstacles on the way, the strenuous contradictions of the New Economic Policy, it requires us to pay tribute to life's happiness, the joy of this enormously difficult advance toward Communism." Yet less than five years later, Mayakovsky shot himself.

Finally, enlarge your proteges' appreciation of the multifaceted character of conviviality. Being popular with pleasant conversation and effervescent personality is the ordinary level of getting along with people, called sociability. Being able to stimulate a group of people to live and work together productively is the institutionally valued higher level, called leadership. Being able always to leave people better off after an interaction is the highest level of getting along with people, called beneficence. It is through this last association that they will receive, without seeking, that wholesome feeling reflecting off the fulfillments they transfuse to others.

62 Cabals Coteries of people with common interests are always present in any organization and are usually beneficial to the larger body. Some of them, however, are more self-serving and harmful. These cabals are characterized by an effectively semisecret mode of liaison. They begin innocently enough as carpool members, coffee-drinking companions, and political-fringe confreres exchanging incidental information about opportunities. Given a coincidence of greedy people a predictable evolution follows. The welfare of the members supersedes the purpose of the institution, of which they are a part.

When operated successfully, cabals often enable their coterie to rise rapidly in the organization. Because of this advantage, there is a strong attraction to joining up. Those to whom professional advancement assumes overriding importance are sorely tempted to align themselves with one of them. In so doing, they implicitly agree to compromise on fairness, integrity, and dignity, since they are obligated to push the worst of their cabal-cousins ahead of the most deserving of outsiders.

Warn your proteges to stay free of these entanglements. Nor cross up cabals for no good purpose.

Where cabals do exist in strength, the chances are that the boss is weak. It might be that he or she does not even know of their existence, like termites eating away at his or her controls. A person attempting to alert the hoodwinked boss may well be looked on by him or her as a trouble-making tattler of tales. Even if the incompetent boss believes the information, he or she probably does not know how to deal with the situation. It will only flare into a worsened state of strife with the informant branded as a stool pigeon by everyone.

Yet there may well come a time when a critical and worthy cause leaves your proteges no honorable choice but to take on one of them. Typical of these occasions is the defense against flagrant injustice being imposed by the cabal on helpless individuals in hapless anguish within your proteges' direct responsibilities.

In this case, groom your proteges well. Train them to be quite clear as to the objective of preventing a specific action on the part of the cabal, as distinguished from destroying the cabal itself. The former is their natural charge; the latter is not. They are to stick to the issues. They are to let it be known privately to a few members of the cabal what they are trying to do and why they have no alternative but to see it through, no matter what the personal cost. At the same time they are to make it clear that they intend no threat to the cabal itself. Furthermore, they are to extend an honest appeal for the cabal's help to resolve the situation without it coming to a head.

In many instances the cabal will cooperate and back down, because the battle that your proteges are obviously prepared to wage is not worth it.

When the outcome happens to be of major importance to both parties, however, your proteges are to be readied for a rough encounter. Let them straightway accept the possibility of losing their jobs. Give it no further thought, and press forward with the instinct and dignity of a samurai fighting his final engagement. Then let Nature take her course.

63 Connections and friends A person needs patronage and connections if he is to succeed on a grand scale. These are not to be confused with friendship. Connections are instrumental in advancing one's wealth and professional standing; friendships in advancing one's goodness and joy. Connections are two-way exploitations; friendships two-way sharings. Connections terminate when either party is no longer of use to the other; friendships go on on their own.

Your proteges come into contact at work more or less regularly with a hundred or so individuals and less frequently with a couple hundred more. Out of these acquaintances might come a handful with whom they share a spontaneous respect for each other as human beings, who know their business, get things done, and put others at ease at the same time. It is professionally worthwhile to keep in touch with such individuals. They will find need of capable collaborators again and again in later life. They will also be asked to make referrals for positions of importance. It is always helpful to all parties concerned if they are able to go over their files of correspondence at that time and come up with several suitable candidates who will constitute a valuable asset on an institutional as well as a personal basis.

Close friends, however, fall into a special group. They enjoy each other's company and widen each other's horizons. Long association does not degrade the initial respect into familiarity. Nor does it render them blind to each other's normal complement of shortcomings. The recognizing without voicing strengthens the bond of mutual support, with a firm and lasting faith. Faith in friendship is expressed, in the words of André Maurois, "by courageously affirming our fundamental respect. I know of a woman who, whenever one of her intimates is attacked in her presence, merely states: 'She is my friend,' and refuses to say more. That, I believe, is true wisdom." The intensity of friendship is, after all, only as deep as that which disrupts it.

The eighteenth century Zen master Sengai leaves a sound piece of advice on the differential associations to be encouraged between professional acquaintances and friends:

> Read poems to those who understand them;
> Drink wine with those who understand you.

64 **Marginal employee** The plight of the marginally gifted, the disadvantaged, and the underdog in a competitive environment was depicted in the story by Rabindranath Tagore about the little goat, who went weeping to the Lord, "Lord, how is it that all creatures seek to devour me?" "What can I do, my child," the Lord replied. "When I look at you, I myself am so tempted."

Admonish your proteges to think especially kindly about the marginal employee. The latter has no place to go for significant help except for a few understanding souls. The extended support often makes the difference between his or her keeping the job or not, between his or her family eating adequately or not.

In considerable degree, the slower-witted is left progressively farther behind because of a reluctance to seek advice. On the few occasions that he or she tries, some of the brighter associates show their impatience and disgust in humiliating ways. This drives him or her farther back into his or her shell. The more he or she retreats, the less he or she learns. Before long, he or she lives in constant dread of losing the job. Life at work becomes more nightmare than sweat.

These difficulties often begin with his or her own lack of recognition of the actual state of affairs, so that he or she can take corrective measures. It may be a simple case of halitosis or a more serious one of looming grounds for dismissal. Considerable empathy, discretion, and skill are required to find suitable conditions for developing the proper prelude of receptivity; to present the facts sincerely, clearly, and briefly; to allow for the natural emotional outburst; and to move the discussion toward a resolution of the problem.

During the critical period of rebuilding confidence, extreme care is to be taken to avoid needless setbacks. His or her ego needs building up. Let us imagine an occasion in which the marginal employee finds himself or herself for once the center of attraction. He or she is carried away in this enthusiasm and newly found spotlight. In the middle of all this, he or she lets out with an amazing statement, which captures the imagination and admiration of everyone in the group—everyone except one of your proteges, who happens to know the facts behind the statement that stand precisely opposite to what is asserted. As a matter of fact, the phenomenon is rather ordinary—nothing to get excited about. Warn your proteges against throwing wet blankets. Let the story stand, so that the marginal employee can relish his or her all too rare rejuvenating hour.

Your proteges need not be hasty even in correcting him or her in private later. They are to allow sufficient time to pass, so that the episode has been fully savored by the marginal employee and his or her spouse and has long been forgotten and devoid of importance. Perhaps some natural way of getting the facts across to him or her without connection to the previous occasion may crop up, in which instance, they are casually passed on. This will save him or her from potential future embarrassment in the presence of another expert, who may not be as considerate.

Situations do arise, however, when it is necessary to correct him or her before others, as in an executive session to determine institutional action. Prepare your proteges by your examples to be extra solicitous in titrating criticisms. The marginal employee is to be allowed to complete his or her presentation without interruption at the point of the misstatement or poor recommendation. He or she is permitted to catch his or her breath and regain his or her wits from stage fright. Begin with a few complimentary remarks, followed by a couple of points of agreement, incidentally slipping in the recommended changes, then quickly go on to spend more time on several other important points of general agreement, even though the latter might not have been explicitly introduced in the briefing itself. By thus diluting the criticisms with the balm of consensus, they become digestible and constructive to the marginal employee.

The marginal employee is to be helped not only with the immediate problem facing him or her but also with techniques of avoiding and dissolving challenges in general. His or her ability is to be improved to the point where he or she regains the confidence that he or she is pulling his or her share of the institutional load and is then able to hold his or her head higher, and life for him or her takes on a brighter hue.

65 **Exasperation** The last shove to the downfall of many an otherwise capable young person is exasperation and frustration.

People without the composure to sail through exasperation and frustration toward the dissolution of a nasty situation often resort to various defense mechanisms. One of these is aggression. Children frustrated at home pick fights at school more frequently than others. Another common defense mechanism is disguising the source of frustration or repressing the related memories, thoughts, and feelings. Although repression may provide time to find a better adjustment, it is potentially dangerous. If allowed to become repetitive, it often leads to distortions in perception in the form of denials, fantasies, regressions, and projections. Facts are masked and reality twisted.

One can get very exasperated in trying to help others. I remember overhearing a doctor's telephone conversation in a hospital lounge not too long ago. There was a long report from the resident on the patient's medical complication after complication, trouble after trouble between the patient and the service personnel, and complaint after complaint from the patient herself, when the doctor finally blurted out: "Goddamit! Why doesn't she get smart and die?" It occurred to me that the doctor might have benefitted from reading the story of Abraham and the old traveler in the Hebrew books.

One day while Abraham was sitting before his tent, an aged and weary traveler trudged slowly toward him. The old man must have been a hundred years of age and stooped over his staff. Abraham invited him into the tent, washed his feet, and fed him. Observing that the traveler ate lustily but did not pray or ask for God's blessing on the meat, Abraham inquired why he did not worship God. The old man replied that he only worshipped fire and did not believe in God. Abraham got so incensed at the unbeliever that he kicked the old man out into the cold night.

After the old man disappeared in the dark, God appeared to Abraham and inquired about the visitor. Abraham explained what had gone on and that he was thrown out because he did not worship God. Instead of the expected compliment, God expressed disgust. "I have endured him for a hundred years. Why can you not do so for just one night, especially when he has caused you no trouble?"

Whereupon, so the story concluded, Abraham went out, fetched the old man back, and entertained him for the night.

66 **Deservedness of aid** The seventeenth century poet, Nilakantha Dikahita, cried out in one of his hymns to the Lord: "If thou has the compassion toward me that I should be saved, save me; why weigh my good and my bad acts?"

But too many lords who ride fine horses have never known to this very day what it means to have sore feet. And so it is that the majority of justices on the United States Supreme Court decreed in 1979 that jailed defendants too poor to raise bail need not be afforded the protection of single cells. Having only ordered people to jail and not knowing what it is to be physically brutalized or sexually harassed by cellmates, they proclaimed the lofty technical judgment that "There is no one man, one cell principle lurking in the due process clause" of the Constitution.

Dissenting Justice Thurgood Marshall exhibited a much more humane yet realistic assessment of the situation, when he said in a subsequent speech on May 27: "For a prisoner in jail, that ain't funny."

67 **Do-gooders** In the rendering of aid, one of the worst things to do is to foist oneself on the poor person in distress and trample his or her last vestige of self-respect, as if to say: "You're so helpless that you don't even know you need help. But whether you like it or not, I'm going to save your wretched self." This approach has been employed for millenia by many people and institutions, especially against the uneducated and the indigent in desperate conditions. Actually, it is not a mission of mercy so much as a masquerade of power.

The do-gooder is particularly careless in disillusioning people—disillusioning in accordance with the do-gooder's own state of enlightenment, of course. He or she does not hesitate about destroying a neighbor's peace of mind because he or she feels the neighbor is practicing a false religion or ideology. The change being actually pressed is not the substitution of one set of circumscribed beliefs for another. It is a matter of uprooting an entire life. Up to the do-gooder's arrival on the scene, the neighbor has been contented in the comfort of divine inspiration and assurance of a joyous hereafter for eternity.

Consider what happens when he or she is overwhelmed by the do-gooder's persuasiveness. He or she alienates himself or herself—not only from his or her former faith but also from his or her former relations. The new faith does not harmonize with the thousand and one facets of his or her former reasonably well integrated life. He or she has to seek new friends, because the old ones are only partial friends now. He or she is no longer an intimate member of his or her family, because the rest can no longer share him or her completely. Suddenly, he or she is an alien in their midst.

Unless the do-gooder is willing and able to substitute a superior life in all of its ramifications for his or her neighbor, who has been living as a fairly wholesome and integrated member of the community, he or she should reexamine his or her motives and should realize that all organized beliefs are divisive of God's people—dividing those who subscribe to one from those who subscribe to another. He or she should look to the model of religious tolerance set by Cyrus the Great, King of the Medes and the Persians (555–529 B.C.). His first principle of governance was freedom of religious worship and beliefs. Instead of destroying the towns and temples, as was the practice in his day, he extended a courteous respect for the deities of those he had conquered and even contributed toward the maintenance of their shrines. Wherever he traveled, he offered pious sacrifices to the local gods with equal reverence. His preserving of the sanctuaries and honoring of the pantheon of the long-resisting Babylonians led them to warm up to him.

Despite lofty protestations to the contrary, callous militancy is the sowing of suffering. The first official record of harm of any kind to human beings sprang from just this sort of disillusionment. Adam and Eve were perfectly well off in their ignorance of evil in the Garden of Eden. God had them living very happily under only partial knowledge of the truth. Everything was blissful in their completely adjusted state. Then along came Satan with his sweet talk and opened their eyes to the difference between good and evil. According to the subsequent chronicles, the entire human race has been in a mess ever since.

68 Decorum It becomes a young person to meld decorum into his actions. Confucius said, "Courtesy without decorum becomes tiresome. Cautiousness without decorum becomes timidity; daring becomes insubordination; frankness becomes effrontery."

There is nothing more irritating than a young zealot for virtue. He or she often begins as a tower of absolute integrity, uncompromisingly unwilling to let an uttered untruth stand. It is not long before he or she finds himself or herself correcting an associate in public and before the latter's boss. If the associate misses the next available promotion, even though the incident had nothing to do with the setback, he or she is likely to hold the young zealot responsible. There is even chance that sweet revenge is already on the way.

This is only one of the many reasons why it is imprudent to correct people in public, unless it is essential for some very worthwhile purpose that it be done right then and there. Improve your proteges' abilities with respect to the circumspect way in which the latter occasion is to be handled. Tutor them how to begin by allowing that they might not have gotten the complete picture. This is to be followed by the admission that the proposition may well be the best option under certain circumstances. But under other circumstances, some modification may be helpful. Does their associate feel that the latter holds in the present situation? If the suggestion is sound, the associate would probably agree and even proceed to explain the revision as if it were a joint clarification. On the other hand, if the suggestion is unwarranted, the statement would not have embarassed your proteges after the subtleties are explained.

In this regard, the former Commandant of the United States Military Academy, Donald V. Bennett, once said that two of the things he made sure were deeply inculcated into the plebes at West Point were (1) when to say, "Why, sir?" and (2) when to say, "Yes, sir."

In general, a person in a very subordinate position does best by not challenging the higher echelons. A popular Polish joke of the 1950s might be instructive in this connection. A Warsaw Jew asked his rabbi to explain the difference between official criticism from the top and from the grass roots. "That's simple," said the rabbi. "When the superior on the second floor spits down on you, he is criticising you from the top. When you on the first floor spit up at him, that's grass-root criticism."

Obsessive militants, however, are not inhibited by such folksy admonitions. The larger the problem with which they are engaged, the greater the sense of importance they feel. Instead of remaining in their own backyard to solve the picayune problems they have been assigned, they thrust themselves into someone else's bailiwick in order to tackle what they envision as a damaging threat to the institution and even society at large. Since nobody is addressing these potential disasters, as is obvious to them from the fact that no progress is being made toward their resolution—so they tell themselves—they are compelled to move out for the good of the larger publics. Nothing is solved, because the underlying cause turns out larger than the institution itself. In the meantime, their own work goes undone.

This does not imply that your proteges are to be discouraged from speaking with candor when necessary or that they are never to attempt major reforms. It does imply that they should be clear as to the rightness of their position, the feasibility of their course of action, the appropriate way of going about it, and the readiness to pay the personal price before setting forth.

The behavior of some of the prime ministers of ancient China may shed some light regarding the practice of public denunciation of exalted superiors. On occasions, one of them would feel so strongly about the need for drastic reforms in government that he would compose an open criticism of the emperor's policies and procedures, together with an urgent call for specific changes. After delivering the formal message with due respect to the emperor, the prime minister would then, in accordance with proper ceremonies, commit suicide.

Needless to say, an extreme ritual of this type is out of place in modern interpretations of decorum in relating to superiors. After all, what chief of state today claims to have received a Mandate from Heaven? Nonetheless, let your proteges take note.

69 Ten proverbs for executives

For planning:

1. The shrike hunting the locust is unaware of the hawk hunting him.
2. The mouse with but one hole is easily taken.
3. In shallow waters, shrimps make fools of dragons.
4. Do not try to catch two frogs with one hand.
5. Give the bird room to fly.

For operations:

6 Do not insult the crocodile until you have crossed the river.

7 It is better to struggle with a sick jackass than carry the wood yourself.

8 Do not throw stone at mouse and break precious vase.

9 It is not the last blow of the axe that fells the tree.

10 The great executive not only brings home the bacon but also the applesauce.

70 **Ongoing moments** Being sensitive to Nature is relishing the present. Living only partly in the present means experiencing only part of the interlaced totality. Living in the past means experiencing present virtual presences of real presences that exist no more. Living in the future means experiencing present virtual presences of real presences that never did exist and probably never will.

Many ambitious young people concentrate almost exclusively on their profession, trying to get ahead in the most rapid fashion. They keep postponing present pleasantries, which siphon time away from their work. They hope to enjoy them all the better at a later date when they can afford to coast on their laurels. Unfortunately, the pleasant moments of today are gone by then. In such manner do they keep boxing themselves into an infinite regress of sighed regrets.

As a matter of fact, the undesirable consequences go beyond the simple regretting of lost pleasures. All through their twenties and thirties and until their efforts during the cumulative sacrifices are considered repaid, they continue to feel that the world still owes them something. In the meantime, they keep expending additional effort for future compensations, which only add to the list of expectations. Under this arrangement, they are never free from begrudging the world for what it has failed to repay.

Wean your proteges from the much-touted flimsy rationalization that what is important is not so much that one actually lives the good life but that one keeps seeking it. This only misleads them into emphasizing the thrill of chasing rather than the enjoyment of realizing. It is somewhat like the all-prelude and no-finale courting ritual of some of the great crested grebes. They frequently become so vigorously exercised in the process of courting that when the time comes, they are too exhausted to consummate the ecstatic climax.

71 **The democratic constant** Do not be taken in by the popular exhortations about maximizing the efficiency of governments. Recognize them for what they are—moves to make the most powerful institution even more powerful in witting or unwitting subjugation of its citizens. Do not forget the well tested equation for a democratic bureaucracy, namely,

$$PE^2 = k$$

where P is the power legally entrusted to a government agency
E is the efficiency of that agency
k is the democratic constant

The democratic constant is increased during periods of national emergency and decreased during periods of peace and prosperity. The more power vested in a government agency, the less efficient should it be kept through inadequate budget and personnel allocation, so that the citizens can retain a desirable degree of freedom. The less power vested in it, the more efficient should it be, so that the citizens can derive benefit from its operations.

Smile with inner relief, therefore, when you hear the president speak with a tinge of anger in 1978 over the bureaucratic inefficiency of the civil servants. Democracy is safe in America for at least some time to come.

72 **Caring** The world today is in far greater need of caring than any other human quality we can think of. Caring about fellow human beings constitute the only reliable governor over modern man's intellectuality and technology from getting completely out of hand.

When discussing human caring, it is essential to distinguish the social from the personal. One example is the difference between social and individual justice. The former does not necessarily assure the latter; often the former works against the latter. The criminal laws and court proceedings are by and large representative of a high order of social justice. But their application to individual justice is rather cavalier in the case of the woman who was kept in a Washington, D. C. jail in 1970 for twenty-eight days while awaiting trial for an alleged traffic violation because of inability to raise the stipulated $300 bail—only to have the charge dismissed by the judge for lack of evidence. The sheer inertia of large organizations lulls the authorities into the moral complacency of social justice. But social justice is only an abstraction of justice; it is not flesh-and-blood justice. A society can be considered just in the complete sense only when its social justice is brought reasonably close to its individual justice. In contrast to social caring, individual caring is minority-oriented—a minority of one if needs be.

The distinction between a human being as a social abstraction and as a human reality is portrayed in the following incident described by Sören Kierkegaard: In extolling those glorious individuals who sacrifice themselves for the truth, the parson usually assumes that no one in the attentive congregation would take his words literally and duplicate the heroic feat. "When he is sufficiently assured of this by reason of the private knowledge he has of the congregation as its pastor, he preaches glibly, declaims vigorously, and wipes away the sweat. If on the following day one of these strong and silent men, a quiet, modest, perhaps even insignificant-looking man, were to visit the parson at his house announcing himself as one whom the parson had carried by his eloquence, so that he now resolved to sacrifice his life for the truth—what would the parson say? He would address him thus: 'Why merciful Father in heaven! How did such an idea occur to you? Travel, divert yourself, take a laxative!' "

The next three examples show how social policies and practices can be related to the thesis that the minimizing of suffering is the criterion of good and the dispensing of good is the index of caring. These concern social welfare, computerization of operations, and educational structure.

With respect to social welfare, the attempt of the American government to "cool the economy" during the early 1970s as a step toward controlling the inflation of its currency is typical of institutional priorities. In the judgment of the policymakers, it was preferable for five percent of the population to be without employment and the families depressed below the poverty line than for the upper fifty percent to forego some of their luxuries in the form of sizeably reduced income for a short period of time or for the employed ninety-five percent to decrease their income a few percentage points for the time being. The government then deliberately launched a series of moves to bring this unemployment about. The national unemployment went over six percent and the local rate in some places went over thirty. After four years of the same policy and worsening inflation, a new president took office. He called a summit meeting of leaders from all sectors of the American people. But the immediate circle around him belonged to same economic and ethical school. Again the new president adopted basically the same approach as far as impact on unemployment was concerned. As always, national policies are more oriented toward social caring than individual caring.

With respect to the computerization of operations, the following two considerations represent some of the more subtle kinds that cross the minds of responsible executives with human-caring orientations.

1 Loss of privacy.

Traditionally, privacy infers one's right to decide what facts concerning himself are to be released to which group of people. The privilege has been eroded as the communications media, surveillance activities, and bureaucratic efficiency came to the forefront. The large collections of information are getting even larger. A Senate investigation of June 1974 revealed that the federal government alone maintained 858 data banks containing more than 1.25 billion records on Americans. These do not include the billions of other pieces of data, such as cancelled personal checks, available in private hands on call for government scrutiny.

Computers add a new edge to the invasion of privacy because of their vast capacity to search, collate, combine, permutate, and do all kinds of things with the data hitherto scattered in various nooks and crannies. A typical concern was expressed in England in 1971: "At present, every hotel guest . . . must sign the hotel register. Suppose the authorities decided to computerize these registers. Suppose also, Mr. Brown stayed in one hotel in Liverpool on Monday, in another in Birmingham on Tuesday and a third in Brighton on Wednesday and if also Miss Jones stayed in the same hotels on the same nights conclusions which would not be conceived by a random examination of the register might be drawn by correlating them." One can imagine all kinds of Sherlock Holmesian possibilities if such information systems are linked with bank records, credit card files, and gossip columns.

2 Callousness with fairness.

Consider the matter of a paid debt. In the computerized setup, the fact that a person had once committed a recorded offense of some kind, even though he has made good on it, is kept permanently in the data bank, not to be destroyed, not to be forgotten, unless someone takes an overt action to erase it. But temperamentally, data bankers are like squirrels, who like to keep the nuts hidden away for some future use or serendipitous rediscovery.

Yet forgiveness is to forget, as the generous fellow says; "Oh, forget it!" Or like the compassionate angel, who runs the computer in the judgment hall of Saint Peter. Once in a while when he comes across a nasty bit of information on an otherwise fine soul, the angel would shed a tear or two, which would drop onto the tape and erase the record. Fair play calls for forgiveness on payment of the debt. True forgiving means forgetting. Retention of a sin in memory is an eternal sentence, an everlasting black book, a denial of a clean slate to begin life anew. A computerized society therefore tends to be an unforgiving one.

With respect to the American educational system, an orientation in which human caring outweighs human learning in value would call for its reexamination.

The present structure and requirements are contributing much to the greatness of this country. At the same time they are also exacting the price of much anguish to a fair proportion of the American people as individuals. If the minimizing of suffering is adopted as the criterion of goodness, a radically different structure might emerge as optimal. Although the following example is not implementable in the United States in the foreseeable future for various reasons, it offers an additional option for developing countries. In any case, it illustrates how compassion can play a role in decision making on a social scale.

The two kinds of suffering induced by the American educational system of concern are: the anguish to the students and the sacrifice by the parents. The question arises whether a relief of the anguish and sacrifice can be realized without adversely affecting the growth of the students, the professionalism of the faculty, and the welfare of the nation.

Delayed manhood is the student's anguish. If neither the age of reason nor the onset of puberty constitutes an acceptable social criterion of manhood, what does? In the United States it is not fighting mortal battles in the defense of the country nor voting for government officials but paying one's way. As long as a person pays his or her way, he or she carries weight. When he or she carries weight, he or she is an adult. It is then that he or she begins to realize himself or herself in his or her fullness.

To be tantalized from the age of six by the benumbing television with all of the goodies that money can buy, from the age of thirteen by the ubiquitous pictures with all the sex that money can buy, and from the age of seventeen by the reverberating speeches with all the prestige that money can buy, yet to have to ask and account for the paltry dollars from daddy that only whet the appetite for the unavailable—such is the frustration and demeaning anguish of the protracted adolescent and enforced dependent for the day of deliverance.

Deliverance comes with a job. Jobs of the kind the young person has been taught to respect come with a baccalaureate degree. The degree comes at age twenty-two. There are few shortcuts through the *rites de passage* imposed by the present educational authorities.

As far as the suffering demanded of the older generation by our educational system is concerned, the parents are forced to forego many enriching pleasures and some basic necessities of their younger days, as well as endanger their health and good living in old age, in order to save enough money to send their children through sixteen and often twenty years of schooling and training. The fact that most parents are more than glad to make the sacrifice does not diminish the fact of deprivation and suffering.

One can readily calculate what it means for the average parents to save enough for the college education for four children. Assuming $5000 per year for each child during the late 1970s, the total outlay comes up to about $80,000. This does not take into account the more expensive professional schools, such as those in medicine with annual tuition fees of $10,000 or more. Does not $80,000 represent a major portion of the financial reserve that the average family is able to generate? If the family encounters one very serious illness, especially in the breadwinner, does this burden not put an extraordinary squeeze on the parents' peace of mind? Does this not mean that the grandparents will have to shift for themselves? How can the average American look forward to a gracious old age under such a financial pall?

The following is one out of many approaches at restructuring the present educational system to reinstate human compassion above incremental technical knowledge in the scheme of societal values.

The baccalaureate degree is to be awarded after successful completion of nine years of basic school and three years of university. All citizens, with understandable exceptions, are required to complete basic school. All qualified students are accorded the opportunity for a tuition-free university education or tuition-free two-year technical and trade training. There will be no interruption by military service during peace time.

The shortening of the educational period is to be achieved by extending the school year to ten and a half months, with forty hours per week at the higher grades. Course content is to be improved. Methods of instruction are to be made more efficient. Recognition is to be paid to the fact that most learning comes *after* the formal education process in any case and therefore it is not essential to encourage the inflationary curricula.

Medical and law schools are to be reduced from four to three years. Interns and residents are to be fully paid junior staff employees of hospitals or clinics, in the same manner as junior attorneys in law firms.

The current graduate schools are to be converted into nonprofit private or state-supported research institutions to pursue research of overall community value and the general advancement of knowledge. They differ from industrial, governmental, and some of the other nonprofit research organizations in the relative freedom of the investigators, the kinds of studies undertaken, and the orientation to more fundamental investigations. Although they work closely with the universities, they are separately incorporated and independently managed. Professors in the universities and teachers in the basic schools, where teaching is paramount, may hold dual appointments in an accredited research organization, where research is paramount.

No further master's degrees are to be awarded. The doctorate is not to be awarded by the university but by an accredited research organization in accordance with strict adherence to professional standards. The research organization may be a nonprofit institution of the kind mentioned above, an industrial, governmental, theological, art, or any other institution, as long as it receives approval of the accrediting body and continues to meet the rigid standards in the respective fields.

Upon graduation from university, young persons of eighteen may join the armed forces. They may become apprentices in a research institution, empowered to grant doctorates. They may enter a medical or law school, in which case they would be eligible to receive a low-interest, deferred government loan. They may work their way up other ladders, like the certified public accountant. In any case, the young person at eighteen is no longer financially dependent on daddy. He or she has become an adult in America in the practical sense.

The financial burdens to the parents and taxpayers are lessened considerably. Decreasing the total lapsed time for the baccalaureate degree from sixteen years to twelve represents the major reduction in the government's subsidy of education and the parents' upkeep of dependents. Lengthening the school year with increasing occupancy hours per day provides additional savings in the cost of capital facilities. A major share of the doctoral expenses will be transferred to industrial, governmental, and other nonacademic institutions, which are compensated by the presence of young and creative minds on their staffs. Expenses for the master's degree will be eliminated.

For once, a temporary respite from the skyrocketing costs of education is within sight. The nation's work force is augmented by four additional man-years for many of her citizens. The tax base is broadened. The mainstream is enriched by the infusion of four of the most enthusiastic and idealistic years of her educated citizens' lives. Although the educational exposure of the youth may be somewhat inferior in conventional scholarship, it will probably be superior in the relevance to adult living. The old folks can look forward to greater chances of graceful dignity. There will more likely be enough money saved so that they can "wear the silk and eat the meat"—as any filial offspring would be pleased to see.

COOPERATING WITH THE INEVITABLE

Some English executive had said some time ago that the secret of his success was: "I seek out the inevitable and I cooperate with it." The most obvious inevitability in your life as an executive is retirement. The most obvious inevitability in your life as a human being is death. This section describes some of the more important psychological and practical steps in cooperating with these two inevitabilities.

73 **Retirement readiness** Retirement without a properly prepared state of mind often activates latent neuroses and aggravates active ones. One out of every two executives experiences some difficulty in adjusting to retirement; one out of every four undergoes real distress. There is a loss of identity, familiar points of references, and social support. Restlessness, depression, resentment, self-depreciation, and/or compulsive doubt frequently follow. For them, life without work suddenly becomes empty. They are disturbed over the loneliness and the nothingness that yawn before them. They are uncertain over the adequacy of funds. They are fearful over the threat of poor health and the nearness of death.

For those who had planned well in advance, however, retirement succeeds active employment as naturally as one bar of music follows another in a beautiful song.

There are many positive ways of looking at retirement. Paul W. Boynton wrote about *Six Ways to Retire.* He listed them as retirement to: (1) a new full-time career, (2) a part-time occupation that will supplement income, (3) creative activity, avocations, hobbies, (4) public service for community or nation, (5) new experiences, the building of new friendships, and the development of personal relations, and (6) understanding, the creation of a mature guiding philosophy, and some answers to what life is all about.

Many practical workers in gerontology subscribe to the activity theory of successful aging. They recommend the maintenance of the attitude and activities of middle age as long as possible and when finally necessary, substitutes for the activities of work, new associations for the work acquaintances, new friends for the ones who pass away. In contrast, others advance the disengagement theory. In this option the person accepts the coming relative inactivity and begins to phase himself or herself out of the actions and associations of work life. Whether or not the person initiates the process, the disengagement is affected by the fact of retirement. The theory suggests that he or she get on with it voluntarily ahead of time, so it does not come as a surprise or an imposition.

We suggest an additional ingredient to be incorporated in both paths. Neither an institutional nor an anti-institutional focus provides a sound reference for good living at *any* age, particularly retirement. What needs emphasis is the continuum of the self that truly is and its harmony with Nature throughout life. Nothing qualitatively essential is to be added or subtracted from one's pattern of life with respect to the self that truly is. The conducive attitude would have regarded work rather detachedly before, and now at retirement it remains no different. It would have looked on the avocation as an important bridge of communion with and enjoyment of Nature, and now it remains no different. It would have considered the relieving of suffering among one's fellow men and beasts as the criterion of goodness, and now it remains no different. It would have maintained doors and windows through the institutional walls to Nature, and now it remains no different. It would have relished communing with Nature in solitude, and now it remains no different.

With this background in mind, it is not too early during your fifties to begin your emotional, as well as financial and administrative, preparation. The following four steps are among the more important.

1 Ensuring financial adequacy.

Even people of relatively high income and intelligence do not always plan wisely for a rainy day. Two examples are sufficient to make the point. One involves the eighty-two-year-old widow of one of the former outstanding justices of the Supreme Court. In 1972 she was on the verge of becoming a charity case in the Home for the Incurables in Washington, D.C. The former law clerks of her late husband had to "pass the hat" and press Congress to raise the pensions of widows of Supreme Court justices to rescue her from insolvency. The other involves a former Republican leader in the Senate and publisher of the Oakland Tribune. He committed suicide in 1974 with nearly a million dollars in debt. If financial insufficiencies can plague the lives of such learned and affluent people and their spouses, say not that it will not happen to you—unless, of course, you prepare properly ahead of time.

As you age past sixty, begin gradually to taper your living habits to your anticipated retirement level of extraneous expenditures. This is to be done, even though you are still holding on to a relatively high-paying position at the moment. Your transition comes about much smoother than otherwise.

2 Strengthening close friendships.

Take a good look at the individuals with whom you come into daily contact at work. In all probability, they also account for most of your social life. Expect that practically all these associations will evaporate on the day of your retirement. Even if some of them would like to continue their occasional get-togethers with you, they are so swamped with work that they will be unable to find the time for activities that do not contribute directly to their professional responsibilities and advancements. This is quite understandable. After all, you yourself are currently whirling about in the same kind of maelstrom.

Consider yourself fortunate if you can count nine couples as close friends to you and your spouse for the rest of your lives. If they number less than three, do something about it right now. Begin by asking yourself whether your own behavior is deserving of any close friends at all. It takes nearly five years for casual acquaintanceships to blossom into intimate friendships, which can never be forced. There is not much time left for the purpose.

3 Lessening ties to office trappings.

It may be that your position at work requires the huzzas of the masses. A public figure cannot do without the applause; a famous personality cannot do without the fans. Understand that these adulations are not directed to you personally but to the office or the fictitious image you happen to represent. They are to be accepted as part of your job. As you step out of the role, however, shed them without regret. Unburden your real self, as it were, as you greet the new freedom.

Start the transition by easing your personal dependency on large numbers of people for a feeling of importance. Diminish your desires for conventional esteems and honors. Get yourself gradually accustomed to the wards of obscurity. Let those associates who crave public attention deliver the speeches in your place. Let the younger subordinates who need the recognition for reputation and promotion enjoy the exposure.

4 Forgetting old debts.

Take preliminary steps to round out your life in its wholeness by repairing the damage to others you have caused, repaying kindness extended to you and your family, and ripening that special benevolent and courteous civility that befits your later years.

End your working phase on a positive note, a graciousness that forgets all debts. The seventeenth century scholar Chin Sheng-tan had set a good example: "Having nothing to do after supper, I rumaged through my old trunks and came across hundreds of promissory notes from old friends. Some of them have long passed away and some could not have been repaid. So I gathered them together into a pile in the backyard and quietly lit a match to it. I watched the smoke rise straight up into the sky until the last traces disappeared. Ah, is this not happiness?"

74 **Withdrawal and return** In some respects, the proper combination of avocation and work gives rise to a refreshening, which is often seen in the withdrawal-and-return cycles of creative individuals and minorities. In Arnold Toynbee's characterization, when creative personalities follow the mystic path, "they pass first out of action into ecstasy and then out of ecstasy into action on a new and higher plane." By withdrawal from external society, the personality is able to realize its inner powers that had remained dormant through lack of exercise.

The Syriac myth of Moses ascending the mountain alone to communicate with Yahweh is a classical exemplification. Buddha's seven years of wandering in search of enlightenment, Jesus' forty days in the wilderness, and Mohammed's retreat from Mecca for seven years were the periods of self-renewals of the founders of today's three largest religions.

You, too, can be rejuvenated by regular withdrawals from the workplace into the avocational sharing with Nature. Your work itself is benefitted from your nonwork. For you, the avocation is performing a function in today's technocracy analogous to that of Christian asceticism in the later Roman Empire. It has become your personal manifesto against the idolatry of the virtual gods.

The overt expression of freedom is dissent; the subliminal expression is avocation. Both forces are necessary for the welfare of the person. They are to be varied, depending on the circumstances. While vigorous dissent is usually not tolerated by a tyrannical institution, the avocation is rarely considered a threat. You can almost always count on it as a safe haven for your own thoughts and feelings. When the prevailing disposition of the institution is ready, it will be moved by the silent message of the many individuals who have kept the self alive. The sense of freedom will then express itself in explicit social form. The institution will accordingly respond by creating a set of new virtual gods of a more reasonable character to preside over a slightly freer and a slightly more human-hearted equilibrium than before.

75 **Man's true setting** Visualize yourself at retirement. The first day brings a sense of relief from the burdens of decades. You are free from the demands of supervisors, the routines of schedules, and the certifications of performances.

Yet there is a reluctance to leave the surroundings with which you have become so accustomed. You look forward with mixed emotions, a welcoming anticipation of doing the many things you had in mind for years, yet an apprehension of how you are going to make out. You have just left the world of the competitive crowds for a cloister of your own. You are to find new activities to fill the vacuum voided by the absence of work. New regulating forces for your pattern of daily activities are to be fashioned. A new identity is to be sought. New experiences are to be evolved.

Contacts with your former professional colleagues rapidly decrease. When you occasionally bump into your old associates, it is always a pleasant affair, a homecoming in miniature "Why don't you drop by the office, when you have time? Sure like to chat with you again," they would say as you part. But the tone does not ring the same as it used to. Perhaps it is just your imagination. But somehow you get the feeling that he or she appears to be speaking to an outsider—someone who does not belong to his or her circle, someone who cannot do him or her any good.

Still you are not certain. You remember very well the words of your chief at the retirement luncheon. "I know we can count on your continued advice and help. We shall take every advantage of your willingness to assist us in the future." You recall how warm the farewells were, and you feel that your co-workers would like to see you again.

How boisterously your associates laughed to blanket the tension of not knowing what to say. And in your own thoughts you feel some concern about your successor's ability to fill your shoes. So on the next occasion of your being in the vicinity, you drop in on your former close-working subordinate.

He was deep in a pile of papers as you walked into his office. On seeing you, he jumped out of his chair, reached out to shake your hand, and patted you heartedly on the back with a "How are you? Sure glad to see you, you old son-a-va-gun! Keeping busy?" So you while away ten minutes or so, sensing all the time that his mind was really not on you but on that stack of cases on his desk. You abruptly broke off the conversation with a "Well, I've chewed up too much of your time already. I'd better be chasing along." He disagreed but walked you hurriedly to the door with a "*Do* drop in again the next time you're in the neighborhood again, won't you?" You wave a forlorn "So long."

As you walked down the corridor toward the elevators, you thought of his heaving a sigh of relief that you had not wasted too much of his morning as he dove back into his papers. Suddenly the vision came to you of that look on the faces of the younger people at the retirement party—the look of gladness to see the old man go, of opportunity for a chain of promotions, of new ideas to take over. You decided not to bother your former associates any more. You have not heard from them since.

So you leave work and the work crew behind with the rest of the severed yesterdays. You are no longer concerned over the immortality of your past contributions. You realize that this fantasy only represents extrapolated ambition, competing for honors in absentia, as it were, attempting to deny the living the mantle of greatness by hanging on to it yourself.

Your day-in, day-out coterie dwindles to a handful: your spouse and close relatives, a few couples of friends, the mailman, the grocer, and the neighbors weeding next door. It now dawns on you that retirement is not so much a withdrawing from responsibilities, as it is assuming a new kind. Sherwood Anderson put it this way: "Many men I know who are without leisure constantly cry out for it, not knowing the responsibility of leisure. Responsibility to whom? To oneself, alas."

Gradually you begin to regain the touch of the things around you, which had been obscured from view since childhood by social concerns held close to your eyes. Natural sentiments begin to flow more poetically and moral values fuse into common sense. You begin to hear the soft voices of Nature, as they are no longer drowned out by the shrill noise of competition.

A new aspect of God is intimated to you—an aspect quite different from that from which you used to draw utilitarian parcels. Somehow you sense that this transcendent kinship is the true setting of man. Up to now, you had enjoyed only a part-time association with it. Now, it can be practically full-time.

76 The masterpiece of wisdom "You know," you hear yourself saying one morning as you look in the mirror. "I *am* old!"

Perhaps, only then are you ready for Henri Amiel's test: "To know how to grow old is the masterpiece of wisdom, and one of the most difficult chapters in the great art of life."

77 Joyful steadiness In your retirement, worry no longer over the state of the world but be pleased with the simple smiles of the persons before you. Waste no emotions over iffy and distant issues and diffuse an unflickering joyance to your immediate company. Calm the troubled waters flooding the young by an easy manner, assuring tone, understanding look, and refreshing expression. Convey a shared reverence for life—a sharing among all the living, as you feel with Issa in his most famous haiku:

Please—kill not the fly.
See how he wrings his hands;
See how he wrings his feet.

As far as your day-to-day dealings with your fellow beings are concerned, consider the principle of net gain. This principle states that other things being equal, conduct yourself in such a way as to result in the least net increase in suffering to the universe, or, if suffering is not in question, in the greatest net increase in happiness. If there is only one cut of apple pie left for desert and it happens to be the other person's favorite, then inconspicuously steer it his way. Even if it happens that the other person does not in fact enjoy apple pie as much as you do but you notice his drooling at the mouth, let him have it nonetheless. A different principle would then be operative—that of magnanimity.

"Every moment think steadily as a Roman and a man to do what thou hast in mind with perfect and simple dignity, and feeling of affection, and freedom, and justice; and to give thyself relief from all other thought," advised Marcus Aurelius. "And thou wilt give thyself relief, if thou doest every act of thy life as if it were the last, laying aside all carelessness and passionate aversion from the commands of reason, and all hypocrisy, and self-love, and discontent with the portion which has been given to thee. Thou seest how few the things are, the which if a man lays hold of, he is able to live a life which flows in quiet, and is like the existence of the gods; for the gods on their part will require nothing more from him who observes these things."

In so doing, the sense is sustained that at any given moment you owe the world nothing and the world owes you nothing. This omnidirectional absence of indebtedness is the beginning of joyful steadiness.

78 **Things to avoid** A checklist of some of the more important items to avoid during retirement is the following:

With respect to health, do not eat indiscriminately. Nor fall into poor sleeping schedules. Do not succumb to the exaggerated anxieties of so many old people. These hypochondriacs are preoccupied with gloomy extrapolations of mild discomforts, which are quite normal. The symptom is frequent among those without satisfying interests. They sit around in boredom, waiting for something exciting to pop up. Nothing happens and they get tense. They feel neglected, persecuted, and finally sick. So life becomes miserable.

With respect to financial reserve, do not fritter it away by succumbing to what Leland Cooley referred to as "money magnets" and "subliminal salesmanship," such as those inducing euphoric purchases of overly expensive homes in retirement communities. The golf courses, swimming pools, and other accessories become progressively more useless to you as time goes on. Nor should you consign your fortune to your beloved relatives or favorite charities too soon. Long experience has shown that old people who have money to hand out are more likely to be treated as charming persons, whereas those who are known to have given it all away are more likely to be treated as old crocks.

With respect to a place to live, do not be too isolated. Find a house that is not more than three level blocks or so from public transportation. Do not live too far from stores, churches, and other places of frequent visits. Avoid areas with high crime in adjoining districts, which is likely to diffuse into your vicinity within a decade or so.

With respect to kibitzing, do not second-guess your friends. Nor offer gratuitous advice to your children as to how to bring up *their* children. Above all, do not recount how *you* used to do things in *your* time. If you happen to be living with your children, do not join their parties or hang around the living room when their friends are visiting. If invited to do so, stay a short courteous while, then graciously disappear into your own quarters to let them have a good time in their own fashion.

With respect to contentions, do not be caught in the middle. It has been said, for example, that there is a Sacred Footprint in the rock at the top of Adam's Peak in Sri Lanka. The impression is venerated by the Buddhists as having been made by Buddha, by the Hindus as having been made by Siva, and by the Moslems as having been made by Adam. Why should you, a Christian, take sides?

79 **Things to do** A checklist of some of the more important things to be attended to during retirement is the following:

With respect to independence, rely on yourself rather than others for happiness. They are too busy with their own problems. The government, the church, the community, the "planned happiness programs," and your children are able to augment your good life by way of some physical assets and occasional opportunities. But they are not able to provide the basic conditions of satisfaction and joy. These can only come from within yourself.

With respect to selection criteria, adopt those that fit your own circumstances in place of those conventional for the public at large. In the purchase of a home, for example, preference is to be given to a moderate-size, one-story house on a level lot with ground-floor entrance and a small lawn, single-mixing faucets to prevent scalding, step-in tub with a nonskid base and grab-bars anchored in the wall, and low-maintenance auxiliaries.

With respect to finances, readjust your investment portfolio to emphasize security of capital with a reasonable return. Adhere to a budget plan so that you are able to save some money even from your current income. The savings serve as an additional hedge against inflation and emergencies. Continue to have inexpensive house parties for your close friends and pick up the tab for a round of drinks now and then. But do not splurge money on frivolous activities or dribble the income away in nickels and dimes.

With respect to your will, keep a clearly written one, which leave little room for later contesting in the courts. Select a dependable person with good common sense as executor. Stipulate a major portion of your estate for your spouse to ensure financial independence. Then make provisions for others still dependent on you. In this regard, bequeathing drastically uneven amounts to the children tends to generate friction among them and break up their previously close ties. Leaving items of sentimental, artistic, or historical value to the favorite is much less disrupting. As far as charities go, look favorably on those that directly alleviate the suffering of the destitute.

With respect to overall orientation, maintain a constant clarity with regard to the prime reference. This is the harmonious union of your self with the totality of Nature. Whatever augments this augments your joy. Whatever detracts from it detracts from your joy. The final tuning of your harmony should go beyond the narrow interpretation of God's will by most institutions. It should include an empathy with all of God's creatures and creations—a peace with the stars and the moon, a feeling for the land and the trees, a shared merriment with man and beast . . . . all that is mutual and spontaneous . . . a placid ease all around.

80 **Death, serenity, and "no big deal"** Living oblivious of death is like playing a football game and refusing to watch the clock, listening to a symphony and refusing to hear the finale, or lighting a candle and refusing to admit the concluding darkness. Most of us find it hard to accept the naturalness of death and so we mourn when our loved ones pass away.

It took Chuang Tzu himself many years before he finally gained an intuitive sense of where death fits in the scheme of things. He was seen drumming on an inverted rice bowl on his knees and singing by his friend, who had come to comfort him upon the death of his wife. When his friend expressed shock at the behavior, the philosopher said, "You judged me wrongly. When my wife died, I was in deep sorrow, as any husband would be. But then I got to thinking about the meaning of death. I began to realize that there is nothing extraordinary in it. In the beginning we are nothing but an amorphous featureless mass with neither life nor form. Then there came a time when mass gave rise to spirit, spirit to form, and form to life. Now life in turn has given rise to death. Like Nature, man too has his seasons. If a person is tired and lies down to rest, we do not bother him with lots of wailing. My wife too has lain down for some rest in the Great Inner Room. For me to disturb her with lamenting and bawling would only mean that I have not yet grasped the elementary features of Nature's Law. That is why I no longer mourn her passing."

One's own life too is to be lived and embraced in its natural progression. The very definition of one's life includes birth and death as the bracketing events. "It is not how many years you have left that counts," said the late Vice President Hubert H. Humphrey, "but what you do with it." Whether the remaining span is forty years or forty minutes, the formula remains the same.

If one does well with what is left at all times, then he would have built the enormous good will of which Marcus Cicero (106–43 B.C.) spoke. One of the most delightful feelings that comes with old age is the sense of a life well spent and filled with many worthy deeds well done. A man who had cultivated the principles and practices of virtues throughout his life therefore possesses "the most suitable defenses" of old age. He would have no fear of death. Furthermore, it is perfectly natural for the old to die. For "when old men die it is as a fire gone out without the use of force and of its own accord, after the fuel had been consumed; and, . . . when ripe and mellow fall of themselves so with the old it is the result of ripeness. To me, indeed, the thought of this 'ripeness' for death is so pleasant, that the nearer I approach the more I feel like one who is in sight at last and is about to anchor in his home port after a long voyage."

The superior person, therefore, does not shut the idea of death out of his daily living. Like Yasunari Kawabata's sixty-four-year-old Shinzo, he continues to relish the rasping sound of the locust, the pale moon above, and the wonder of the seasons, as the sound of the mountain in the back of the garden reminds him of death approaching. To the superior person, there is nothing special about an equanimous incorporation of the end as part of the extended present. It is the most commonplace common sense that one can think of. His outlook reminds me of a little episode that took place several decades ago in a Chinese cemetery in Honolulu.

In accordance with Chinese custom on Chinese Memorial Day, members of my family and I visited the graves of my father and mother. The ritual involved the placing of specially prepared dishes of rice, fish, chicken, pork, soybean curd, lotus root, oysters, and so on, together with cups of tea and whiskey on a little stand before the grave site. After the punks and candles were lit, each of us in turn invited the parents to dinner, clasped our hands in reverent gesture, bowed three times, touched our foreheads on the ground three times, and poured the tea and whiskey before the grave in symbolic serving. We then lit a string of firecrackers in celebration of the happy occasion. As we began to leave, another large family group had gathered nearby to pay like respects to their ancestors.

It was a beautiful day. The air was festive with a picnic-like exhilaration for the youngsters. They romped all over the grassy plots, while the fifty-five-year-old lady was arranging the dishes, punks, candles, and so on. When she was halfway through, she noticed that none of the younger members of the family group was watching how she was going about it. So she stood up and called out in a high-pitched cheerful voice: "Come on, boys and girls. Come here and let me show you how to do it. You better learn how. Because when I'm down there, I don't want to be just smelling flowers once a year, you know. I want a real good meal. And served in the right way."

There is much about the good life that sophisticated executives can learn from the matter-of-fact cheerfulness in which this simple lady threaded the theme of her own death into the activities of her daily affairs. She did not make a conscious effort at it. It just came on its own. In the American vernacular, "It's no big deal."

Of all of the suggestions made in this book, perhaps the most difficult for the average executive is the intuitive acceptance of things that ordinarily bother him as "no big deal." It is the "big deals" that send waves of excitement through the executive corridors. It is the "tough decisions" that elicit whispers of adulation from the subordinates.

At the same time, it is just such "big deals" that obstruct your vision of many a beautiful thing happening around you, preclude many a fine feeling waiting to enter your being, and smother many a foci of composure spreading within you. See through these "big deals" in the jousting arena of power for what they are—the bewitching brew of The Demon. Drink them?—yes. But get drunk on them?—of course not, for they're really "no big deal." When death itself is unexcitedly assimilated into every second of your living self as "no big deal," how can anything else be a "big deal"?

And so, for the philosopher-executive, serenity itself is "no big deal." There is no seeking. He or she doesn't even give it a thought. It naturally comes on its own. And just as naturally, serenity stays.

81 The Land of Keikitran and Eleevan

THE LEADERS

1

"Welcome to Chianglai!" The gentle voice at the foot of the ramp beside the plane sounded just like that of my skinny roommate of some thirty years ago. It now belongs to the National Administrator for Policy and Planning in the youngest nation in the world.

Dao led me directly to his car and handed my passport and three baggage checks to the aide. "Your bags will be delivered to the guest cottage, J. C., where you will be staying for the next four days or so. It's surely good to see you—after all these years! I know you love wine, used to anyway. So I've collected samples of our finest for our little private celebration of your visit. By the way, did you remember to repay the rent we owed? If not, we ought to wire some money to our embassy in Paris right now to take care of that kind landlady, her son, or somebody. You had? Wonderful. How can I forget those days! Especially with you, my good friend, who shared his last sou with me." At the house I tried to discuss the work planned for the trip. But he would not listen. "Business? Not tonight. Tonight is for warm friendship . . . for the spirit. More wine, J. C.?" So the night went, just like the old times—reciting verses, nibbling sausages, sipping Beaujolais in our dingy attic flat in Montparnasse.

Turned in at 4:40 A.M. Thursday.

2

Got up a little after nine. What paradisiac surroundings! Bedroom windows overlooking bend of clear pond. Two-horned frogs floating dreamily on lush round trays of lotus. Chaste buds rising foot above still surface, broken now and then by splashing tails of mullet. On the banks, pandanus laced with strands of morning glory's green and funneled pink. And farther back, a stately stand of hundred-foot teaks—waxen, large, and oval leaves, and flowering white candelabras. Finches warbling. Gentle breeze, perfumed by blends of jasmine-ginger, brushing by my freshened face. Ah . . . life can be so beautiful!

On the dining table was *Le Figaro*. Beside it was a note from Dao. He hoped that I had slept well, asked that I enjoy my breakfast leisurely, and said that my assigned aide would escort me to his office when convenient. I downed the ham and eggs in gulps and wasted little time in getting there. After reminiscent pleasantries, he offered an agenda, laid out on the map below, for my approval. Two days here at Terkung, for intensive briefings and discussions with the top officials. Saturday and Sunday sightseeing around the capital. Two days at the Community Prakung, to get a feel of Laians at the grass roots. Three days in the Saikung Region, taking in a university, a modern manufacturing plant, court and prison operations, and a teaching art museum. Weekend horseback outing in the nearby national park. Two days at

Itinerary in Chianglai

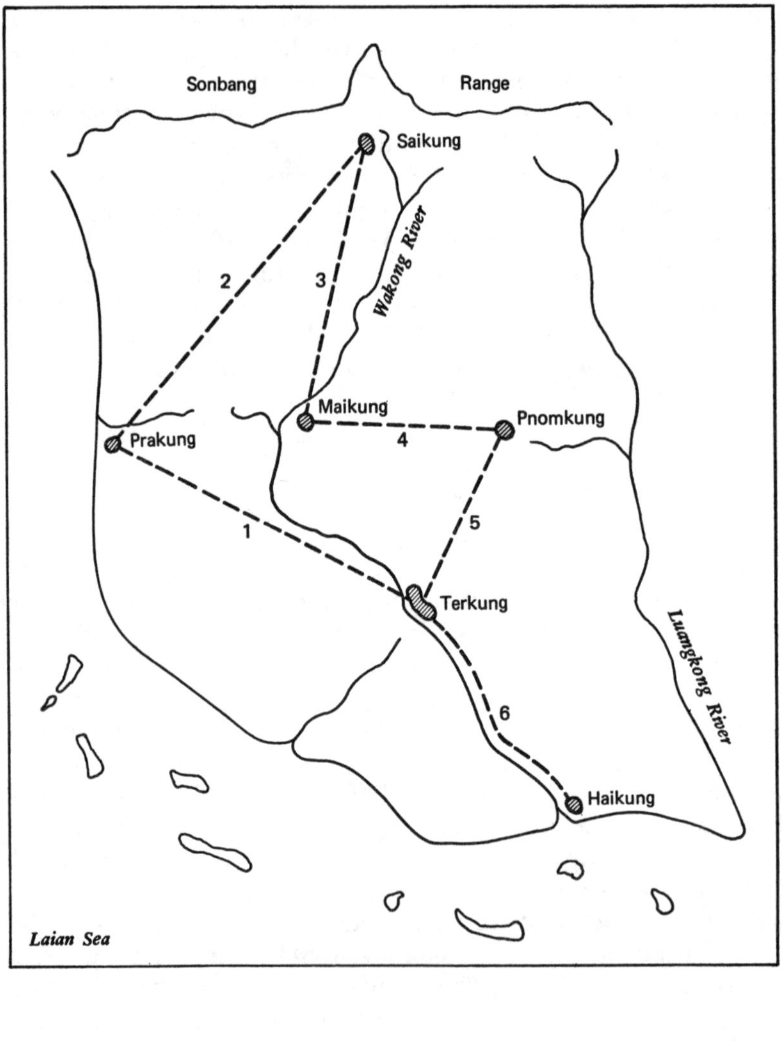

Maikung, inspecting agricultural activities, a center for research, an agency for city management, and an environmental bureau. Two days at Pnomkung, to call upon the Eastern Sector Military Headquarters. One day at Terkung for debriefing. Overnight cruise down the Wakong River to Haikung. Then home.

All of my desires had been anticipated. There was nothing further I could suggest.

3

Dao himself presented the orientation briefing. I had a rather difficult time understanding his philosophical preamble. It was extremely vague. Profuse allusions about not carving out abstractions from the Uncarved Unity. About not splitting the human being from its natural belongings. Yet he seemed to have no problem getting down to earth when it came to specific governmental policies. A strange combination of the mystical and the mundane. As far as I was able to make out, the Laians seem to place a kind of religious emphasis on their ties to Nature. Dao expressed the hope that at some time in the far future the entire world would be subsumed within this enveloping brotherhood, in which boundaries dividing nations would no longer be necessary. Peoples everywhere would then live in harmony with each other, as he put it, within the One.

Highest stress is laid by the Laian government on nurturing the people's harmonious associations with the One. What Dao referred to as the Great Domain is treasured with the greatest care and preservation. Nothing causes more dismay to an onlooker than the despoiling of the outdoors. Violence to the natural environment and public places is regarded as a crime against the Uncarved Unity itself. As one of the inseparable elements within the One, man, too, is as sacred as the wildlife of the forest and the trees along the alleys. Government practices are shaped accordingly. A minimum of material goods and cultural services is guaranteed everyone in Chianglai—employment, shelter, nutritious sustenance, high-school education, medical attention, safety from external and internal dangers, and decent burial—not because of some political or social doctrine, but because it is the natural and reasonable thing to do.

As we left the conference room, Dao grew serious. "After you have seen our country and talked to our brothers, J. C.," he said, "I would immensely appreciate all the advice you can give us as to how we can do better by our people. I would be especially grateful if you will answer two questions I would like to put to you. No explanations, J. C.—just yes or no. First, do you feel that everyone of the officials you met is trying to follow these principles and aspirations? Second, do you think Chianglai will achieve these aims within our lifetime?" I responded with a nodding promise. Whereupon he broke the solemn silence, which began to set in. "Well, so much for business! Let's have some food. Some delicious food, which I know you love, used to anyway. Oh, incidentally, I meant to tell you. Chairman Nam had just invited us to dinner. Nobody except the three of us at his chalet. You'll like the chairman. He's a good person."

4

As Dao had rightly anticipated, the food was absolutely delicious! The entree was *canard à l'orange*—orientalized. It had a tasty, crispy, golden brown skin that I savored only once before in my life in a little restaurant on a side street in Peking. Nam was an engaging conversationist, with a twinkle in his patient eyes, set in a kindly face which rose from a determined jaw. He was completely genuine and open, as I tried to understand his preoccupations as the leader of a technologically underdeveloped country.

I began by inquiring about his concern of highest priority. "It is the sustaining of an undying faith among the Laians, a stability of confidence, an anchorage into the very bowels of the land," he replied without the slightest hesitation. "It is the love of mountains, rivers, animals, trees, people—places where their ancestors lived, birds and beasts they tended, hills they terraced, fields they plowed, old men they venerated. This is where the Laians came from. This is where they will return. Chianglai can only be this. This is they." He cogitated for a moment, then went on: "With such a dedicated sense among the people, young and old, no army will be strong enough to conquer us. With such a dedicated sense among officials, high and low, no human being, tree, or creature in Chianglai will be maltreated." Nam felt strongly that his principal responsibility is nurturing this shared identity. To him, operating the machinery of government is of purely secondary importance. "An administratively inept department with a sincere love for all people and kindred Nature is preferred by far," said he, "to coldly efficient bureaucracies with impressive charts and neat figures."

He was equally certain in his belief regarding the greatest potential danger facing his country. "This is the displacement of the traditional love of Chianglai as a means of brotherhood in Nature by a kind of sophisticated chauvinism in which Chianglai is to serve as a means of massing personal possessions." Since the latter attitude is so prevalent throughout the world, Nam feels that Chianglai must be extremely cautious about indiscriminately enlarging her associations with other countries. The extent of cultural contacts is to be kept at a rate commensurate with her capacity of orderly assimilation of the good without most of the bad. "If not," he spoke with an air of determination, "our country will soon be reduced to nothing but a backwater of churning restlessness. I am not too afraid of an invasion of a military character as much as an ideological one, ostensibly to raise our level of scholarship or jurisprudence or management or standard of living or worship of God or some equally worthy purpose. The former we can see and counter. But the latter is much more insidious, especially the pitting of one citizen against another in immoderate competition, whether it be for the concrete gain of material goods or for the mythical glory of sheer winning. We do not set brother against brother. Laians are not divided into competitor-we and competitor-they. We accommodate in reasonable caring for each other. If life among the Laians is to continue with an abiding meaning, such an atmosphere must permeate our land as naturally as the oxygen we breathe." On that note, we bid each other goodnight.

5

Early Friday morning, I was introduced by Dao to Naaouk, Chief of National Planning. Referring to the four charts shown below, Naaouk explained the government procedures in Chianglai. He seemed particularly eager to ensure that I receive a lucid exposition, and he watched my eyes for clues of progress very closely as he went along. The country is divided into ten administrative jurisdictions, known as regions. Each of these has two to ten million people, organized in

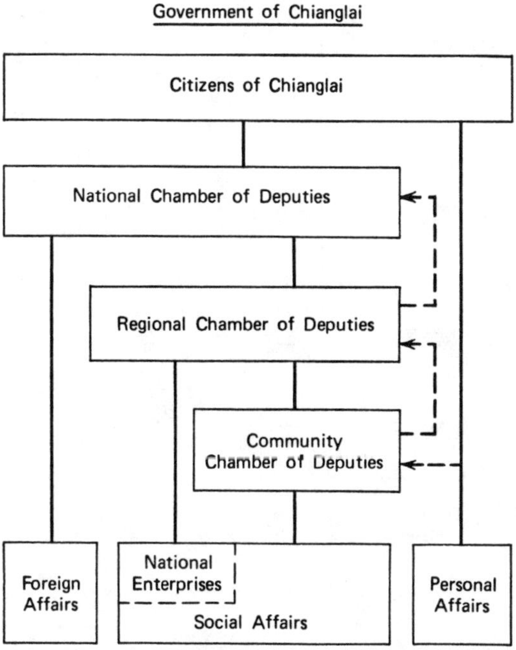

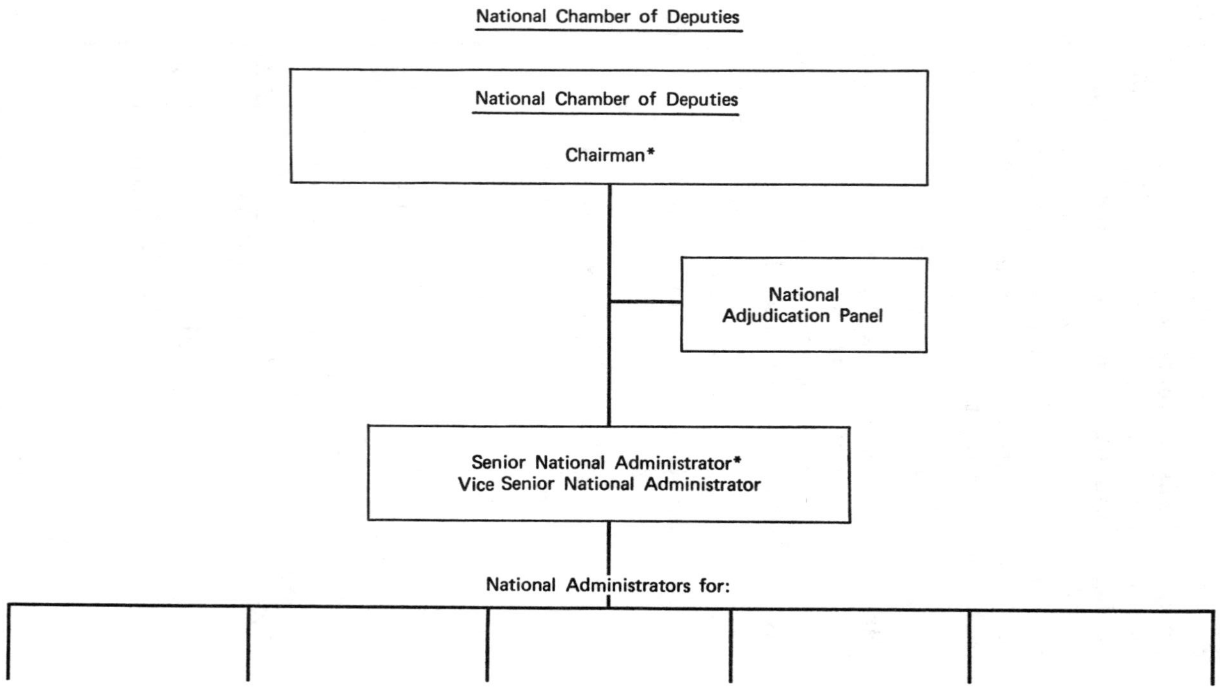
National Chamber of Deputies
National Chamber of Deputies
Chairman*
National
Adjudication Panel
Senior National Administrator*
Vice Senior National Administrator
National Administrators for:

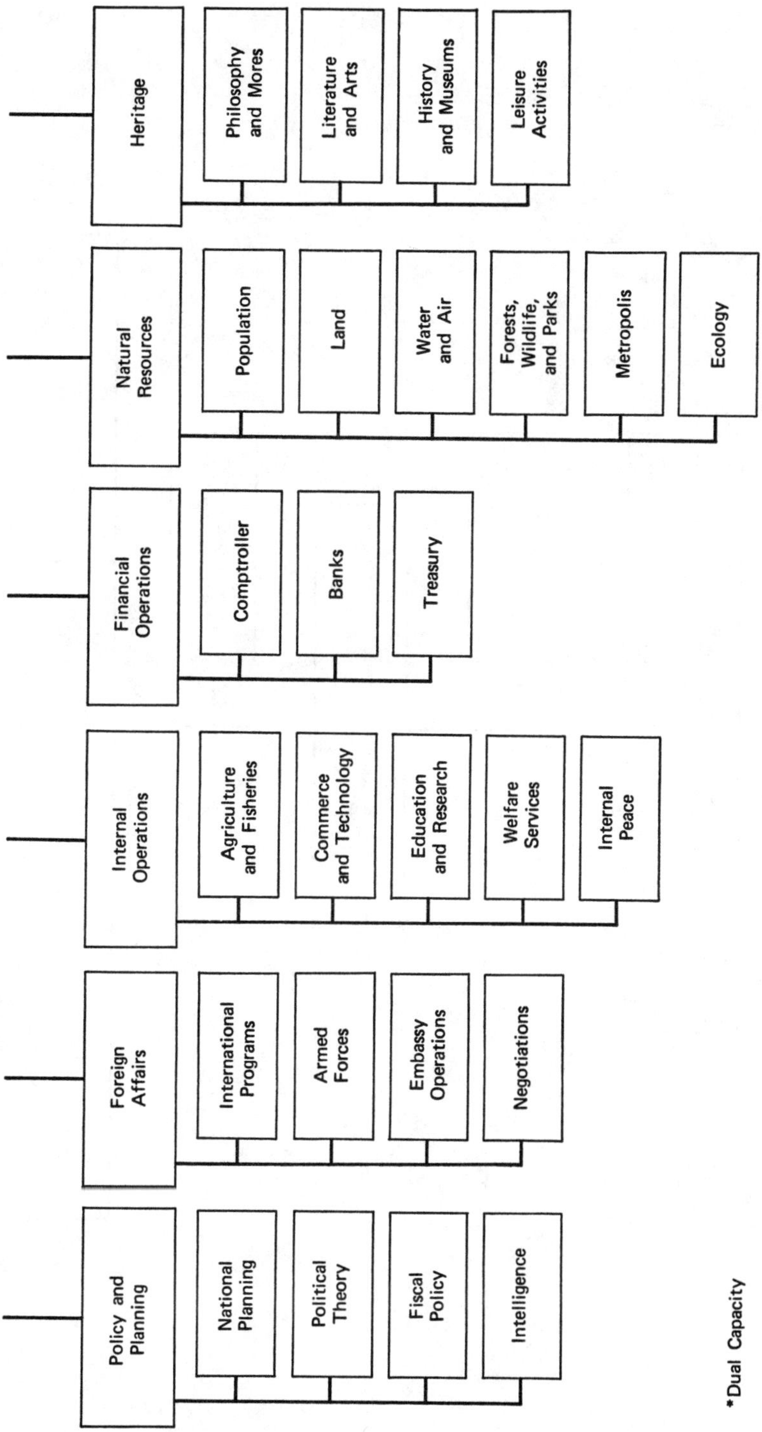

*Dual Capacity

Regional Chamber of Deputies

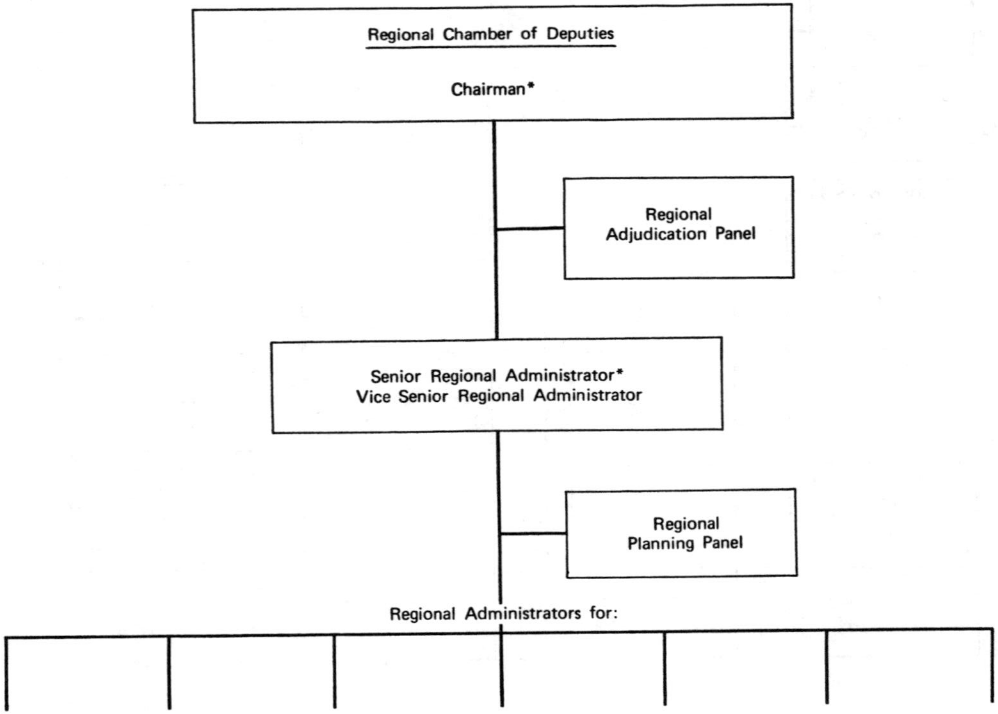

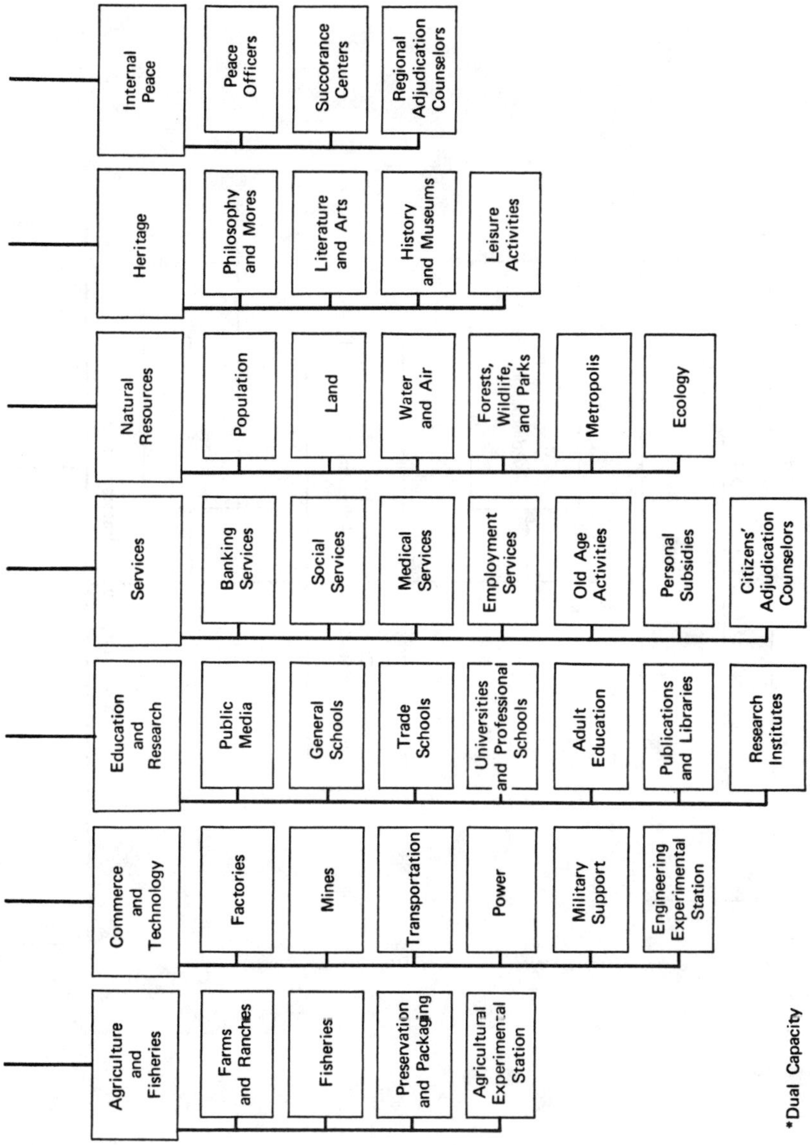
Agriculture and Fisheries
Farms and Ranches
Fisheries
Preservation and Packaging
Agricultural Experimental Station
Commerce and Technology
Factories
Mines
Transportation
Power
Military Support
Engineering Experimental Station
Education and Research
Public Media
General Schools
Trade Schools
Universities and Professional Schools
Adult Education
Publications and Libraries
Research Institutes
Services
Banking Services
Social Services
Medical Services
Employment Services
Old Age Activities
Personal Subsidies
Citizens' Adjudication Counselors
Natural Resources
Population
Land
Water and Air
Forests, Wildlife, and Parks
Metropolis
Ecology
Heritage
Philosophy and Mores
Literature and Arts
History and Museums
Leisure Activities
Internal Peace
Peace Officers
Succorance Centers
Regional Adjudication Counselors
*Dual Capacity

Community Chamber of Deputies

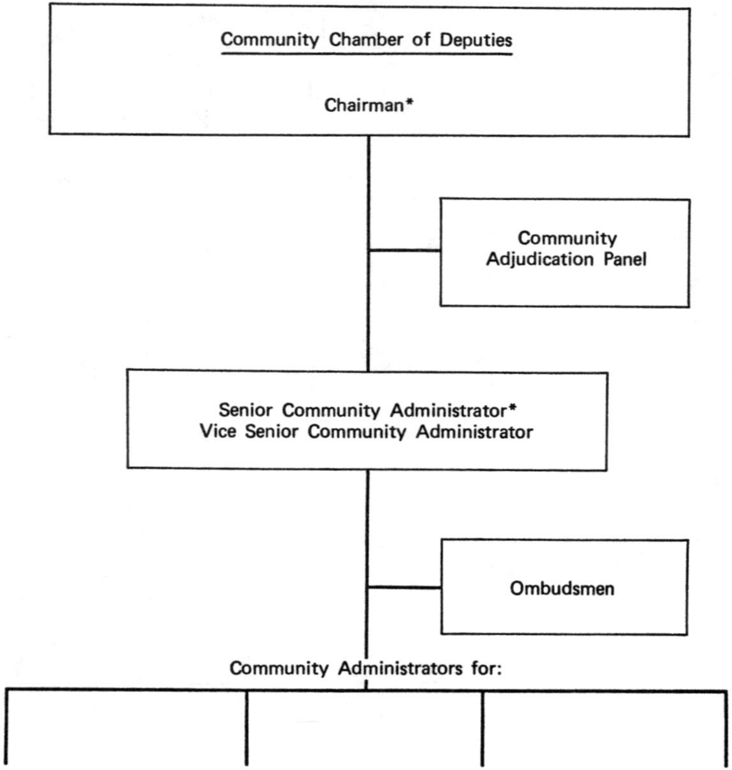

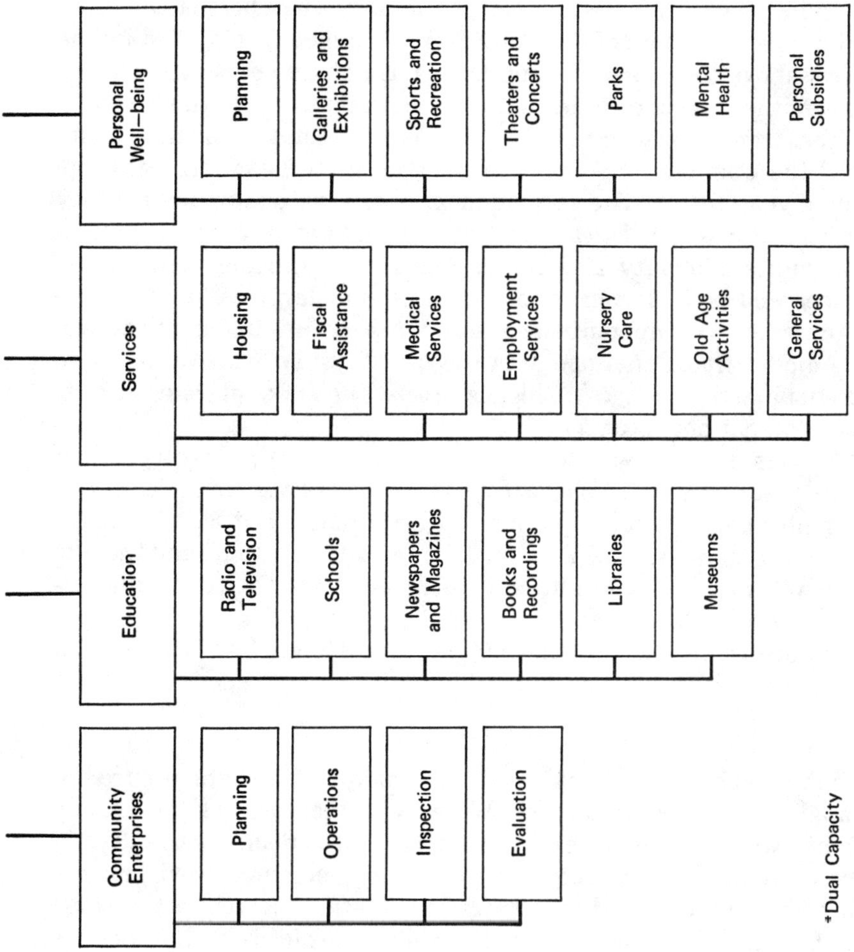

*Dual Capacity

roughly 200 communities. This calculates out to be about 50,000 in the basic political element. The highest governmental body is the National Chamber of Deputies. It manages the international affairs and plans and supervises all internal social programs. Personal and intrafamily events are left as private prerogatives of the person. The ten Regional Chambers of Deputies administer the national domestic enterprises and review the social programs of Community Chambers of Deputies. The hundred members of the Community Chamber are elected by the citizens above the age of sixteen for a term of six years. The elected members then select a chairman, their representative to the Regional Chamber from their own ranks for a six-year term, and the nine members of the Community Adjudication Panel from the citizens at large for nine-year terms. The chairman also acts as Senior Community Administrator who is chief executive in charge of program execution. He appoints a deputy and senior aides from the members of the chamber and ombudsmen from the citizens at large. Administrator-designees, in turn, appoint successors for their own unexpired terms. The Adjudication Panel operates the court system with rather wide discretionary flexibility. Analogous proceedings take place on the regional and national scene.

There is no other way to major social power in the country. All of the significant resources that can serve as power base are under public ownership. Land, for example, cannot be purchased; it is only loaned for use over one's lifetime. Although some writers, artists, and the like might well become quite affluent, their wealth is limited to that directly tied to the endeavors of the family alone.

"Where is freedom for the individual in Chianglai?" I injected a discordant note.

6

Naaouk tried hard to explain how freedom is provided and assured in Chianglai. But it was of no use. We were communicating on entirely different wavelengths. In his indoctrination, freedom is derivative of concrete living. It is not a postulated principle for which provisions are then to be found toward its realization. Round and round the same track he went. Each time he would speak more slowly and pronounce his French words more distinctly, thinking that my obvious dissatisfactions must have originated from misunderstandings due to his imperfect accent. But we would always end up where we began.

"Now, the worst kind of existence is the stupor of the conquered and oppressed. Would you agree, sir?" I nodded. "Equally pernicious is starvation, sickness, and deplorable deficiencies. Would you also agree on this, sir?" And again I nodded. "That is why we place the freedom from these two fears as number one and number two on our national priority. Does this make sense, sir?" I kept nodding yet a third time. "Well, our country is poor. Many of our people are uneducated. It is easy, as you can see, for a cunning man to steal the clothing off their backs if he were given license to do as he pleases. There is no one who can more effectively protect the poorly endowed and the suffering from the more talented and insatiable than the government . . ." By this time I gave up and girded for a long harangue. "The people here are brought up to yield to the exigencies troubling their brothers," he caught his second wind. "They become very distressed when confronted, sir, with an uncompromising either-or alternative. This is the reason for the very wide latitude you will observe, sir, within the operations of our adjudication panels, as they go about fitting the sentence to the particular person's extenuating circumstances." At this stage, Naaouk must have felt that he was finally getting his points across, for I had stopped arguing for some time. "Before the hearing of a case," he persisted with increased alacrity, "counsels representing both sides formally attest to a sincere commitment to the truth as they see it without intentional distortion in degree or kind for any purpose whatsoever. Then after hearing evidence from all points of view, both sides and the adjudicators come to an agreement as to a reasonable and acceptible judgment. In this way Laian jurisprudence guarantees our freedom from the clever extremist." He paused for a short breath and went on. "Still another point, sir. Laians are most trusting with each other. They are happy in their pleasing one another. You can well imagine how distraught they would be if subjected to conflicting orders by different officials. If we allow this to become normal practice, the people will gradually become a dissembling, litigious, and hard-hearted race. Then they would no longer be Laians. For us, this would amount to spiritual suicide, sir, and our humble ancestors will be most displeased. That is why we take considerable pains to shield our people from dilemmas of this kind. We limit the social power to the single political system governed by the Laians themselves. To ensure that no one holds control too long, encumbents in high government offices are not allowed more than one term at a given echelon. This is also the reason why we do not permit any foreign institution to give orders to our people, or vice versa, of course—whether it be economic, cultural, political, or other forms. A person may believe or think whatever he desires. But there is a definite restriction to his issuance of commands affecting others. In this way, sir, we provide to our people the freedom from bewilderment." And so the session lasted on and on.

All this must have seemed quite logical to Naaouk, for his eyes beamed with enthralling dedication. But to me it smelled so much like Marxist tonic being squirted out of a totalitarian machine. Yet, Naaouk and his staff were most considerate and courteous through what must have been a somewhat exasperating morning from their standpoint. For my own part, I tried to reciprocate as best I could. However, I fear my ill-bred manners and antagonisms must have shown through.

7

Seeing that there was no point in attempting to appreciate their rationale, I shifted my attention in the afternoon to those specific areas that may have application in a wide range of political philosophies. Perhaps, I thought, I might just learn something worthwhile. Laian justice had been covered in the morning period. The emphasis on culture had been clarified by Nam last night. The one on planning follows from Chianglai's own trans-socialist foundations. So I decided to begin with their unusual alignment of the armed forces, reporting to the chief of international affairs.

"We did that to unify our dealings with the outside," Naaouk stated. "Military force is only one of the many instruments of international relations, as you know, but which we hope will not be a factor in our own associations with other countries. ... No, sir—Senior Administrator Nam is *not* the commander-in-chief of the armed forces. He does control them, of course, but only through the National Administrator for Foreign Affairs. We see the Senior Administrator's primary role as optimizing the integrated wholeness of the national well-being, which transcends that of special functions. We feel that loading him with a specific operating mission might prevent judicious allocation of scarce resources because of his subconscious ties." Naaouk admitted to great advantages in the arrangement of having the head of state also command the armed forces. But he insisted that these are limited to situations of potential revolts by the military or to aggressively expanding empires, which he did not think hold for Chianglai. I then probed the role of religion in the Laian society. "Religion is a personal affair. The government does not speak on the subject," he asserted. "As far as the churches themselves are concerned, there is no official religious leader for any of our fifty-six denominations. Each community has teachers and ministers of its own. Before long, one of them becomes nationally revered as wise and virtuous. He then becomes accepted through consensus as the teacher-primate of the country. He is neither designated nor elected and has no authority to dictate dogmas or beliefs. Yet his instructions carry weight as if he had been given formal leadership. . . . You asked about funds, sir? Most of the pastor's pay come from the government and the rest from donations. All of the construction funds and two-thirds of the upkeep also come from the government." Then I asked about the ombudsmen. "They have been of greatest value," Naaouk smiled with pride. "The wise, compassionate, and patient are appointed to these posts, sir. They can call on any office for assistance on a case. They even take pains to arrange a match for lonely Laians on request. When confronted with what they consider to be an unresponsive reply, they would appeal to the Adjudication Panel, which can pass judgment resulting in swift action. The ombudsmen are so effective that we know of no one in Chianglai who feels completely helpless." One of the blocks on the chart, entitled "Personal Subsidies," caught my fancy. "What's that?" I inquired. "That is where a man can go to get financial help beyond those stipulated in the standard social programs. There are not many instances of this kind. If they do show up, however, we would want our brothers to feel that no matter what the problem, we *do* care about them. For example, I read a Prakung report this morning about a poor young man who lost his wallet while arranging for hotel and transportation reservations for his three-day honeymoon. I am sure you would be pleased to learn, sir, that the Personal Subsidies Office reimbursed him right then and there."

"What a satanic mousetrap," I shuddered in my mind, as the discussions ended for the day. "The wretched Laian is owned body and soul by the state."

8

Friday evening was one of those occasions for warm friendship . . . for the spirit. I was guest of honor at a banquet at the famous Ehahai. The members of the National Adjudication Panel and the Cabinet were there. So were their spouses.

Dinner started with a toast by Dao: "To the joy-filled longevity of the beloved brother who gave up his last possessions for the survival of a poor Laian—to J. C.!" His comrades joined in unison: "To J. C.!" I was deeply moved, having just learned at cocktail that my friend had spoken often of our trying times in Paris and made me into a hero for the children in Chianglai by recounting how I had sold the last thing I owned of any value—great-great-great-greatgrandfather's gold watch—to buy some medicine for him, as he laid deathly sick in bed. So overwhelmed was I that I was barely able to respond with: "To Chianglai!" The rest repeated: "To Chianglai!" Thirty more toasts followed throughout the dinner: a reciprocal greeting with each of the other members at the table and a group welcoming of each new dish as it was served. Most of the dishes were exotic ones, which I have never seen before. One example: large precooked dried oysters, resoaked overnight in water; partly sliced like a hot dog bun; filled full with kneaded fish meat, mixed with chopped ham, peanut, water chestnut, strips of bamboo shoot, with some salt, spices, sugar, and a sauce called nuoc yeou; wrapped in pig mesentery; dipped in scrambled egg with herbs, and rolled in cracker crumbs; then deep fried in a vat of chicken fat. The pieces were arranged artistically with some sprigs of parsley, rising from a large green platter like a majestic miniature mountain with wind-blown pines, jutting out between the boulders on the steep face.

I had difficulty sleeping. I was troubled by my inability to reconcile how these fanatics I had pictured operating the dictatorship described in Naaouk's briefing could have been the very same friendly and gentle individuals with whom I had just spent one of the warmest evenings of my life. I must have been mellowed by the wine.

9

Sightseeing with Dao on Saturday consisted of a drive around the downtown area, a look at public monuments, a stroll along the promenade, a stop at a sidewalk cafe, and a walk through a museum. Having visited innumerable cities, I was quite blasé about the tour as we began. But Dao's companionship was most enjoyable, as always. As the hours wore on, I gradually stopped thinking about what I was seeing and simply let the Laian setting soak in as it will. Then just as imperceptibly some pervasive something, rather pleasant, began to envelop me like a dream. It seemed as if I was floating with an airiness of mystical belonging. Could it be what Nam was hinting at? But as soon as I thought about it, it disappeared.

We spent Sunday riding in an open horse-drawn carriage through the Terkung Park. As we were leaving, an intriguing monument attracted my attention. In the center sat a powerful man, looking down at a small cat. The cat seemed in some sort of pain. Beside them, stood a bird and farther back, a goat. They were encircled by a large group of dejected animals and drooping trees. It was the monument to Keikitran and Eleevan.

"Now, if you can really feel the spirit of that bronze sculpture," Dao said softly with his eyes looking into the distance, "you will grasp what—how do you Americans say it?—yes, what makes Chianglai tick." "Who is . . ." I started to inquire. But it was evident that Dao was speaking not so much to me, as to himself. So I decided not to interfere with his own meditation of the moment and postponed my question for another day.

THE PEOPLE

10

Monday morning. After circling the dirt airstrip, bordering a beautiful wide beach, our Piper Cub touched down and taxied over to the waving crowd of two hundred. A delicate old man with white and flowing whiskers came toward us and smiled. He bowed and amiably greeted me: "My honorable elder brother. Welcome to Prakung." The Senior Community Administrator Olunol then introduced me to the members of his cabinet. I waved back to the friendly people, as we walked to the nearby pavilion. Thatched roof, freshly painted wooden posts and floors.

During tea and cookies, Olunol assured me that it would be a great honor for Prakung if I would think of it as my own home. I should feel free to do whatever I would like. He and the people were at my disposal. "And what is your pleasure, honorable elder brother?" he inquired. I said that I would like to get a general idea how a typical community is governed, to hear what senior officials feel to be their major problems and goals, and, most importantly, to get to know some of the people. He was specially pleased with my reference to people. "As my honorable elder brother so wisely put it, people are the most important." Our schedule was accordingly set. Monday: meeting people randomly as they go about their daily routines. Tuesday: visiting an elementary school, a Catholic church, and a Buddhist wat and receiving a formal presentation on the government apparatus.

"My chauffer and car are at your service, honorable elder brother," Olunol said. "Your aide, Paalol, was born and raised here. He still has many friends and relatives in the community. He can care for you quite nicely. I have not assigned any escort from my own office, because I believe people in general tend to be more spontaneous in the absence of government representatives. I am sure that you, in your perceptive insight of human behavior, will not regard this move on my part as inattentiveness to your honorable person but rather as an indication of our earnest desire to make your visit here as worth your while as possible. I would be deeply indebted, however, if you would phone me right away should you need any help at any time. Do promise me that, would you, good Paalol? Excellent. Do these suggestions meet with your approval, honorable elder brother?" I thanked him. We shook hands all around. My aide and I drove off in Olunol's old Citroen.

11

Everyone seems to be going about his rounds at a steady pace in this quaint place. An unlabored nonhustling gaiety of heart. Yet there appears to be no loafing on the part of anyone in sight. Whether we discussed important matters of state or simply exchanged light banter, the Laians never showed the slightest indication of annoyance at my interrupting what they happened to be doing.

Sixty-eight-year-old man planting saplings in the public square—a part-time worker for the Old Age Bureau; carver of rare native hardwoods—a direct descendant of a long line of respected carvers; couple on a three-day honeymoon—thanks to the Personal Subsidies Office for replacing their lost money; Paalol's friends at the cooperative—who invited us to share their lunch of salted giant sea perch, white cabbage, rice, and tangerines. Each individual was refreshing in a unique way. Yet they all appear to have the same kind of instinctive friendliness. A little boy with a small kitten—black, with a white cravat, a white streak down the chest and belly, and white chin and paws—kept following at a shy distance. After fifty yards or so, he edged up to Paalol and exchanged a few words. He then stood back and beamed with a kind of loving gratitude in his big brown eyes. I smiled to him and walked on.

It might have been the infectious cheerfulness of Prakung. But somehow I strangely felt much more at ease with my own self than I have had for quite some time.

12

"What did you two talk about?" I casually asked my aide just to make some conversation. "Something he learned in school," Paalol answered and went no further. The faint but noticeable blush on his face aroused my curiosity. "But what *specifically* did he learn in school?"

"He had learned a story about a white man, who helped a sick Laian whom the people dearly love." I felt a little lump enlarging in my throat, as Paalol continued. "He asked me whether you are the good brother from the far West who gave everything he had to do it." "And . . . what . . . did . . . you . . . say?" "I said that you are indeed the good brother, who saved Brother Dao's life."

Something in me oozed out as a tear.

13

Monday night was yet another one of those times for warm friendship . . . for the spirit. But on this occasion, it was purely trans-socialist! The community feast was attended by as many as the farm cooperative's produce hall could hold. It was cleaned out for the affair, because it was the largest building in the area. The senior officials and a thousand others drawn by lot had been invited.

Olunol opened the feast with a brief one-minute remark to the effect that they were most honored and pleased by my joining them in a simple family meal. That was all as far as speech-making went. Every item in the meal itself was locally produced: pork sausage, chicken pot-roasted in nuoc yeou, cuttlefish with bamboo shoots and mushrooms, chive and crabmeat duck omelet, vegetables, rice, mangosteen, and *vin ordinaire*. Many of the women guests helped for over a day in its preparation. Others pitched in during off-hours. I was fascinated by their game of menagee, which took place at practically every table throughout the dinner. Two men stood with right arms drawn back, then extended them, while putting out some fingers, shouting what they thought to be the sum on both hands at the same time. Two arms darting back and forth, then faster and still faster. Voices sing-and-songing, then louder and still louder. Until one guesses right. Shrill cheers and laughter, as the loser downs his glass of wine.

At the end of the festivities, I counted no less than a hundred jolly losers wobbling through the doors, amid the understanding chuckling of their friends. About a score could barely navigate. We packed as many in our Citroen as we could. After seven round trips, finally, we bid the last of them goodnight at midnight.

14

Visited the General School Tuesday morning. Spartan is the word, as far as equipment and facilities are concerned. Small sturdy wooden chairs, few pictures here and there, but everything in place and clean. The bright and vivacious headmistress explained the Laian view of academic education in the scheme of things. All Nature is our teacher and every encounter is a lesson. Education takes place everywhere and learning continues throughout one's life. The schools constitute only one, although very important, place where much of these experiences occur during the formative years of a Laian. The General School is a combination of our elementary and high schools, compressed into nine years. Its main objective is to inculcate a sense of wholesome living through self-confident reliance on the heritage of Laians, the strength of their united efforts, and the basic goodness of the human being. Major secondary aims include the fundamental skills of our three R's. The schools do offer courses in the creative and performing arts, but these are given after hours and are not required. The churches similarly sponsor sessions on personal ethics and religion. But, in general, morality, art, and leisure activities are looked upon as falling within the primary responsibilities of the person and the family.

There are no explicit rules on discipline, although, traditionally, the principal possesses almost unlimited authority in school. It is rare, however, that he has been known to have raised his voice or laid his hands on a student. Such an action would have been interpreted as a public confession of failure on the part of both principal and parents.

Just before leaving, we sat briefly in a class on literature in the sixth grade. One of the pupils was reciting Mechit's patriotic poem, entitled "Watering the Land":

> Lone elephant in chains clanging,
> Overpower'd by conqueror's herd.
> Taught hiss of asp, his trumpeting
> Wheezes like frail consumptive bird.
>
> Ancestors, grandsons! Ought I
> Seek success with groveling hand,
> Or for Chianglai, the foe defy?
> Let my blood water our parched land.

15

After saying goodbye to the headmistress, we were attracted by some yelling from an open clearing. A group of boys and girls were scrambling about kicking something in the air. According to Paalol, it was their national game of naloeen (flying swallow). Other popular sports include gymnastics, swimming, and racing water buffaloes through rice paddies. Contact sports involving intentional assaults, like boxing, are prohibited.

In naloeen, each of two teams is made up of five individuals standing on the opposite sides of a net that is two meters high and strung across a field six by ten meters in dimensions. Something like a badmington shuttlecock, called the swallow, is used. The base consists of a flat rubber disc, eight centimeters in diameter and one in thickness. Feathers are attached to the topside. This keeps the disk floating downward in a horizontal attitude. The object of the game is to fly the living swallow over to the other side with three passes or less, as in our game of volleyball. Only that part of the foot below the knee is permitted to touch the living swallow. The most common of the techniques are the cross-kick by means of the side just above the instep and the upward-forward motion with the top of the foot. The great players, however, are skilled in a wide variety of moves. We saw a sprightly little fellow flip a somersault and, while still upside down in midair, slam the swallow over the side with a swift kick on one occasion and bluff with a quick flick on another. The side that fails to keep the swallow flying has a dead bird on its hands and loses a point. Twenty points comprise a set and two sets a game.

Since the next two persons on the docket spoke both French and English, I excused Paalol, who dashed off to visit his aging parents.

16

Lively Father Cushing hailed me with a heavy Irish-American brogue. Impressive six-footer. His parish numbers 200 communicants and 400 of what he called associate communicants. He has endeared himself to the non-Catholics as well as Catholics for his tenacious defense of Prakung residents against outsiders, both religious and political.

Seeing that the Padre was brought up in Boston and American directness, I came right to what I had in mind: "Did severance of your financial and institutional ties to the Vatican disrupt your mission badly?" "It depends on what you mean by badly," he was equally outspoken. "It was hectic sledding at the outset. Nobody had any money. I was absolutely broke, as you can well imagine. Couldn't float a loan from home base. Now, we're able to obtain some subsidies from the political authorities and things aren't too bad, as you can see. We have a little church but a devoted congregation. Wouldn't swap it for Saint Paddy's. You can't find more deeply religious people anywhere else. I'm not referring just to the Catholics here in Prakung, but to the rest as well. Even the agnostics here are not like those repugnant intellectuals in New York City with their cynical superiority. The local brand appears to be religious in their own way. Sometimes, I'm not sure that they're true agnostics in the light of their genuine respect for the mystical. But I suppose that by the book we'll have to call them agnostics. I don't think that there are any real atheists around though." He paused and drew a few puffs on his cigarette. "In any case, they're all first-rate, with religion or without. Since I am not much of an empire builder, I am perfectly contented preaching our Lord's Gospel in the way I'm doing now. In fact, I don't have to debate with those nit-picking nincompoops in the old bishop's secretariat in Terkung or tangle with the Vaticrats in Italy anymore. Quite a relief in many ways. Bureaucracy's the same all over. Rome is no exception. I continue to receive encyclicals and all that, of course, and I follow them meticulously. I myself am one of those old-fashioned priests out in the boondocks, who believe in Papal infallibility, celibacy, and so on, although I must admit I *do* love that fine local wine—that wonderfully tasting stuff. They call it mei jiu. Have you tried some?"

"How about the moral leadership of Christianity in Chianglai?"

"Y'mean political involvement? Power of the Church? Wiped out! Gone!" Again disarmingly forthright. "You can preach to your heart's content, so long as it pertains to personal morality, your own belief in God, relationships within the family, and the enhancement of a person's virtues. When it comes to social matters outside the familial preserves, however, that's where we preachers have to be careful. I have no difficulty at all recognizing the thin line of demarcation, since I understand their rationale. But it is very fuzzy for the folks back stateside. Anybody is permitted, even encouraged, to discuss man's proper conduct in society. The moment you begin to tie a penalty of any kind to deviations from the propositions, that's when the political boys step right in and say: 'Uh, uh! That's our bailiwick.' Obtaining compliance by incarcerating someone, firing him from a job, threatening him with eternal hellfire, or enticing him with money—all are instruments of power in the regulation of the social order. People shouldn't be bossed by many sources telling them to do conflicting things. So only the deputies, empowered by the people should be permitted to do any coercing. No outsiders, no self appointed person—no one not elected by them is to order them around!" The Padre stood erect, declaiming eloquently. His huge face began to flush. But then, he instantly erased it with a smile. "So far, however, things have not gone badly from my personal standpoint. I have never found a moral doctrine that I wanted to preach that was contrary to the Laian laws. Besides, I go easy on that reward-and-punishment-after-death theme, which is the main staple of many religions, as you know. In Prakung, though, that kind of appeal does not work as effectively as elsewhere. People do things just because they feel right in doing them. This is what makes life so happy for me as a priest here. As to what I would do if the officials come out with laws on, say, abortion, I . . . But—knock wood—that seems quite unlikely in my lifetime." He reflected for a couple of seconds. "But this does not mean that Catholicism will be gradually squeezed out of this part of God's world. This frail seedling of true faith that I keep tending in this lovely pasture will most surely blossom out again one of these days. Our Mother Church has been around a long time—much, much longer than this twenty-seven-year-old government. And with the Grace of God, we'll outlive them all!" He winked at me with a broad grin as I got up to hurry to my next appointment.

17

Abbot Minh was waiting on the step of Prakung's largest wat, when I arrived some forty minutes late. The pagoda was built six centuries ago. Its gold-leafed statues and ornate spires constituted glittering reminders of the Buddhist eminence of former times. Minh had come from quite wealthy parents. He is versed in English, French, Chinese, and German, and completed post-graduate work at the Sorbonne. He remains one of the leading scholars on comparative religion.

As we sat on a bench beneath a banyan tree, I solicited his views on whether he thought the religious spirit of people around the world was waning. "Well, no and yes." Then he elaborated at length on an unusual theme, unusual for me at least. He defined the religious spirit roughly as "a Sharingness among the living, the livinged, and the living-to-come." The extrapolation of this Sharingness in both directions would lead to what we commonly refer to as God, the Alpha and Omega. A religious spirit of this character is not diminishing. To him, this Sharingness is not determined by the presence or absence of obstructions, which hide it from view. No matter how thick the encrusting or confusing the distracting, it is still there. "But regretfully," he slowly shook his head, "there have been many hidings and distortings over the centuries. Instead of letting Sharingness be with our being in it, as it is to be, many religious leaders have been overzealous in their eagerness to make this God of ineffable Sharingness understandable to the average disciple. They therefore attempted to precipitate this universal presence into a concrete thing, thereby converting this uncongealable Reality into an artificial image of man. By such a metaphorical stroke, Sharingness was converted into a kind of Father, and everything became easily explainable. The ministers can then draw innumerable analogies to the relationship between an awesome father and his children. Sharingness with plants and animals was simplified away by the idea of our being the Father's only child. As time went on, certainty and convenience of administration were added factors leading to the stipulation of explicit places and instructions for communing with this God. Still more of Sharingness was simplified away. Before long, man sensed his becoming self-alienated from the Sharingness Itself by these intermediaries. He began to feel that somehow the continuum of belonging that flows between him and Nature is being dammed up by these man-made artifices. And he is restless in his imprisonment. The resulting irreverence for established dogmas and rituals is interpreted by many as a decline of religious fervor. Yet from a certain point of view it may be seen as an encouraging sign. It suggests an earnest searching for the fundamental Sharingness, by questioning our own naive reliance on the crutches that have been offered to prop us up in our spiritual indolence. I see it as a seeking beyond the man-made obstructions for a return to our true belonging, which is Sharingness."

I then asked if he would consider his own religion as a beacon toward the rediscovery of Sharingness. "I don't think so," he confessed with candid modesty. "We too have embroidered our beliefs. We too have simplified much of Sharingness away over the centuries, although perhaps not quite as much as some of the more militant religions. Our very dominance in local regions, however, have induced a lot of us to think that we are somewhat more acquainted with the truth than others. We forget, alas, that Sharingness denies priority to any single component. There is no pecking order—only sharing. So in answer to your question, we hope to contribute first by rectifying our own selves. By rectifying our selves we may thereby become that much more deserving partners in Sharingness." When I suggested that he might consider leading a crusade to bring people back to the true God, he replied that from the viewpoint of Sharingness, crusades are self-defeating. Instead of resonating with others in Sharingness, crusaders disrupts the harmony by imposing their own wills. "Of course, we will be more than pleased to share our own experiences. It is our hope that by heightening each other's awareness of this Sharingness, which binds all creatures together, we may reach a more lasting peace on earth than by fragmenting it and nationalizing the pieces."

18

As I left the Abbot, my arrogant attitude at Naaouk's briefing came to mind. Yes—*I* knew *the* way. I reflected on what Minh had said about crusaders and about first rectifying one's self, and I felt ashamed.

But as I thought more of his unassuming sharingness, something rejuvenating began to saturate the atmosphere, and I felt much better.

Yet his Sharingness is so difficult to grasp. Come to think of it . . . so is God.

19

At lunch, Olunol showed an absorbing interest in learning more about America. He had studied Jefferson and Emerson. He mentioned that the people in Prakung refer to the United States as the Golden Valley. "How has your distinguished government been so successful?" he asked. "Can you instruct us, honorable elder brother, how we can improve our management so as to bring my own brethren a bit closer to the good life you all enjoy in your great country?"

When I said that millions of Americans are unemployed, he was surprised. When I added that some even starve, his eyes popped, shocked. But he composed himself, apologizing for his slowness to observe that such self-deprecation was the courteous expression of deep modesty in "my most esteemed elder brother."

I decided not to disillusion the old gentleman and changed the subject abruptly.

20

"Mr. Administrator," I rechanneled his line of thought, "I have been much impressed with the good life of your own brethren here in Prakung. You must work quite hard to bring about such a condition. I was wondering what facet of the total program occupies your prime attention." As he bit the bait and started to reply, I heaved a sigh of relief. I could imagine how he would have collapsed had I been forced to talk about the state of our medical service.

"You are so kind with your generous remarks, most worthy elder brother," he demurred, insisting that he had contributed extremely little. The good life for the people results from something much, much larger than a single man or a single species. "Happiness does express itself through the individual. However, the individual is only the confluence of many, many people, who lived long ago and who are living today. The happiness which springs from a person's own self is nurtured by the rest of Nature. Now, if everyone is dedicated to this kind of mutuality, a tradition evolves which furthers the universal joyfulness. The longer it is enriched, the more imperturbably is it capable of standing in the face of the normal hardships that arise in everyday life." Olunol spends most of his energies, accordingly, in encouraging this quality through concrete exemplifying actions. He is convinced that the little things that one does for his neighbors are as important in fostering the kindred spirit as the big cooperative projects. A number of the Laians with whom I had talked yesterday had mentioned having seen Olunol extending a helping hand to some old lady with her load, removing some thorn from a dog's paw, and propping up some leaning tree along the road. I was told that he never lectures or admonishes anyone. He simply nudges very amiably through examples of his own, praising those who succeed and comforting those who fail.

His comments about human confluence and Nature's infusions sounded quite familiar. "Do you belong to Abbott Minh's church?" I pursued a hunch. "I am afraid that I am not acquainted with the views of the revered Abbott, honorable elder brother," he replied. "You see, I happened to be an agnostic."

21

The official briefing followed the identical arrangement as the one presented at Terkung. Most of it was pretty dull, as such things usually are. But I was intrigued with their unusual approach at handling radio and television.

I began the question period with: "Why did you place radio and television activities under the Community Administrator for Education rather than under one of the other three administrators?" In her reply, the Community Administrator for Services called attention to the fact that it was listed in the first position on the chart. Because of the capacity of radio and television to reach the entire community at one time, the government regards them as the most important means for educating the country as a whole. Social education, then, can be conducted most effectively by radio and television, as contrasted to the individual instruction in the family and school and peer-group education in the institutions of employment, worship, and the like. Whoever dominates the radio and television dominates the education of the community as a community and of the country as a country. Thus education has been designated as their principal function. Next comes information, which may also be regarded as falling within the scope of education. Cultural enrichment follows next in priority. Entertainment as such ranks a low fourth.

I expressed some difficulty in reconciling the pervasive cheerfulness that I had seen among the people with such a deemphasis on leisure and entertainment. "On the contrary, sir," she assured me. "Leisure is considered an essential part of wholesome living. It is guaranteed by long tradition. Even elephants in our teak forests are provided four months of vacation every year, as you may know. But we encourage the participatory kind of activities, in which there is direct personal association, such as concerts, plays, and sports. We do not encourage the impersonal variety, such as movies. It is our belief that each time an inanimate device is inserted in the chain of communication, human warmth becomes attenuated just that imperceptible much. Warmth, of course, is what makes for a humane society. If people learn to operate without it, society then turns cold. We try to keep that uppermost in everything we do—as I hope you have gathered, sir, in your own meetings with our brethren during the past two days."

22

"Where does the intrinsic power of the government come from?" I posed a leading question. "From the people," came the cliché, as expected. "Can you tell me how this is attained in Prakung?"

The young lady continued in her personable way, completely unaware of my intended challenge. "Every person over sixteen is required to vote in the elections for the Deputies. This is the first step in their exercise of power. But that is not all, sir. A vote of confidence is held midway through the term of office. Those encumbents who receive below the sixty percent threshold are invited to resign. Comparable proceedings are in effect with respect to the administrators and the representatives to higher chambers. This makes it very clear to everyone that the deputies work for the people and that they should do their very best. To be invited to resign is such a shame! Did you ask whether there had been such an invitation, sir? No, fortunately, no. The lowest vote on record so far is sixty-six percent confidence. And furthermore, since there is a limitation of a single term of office at a given echelon, there will be a greater chance among the citizens at large to share political power. Finally, electoral divisions are so small that the candidates are personally known to most of the voters and even to the children of the area. In other words, we vote for persons whose behavior we have observed firsthand for years." She then moved on to the legislative process. Referendums are held twice a year on major issues. The deputies are not obliged to follow the majority opinion. But justifications for their contrary positions have to be explained much more convincingly than otherwise.

By this time, we were retracing old grounds, and my interest began to sag. So I asked for the opportunity of visiting one of the other administrators—say, of Personal Well-being. Noting that we had only an hour left, the briefer promptly terminated her discussion and escorted me to the next office.

23

We showed up at the administrator's office unannounced. She gracefully rose from her chair and expressed appreciation for the honor of my presence.

"In the main, sir, the function of our office is two-fold," she summarized her own responsibilities. "First, research on factors affecting the quality of living. What excesses in one phase of life affect personal well-being adversely in another, how can enabling means be provided for improvement at the time and place of need, and so on."

The administration of operating programs was the second aspect of her job. "We pay considerable emphasis on art, music, drama, sports, and the like. These are essential nutrients to a satisfying life. After all, what is a human being without cultural expression?"

24

At that point, my aide entered excitedly, apologized for his interruption, and informed me that I must be at the airstrip forty minutes early because of some unforeseen development. I shook the administrator's hand and dashed downstairs. Olunol was there waiting to accompany us to the plane. As we approached the field, I saw a large crowd gathered around a hastily constructed platform. There must have been at least 5000. Olunol introduced me to a Brother Akanna, whom I immediately recognized as the ebullient menagee player at the community feast last night. Beside him stood the smiling proprietor of the small carving shop with whom I had spent an enjoyable hour. The pair led me onto the platform. Olunol insisted on staying back.

"Honorable elder brother," bowed Akanna. "You come from far away. You talked with us when we were happy. You took care of us when we were sick. We like you. Now we know that men from far-off places can be brothers. We have one ourselves. We thank you much for it. Your Prakung brothers like to give you something. This was made from old, old Prakung tree, 400 years old. Loianol here did the work. His ancestors lived in Prakung for over 1200 years. *Bon voyage.*" There was a loud sustained cheer as he handed me a beautiful large wood carving of a plant and animal group. I was so overwhelmed that when I tried to express my gratitude, I only choked. I then bowed to Akanna, then to Loianol, then to Olunol, and then to the people. I waved as I stumbled off the platform, walked falteringly toward our plane, respectfully shook Olunol's hand, bowed again—and deeply this time, much more deeply felt—to my new Prakung brothers.

As we taxied down the strip, I peered through the window for a fond last look. And there, along the far edge of the multitude, stood a little boy, waving, and at his side was a kitten—black, with a white cravat, a white streak down the chest and belly, and white chin and paws.

REGIONAL OPERATIONS

25

We arrived at Saikung at six, Tuesday evening. The Senior Regional Administrator Mahanouk greeted us and invited us to use his guest house and have dinner that night with him and his father at his home. While we unpacked, my aide gave a run-down on Mahanouk, a young brilliant executive, and his seventy-six-year-old father, who is one of the most respected men in Chianglai.

The meal was quite simple. Five courses with some wine. In the after-dinner conversation, I asked my standard question for occasions of this kind. What was his chief preoccupation as Regional Administrator? He acknowledged that although he did not have the slightest difficulty in identifying it, he felt he was far from any satisfactory solution. It involves the optimal balance between material progress for the region and wholesome living for the individual. "What is the optimal Laian rate of technological change?" he asked rhetorically. "On the one hand, our country is materially so far behind that we would like to catch up within the shortest time. Our younger managers, especially those trained in America, are of this leaning and want to propel ahead full throttle. They are getting impatient with our more deliberate human-oriented programs, which they consider as wasteful inefficiency. Given full rein, they can easily increase our gross national product at a rate twice the ongoing figure. On the other hand, the good life for individuals rests on a measured pace in all things. This cannot be attained if we are dashing all around the place all day long. We would wear everyone out in the process and anxiety will gut the masses." He meditated for a moment, then continued, "I suppose, this would not have been such a strong concern for most of us, had we not been brought up in moderation and compassion. It would not have constituted such a central focus for the country's leaders, had they shown the slightest willingness to sacrifice some individuals for the prosperity of others." I could see that Mahanouk had given this particular dilemma much deliberation. It was equally obvious that he was still much bothered by the unresolved problem.

The line of discussion led naturally to questions on materialism and depersonalization. I inquired as to his feelings about Chianglai's ability to resist the worldwide trend. He replied that he was not clear on the issue and referred the question to his father. "My humble opinion is that our leaders here will not succeed in keeping this engulfing wave away from Chianglai in the coming several decades," the old man said. "As you know, the pendulum of culture swings continuously from one extremity to contrary extremity. At present, it seems to be moving away from the gentle and human love toward the militant and materialistic greed. Yet it will begin to swing back after an ephemeral display of evil. So the crucial consideration becomes: When it returns in our traditional direction, will the people here be able to inject the wisdom born out of the intervening suffering into the mainstream of Laian heritage, so that they will ascend onto a higher plateau of integrity? Our elders and leaders would not have failed their countrymen through an inability to stop the natural swings of the social pendulum. They would have failed if they have not nurtured the sturdy stock that makes it possible for future generations to attain a fuller life with each swing of the pendulum. If they do not succeed in this, then their descendants will be subjected to the aimless endlessness of a reversing treadmill, now in one direction, now in the other, ever moving faster, but always getting nowhere—an eternal, pointless, terrible befuddlement. It seems to me that this befuddlement is causing much of the anxiety of meaninglessness and of emptiness in many lives today. But when the people have the requisite faith in their fundamental values and the knowledge of the necessary strands that must remain unsevered, whatsoever may be the enticements of expedience, they will retain the basic strength of perseverance in adversity. I am deeply grateful for the feeling that the leaders in Chianglai are providing this abidingness and that accordingly their adjustments to the onslaughts of materialism and of depersonalization are succeeding."

26

The orientation briefing was presented by the Chief of Regional Plans. It was the expected bureaucratic recitation. After half an hour, I interrupted the boring series of charts and statistics: "How do you determine where to start in planning? Are there standard government directives on operating procedures?"

He replied that there were prescribed forms for recording and transmitting the results to others in order to produce a coordinated regional document. But he did not see how directives can be issued on the essence of the process. Planning itself is creative. It is a personal affair, varying with the situation and the factual voids. "To be honest, sir," he confessed, "I have never thought about how I did it myself, until you raised the question just now." Then he tried to reconstruct his approach, thinking as he slowly recounted the process: "In my case, I ostensibly begin by talking with the operating personnel. Nothing specific, as I recall. Just a sauntering reconnaissance, one might say, of whatever may come before the mind's eye. Then I do some reading. Again no particular direction. Only by and large germane to the broad topic being considered. No analytical thinking at this stage. No drawing of tentative conclusions. Only talking, reading, looking, musing. Suddenly, out of the blue, an integrated outline of the plan would burst into the open. There was never a concrete stepwise effort at building it up. It seemed always to arrive in its entirety, sir. Somehow, it reminds me of Athena—full-grown from the head of Zeus, not meaning to compare myself to the Greek god, of course. Only after that episode of an integrated framework that feels right do we embark upon a vigorous and organized study and analysis. Modifications and details are filled in by all interested parties."

I was much impressed with the young fellow after our long exchange on creativity. I doubt that the depth of his talent would have shown itself, had we remained within the confines of the scheduled bureaucratic presentation. I felt good about my part in "giving this bird room to fly." Mahanouk himself seemed most pleased by my laudatory comments.

27

On the way to Saikung University we drove past several men walking with a pole on their shoulder, balancing a twenty-gallon can at each end. At my aide's suggestion, we called out to one of them and ordered lunch.

He let down the cans, removed the lids, and placed some noodles into a pan of boiling water over glowing coals. About three minutes later, he transferred the contents to a bowl, then added powdered chicken flavoring, and stirred the contents with a pair of chopsticks. Finally, he carefully laid three slices of barbecue pork and some parsley on the surface. I was pleasantly surprised by the delicious taste.

In response to my question, the vendor said he was Cantonese. He much preferred the life of an entrepreneur to that of an employee in the government facilities, because he made more money. It appears that Laians have not gone into the business. After we left him, I asked my aide, "Why not?" The chap explained that Laians are not ambitious people by nature. "They're much more contented than even the Chinese!" he exuded a sense of pride in making the comparison.

28

Chancellor Tlak was effervescent and articulate, quite certain of himself, which is atypical of the Laians I have met so far. He was pleasant, however, and I suppose rather warm-hearted. His outspokenness was refreshing, after a week's exposure to self-effacing manners.

The curriculum for the baccalaureate degree takes three years. It is made up of three series: Living, Heritage, and Ecology. The students are required to complete a stipulated series of courses in all three areas. This basic load accounts for three-fifths of their time. The rest is open for electives. Those wanting to go on to medicine or law take an examination at the end of their second year. If they pass, they are accepted and can then expect to graduate in three additional years. Neither doctoral degrees nor masters are awarded. At the present time they are not even recognized. The educational plan for the country calls for upgrading the level of all Laians to a General School minimum before siphoning resources for postgraduate curricula. The question of advanced degrees will be examined in another ten years. They may be instated after that. But intervening evidence may well reveal their social unessentiality. "I personally feel the latter will turn out to be the case," Tlak, who himself holds a Ph.D. from Cambridge, prophesied.

No grades are given in class. But corrections, comments, and the like are freely offered by the professors. Since the graduates are all employed in any case at comparable wages, the authorities did not see any point to universities performing an evaluation service on job applicants for management. Some scholars have suggested that grades serve as an incentive for the students. "But if grades can't even buy a cup of tea, then what kind of incentive are they? To excel competitively? Surely, to show up one's friends is hardly worthy of a gentleman," he argued. "What we on the faculty try to do is to assist each student—I would like to stress the word *assist*—in the maturing of his natural endowments to the maximum within the time available and resources allotted. It is up to him to show what he is able to contribute to society, when called upon to do so after graduation. Since he won't have grades at work, he might as well now get used to not having them in college."

29

The soft-spoken and retiring elder teacher of the living series was a contrast to the Chancellor. "Our offering," Jen pointed out in flawless Oxford English, "is a medley of exposures, first and foremost, to impart a quickening instinctive sense of life." To him, this is the essence of a healthy introduction to maturity. The rest is supplemental knowledge and experience.

Physiology, psychiatry, philosophy, and such are integrated into situational happenings in the course, entitled "Personal Well-being." The professor pointed out that just as beautiful songs come from combinations of innumerable variations of a limited set of notes, which well might be discordant if grouped in innumerable other ways, so can one's own life be made satisfying by the proper blendings of ingredients, which well might be discordant under other settings or in different proportions. One should learn to listen to the piece of music in its wholeness. He should sit back, soaking in the beauty undissectingly. But if, for some reason, it is unpleasing, he might then begin to listen analytically, trying to discover what went wrong. Analogous approaches are adopted in his course. The student is first taught to apprehend life as a whole and, only later, to dissect for pathologic causes, should the wholesome whole seem violated.

Man is not alone, however. He lives in the midst of people—he in them and they in him. So here again, conventional courses of ethics, family responsibilities, political science, economics, sociology, and the like are fused into one course, known as "Social Well-being." The point of departure is the well-being of society. "We learn to sense events in all of their communal impacts," Jen explained. "In particular, we try to stress the necessary resonance between the part and the whole, between the person and the society. We do not believe that personal well-being can be achieved without social well-being, nor vice-versa."

30

"How about the sciences?" I sensed a flaw in their rather strange course structure. "I am grateful you reminded me of this important matter," Jen continued with the same solicitous empathy. "They fall into the third course, known as 'Support Techniques.' This includes trades, languages, and engineering. The title, Support Techniques, was deliberately chosen to impress upon the students the primacy of personal and social well-being. All knowledge should contribute constructively to these ends in actual practice."

After a while his concept began to make sense. Actually, I was intrigued with it more and more as he wove the pieces into a pattern. I became curious as to his description of the overall motif. "It is difficult to verbalize," Jen went on thoughtfully, "since it is a projection of a fine and subtle trait of the superior person. It includes not only what specific impact is delivered, viewed objectively, but also how the impact is received subjectively, not only on oneself but also on others. If we are compelled to fall back on a single term—more as a reminder, of course, than descriptor—I suppose it would be graciousness." He then attempted to convey its nuances through a succession of quite roundabout allusions and suggestive stories. Graciousness appears as a pervasive evocation. It entails much more than one's behavior. It is like a harmonious denouement of reciprocities, whereby the local universe—including persons, things, and all—dissolve in pleasing fitness. It belongs to neither subject, object, nor both—but to the *de novo* moment. Obligations and intentions sublimate together in an atmosphere of mutuality. The giver feels no loss; receiver, no indebtedness. "In other words," I found myself being carried away, "the entire affair is as spontaneously pleasing as the sweet melody of the water ouzel blending with the rumbling chord of the Sierra waterfall."

"What an apt description!" he clapped his hands in delight. Jen then concluded with the Laian proverb: Know the good person by his reasonableness, the superior person by his graciousness.

31

Jen's holistic statements were echoed by the Elder Teacher in Ecology. Originally, she was not in favor of the separation of Ecology and Heritage from Living. "As you know," she said, "the more you break the total apprehension into abstracted bits, the harder it is to reclaim the whole."

She admitted, however, that there were compelling political reasons for the separation. "We have been subjected to foreign domination on and off for two hundred years—seven generations," she explained. "Something had to be done to regain and strengthen the Laian traditional love of the land and respect for deeply rooted values. Accordingly, the curriculum has been divided in part so as to draw attention to the ecology of Nature and the heritage of Chianglai.

Laian scholars use the term ecology without the connotations of an "external environment," as generally used by Americans. There is no disjoining the human being from his milieu. Everything is fused in harmony within a single whole. When a given situation feels disharmonious, man has no intrinsic right to expect all else in Nature to accommodate to his own convenience and taste. The others have as much right to expect responsive adaptation in his behavior as he has on the others. All are one in Nature. The appreciation of this oneness with its delicate relationships among the various diffusions constitutes the principal subject of attention in the program in Ecology.

32

The following hour was spent with the seventy-two-year-old Elder Teacher of Heritage Yuit. He had once served as the Senior Administrator of Prakung. Among his many proposals which had been implemented was the nationwide dispersion of the cultural centers. He had felt that since Laian heritage arose from people throughout the country, especially in the rural areas, rather than from people in a few cities, the major cultural centers should be so situated as to keep close touch with this source. In turn the latter should continue to contribute their steadying influence in the preservation and evolution of that heritage. Following this line of thought the major universities, museums, and centers of the performing arts are fairly evenly distributed throughout the country. Every Laian is within short travel of at least several of these national centers. The local communities take great pride in discharging what they consider to be a sacred trust.

There are no fixed requirements in the Heritage curriculum. The classes are unstructured. Students are invited to compose two essays for each other's reading. They are not required to do so. But so far, everyone has. Weekly sessions, lasting all day, are held in various parts of the neighborhood—a factory, farm, park, jail, and so on. Attendees are divided into groups of thirty. Someone usually starts by mentioning some actual event which struck him as exemplifying certain current trends, desirable or otherwise, in Laian culture. If it does not strike a responsive chord, it fades away as passing conversation. If it does, it leads to an extended exploration of its relevance to traditional philosophy, extrapolation to long-term effects, and so on. Many government officials, including some very senior ones, join the sessions from time to time as a means of keeping in touch with the evolving trends of their fellow Laians.

Yuit himself does not say much at the sessions—questions, now and then; a look of wonderment or puzzlement, perhaps. He does, however, comment liberally on the student essays, spends considerable time in individual and small group consultations, and presents an annual three-hour public lecture in the largest auditorium in Saikung with a seating capacity of 4000. I was told that the place was invariably packed.

33

There are only two professional schools in Chianglai, namely, Political Welfare and Medical Welfare. The rest of the professions, trades, and crafts are taught at work. It is encumbent upon the Adult Education Bureau to ensure that this part of a man's continued growth is not neglected by the agencies and industrial units in their drive to meet production quotas.

I had to cancel my appointment at the medical school, since time was running short. The catalogue described it as a specialty in Personal Wellbeing of the Living Series. In the case of medicine, the usual curriculum of physiology, pathology, anatomy, and other technical disciplines is overlaid with strong inputs on extra-medical factors affecting personal well-being. In addition to the medical techniques per se, the students are instructed in the art of sensing what it takes for the well-being of a person as an integrated individual. The doctor is expected to refer his patients to the appropriate places for the amelioration of the other problems facing them. Only when the individual is recovered in all aspects is he regarded as having been restored in personal well being.

Analogous assistance toward total rehabilitation is provided by ombudsmen, teachers, government officials, and other individuals engaged in personal services.

34

The Political Welfare College is the equivalent of our law school. But the two differ greatly in basic philosophies. In general, Laians are averse to the adversarial approach. This is antithetical to their way of life. The authorities are trying very hard at substituting reasonableness for cunning and litigious legalism, which had constituted the surest path to success in law under the former occupation by Western powers.

The Chancellor believes that it will take about two generations of earnest effort to change this rather deep-seated practice. Others in the legal hierarchy are much more optimistic. In the Senior Regional Adjudicator's last commencement address, he voiced encouragement with his own observation that the American judicial institutions are now moving toward the Laian pattern. The Chancellor recited the keynote passage from memory: "It is neither blind subservience to law nor strict enforcement of its letter that ennobles our society, but reverence for the human spirit. Laws are only approximate and summary reflections of the evolving state of this spirituality. Like all approximations, laws must be interpreted with an understanding reconciliation to the person's peculiar situation and the differential impacts of the same objective pressures on subjective souls. That empathetic easement is what we in Chianglai mean by brotherhood. And it is this and this alone that imparts nobility to our laws and our men of law."

What the college stresses is the art of leading and enlightening one's fellow men. "This is the most sophisticated of the arts," the Chancellor repeated. "Most sophisticated, I believe, because the strength to lead must be accompanied with the wisdom to discern and both blended with the humility of service and the love of man and beast, resulting in actual benefits to all concerned." This is entirely apart, he took pains to emphasize, from ruling. Almost anyone can rule and issue orders, which are backed up by minds and muscles, might and money. Over and over, he described the same fundamental premise in various ways: the purpose of law is fulfilled in its beneficence, not in its vengeance.

35

Next on the schedule was the Saikung Armament Works, which enjoys the reputation of being the most efficient factory in Chianglai. Its major item of production at the time was some kind of a guided missile for the navy. Looks like our 1972 Sidewinder on the outside.

After touring part of the assembly line of typical American design, I asked the manager about the principal difficulties he encountered in industrial production. In his reply, thirty-five-year-old Tanak went out of his way to castigate the bureaucrats at Saikung Headquarters for being impractical idealists. "All this talk about the brotherhood of man, the good life, and the like is fine," he waved his right arm in a wide arc. "But that just does not get the production out. The navy has been putting terrific pressure on me for delivery of this subsystem. National priority quadruple A and all that. Yet when I take steps to cut out the wasteful drainage of manpower, such as personnel development that has nothing at all to do with missile output, obligatory vacation, . . . now, if a guy is so inspired and conscientious that he would rather work than take time off for some unnecessary leave, why do we refuse to let him do it? Where is our freedom? Anyway, as soon as I begin to really get efficient, a directive comes from some clown up there to cease and desist. In fact, I got chewed out just last week for not employing my assigned quota of sub-par I. Q. and handicapped types from the local area and tailor-making sufficient part-time yet satisfying and productive jobs for them. You know, this puts a helluva bind on us shirt-sleeve engineers who have to put out the stuff."

His mannerisms and commitment to efficiency made me feel so much at home. I later learned that he had graduated from M. I. T. and spent some five years at Hughes.

A FAMILY DINNER

36

Nothing was officially on for the evening. My aide and I took a walk around town, turning up an alley. It was lined on both sides with small frame houses, about three meters high. From one of them came the sweet sing-song of a Laian mother to her giggling infant:

> Rhino walking, rhino walking.
>   Clop! Clop! Clop! Clop!
> Egret riding, egret riding.
>   Aark! Aark! Aark! Aark!

Outside, women were busily sprinkling water over dirt fronts, tidying up the place with brooms of loosely tied twigs. Up ahead, a cluster of excited children was all speaking at once in noisy frenzy, now looking at the ground, now trying to comfort a bawling child. We quickly moved to see what was the trouble.

It turned out to be another one of those perennial despairs of tiny tots all over the world. The boy had dropped his only penny through the iron grill into the drain pipe just beyond reach. They looked eagerly as we approached. The child stopped crying. I tugged at the grating. No luck. Rusted. Sighs of disappointment all around. My face lit up with an idea. Ah, encouragement anew—the lads observed my every move, as I reached over for the broom against the wall, untied the bundle, took two of the longer and straighter twigs, inserted them into the small slit, fished the penny out in chopstick style, and gave it with a broad smile to the child.

A triumphant burst of exultation heralded our great achievement! Heads came popping out of doors and windows, as the child ran overflowing into the outstretched arms of his mother. I retied the broom with care and placed it back where it had been. My aide and I took one more glance at the heart-warming picture and resumed our walk.

37

Barely had we gone twenty meters, when we heard fast footsteps back of us. We turned and saw a strapping fellow running after us.

He bowed. Introduced himself as Ikaikorn, the father of the child. He told us that he had never seen his son so happy and expressed profuse appreciation.

"Honorable elder brother," he bowed once again. "My humble family is very poor. Our shack is old. Our food is unworthy of most honorable elder brother. We have just set our dinner table. If honorable brethren will accept our meager meal, it will bring great joy to my wife, to my number one son, to my number two son, to my daughter, and to my humble self."

38

We sat on low wooden stools, made from discarded crates, around a small round table. Supper consisted of cabbage soup; steamed catfish with ginger, nuoc yeou, salt, and sugar; and rice.

The shy mother did not say a word, but cast a grateful glance in my direction now and then.

The little lad sat next to me. He hardly ate a thing but kept his eyes glued affectionately on me. He inched his stool right next to mine and gently nudged against me every minute or two. In response, I sent a friendly wink his way, and waves of loving admiration would sweep over him.

39

Ikaikorn is working in the local steel plant as a member of a labor crew, which handles the buggies transporting the ingots from the blast furnace to the strip mills.

Plans are being implemented to replace the labor crews with small locomotives. In preparing for the change, the men are taking part-time classes sponsored by thc Adult Education Bureau. Ikaikorn is learning welding.

After he completes the training in another two weeks, Ikaikorn expects to be promoted to a welder, joining steel sheets on the galvanizing line. He had already seen his new superintendent and the new location. Wages will be higher, work much easier, and the family much better off. He is looking forward to the opportunity with great enthusiasm.

40

All through dinner I could see that Ikaikorn was looking hard around the room to find a gift for me. But I could also see that there was not a thing remotely suitable, not even as a memento.

As we rose to leave, he searched about with some anxiety. But still, without success. His young son whispered a few words into his ears. The father smiled and nodded. Then he said to me: "My humble son would like to speak to you, most honorable elder brother." I bent down and looked into his bright beaming eyes, which gradually grew solemn.

The boy reached for my hand, slowly deposited the penny, ceremoniously closed my fingers over it, and hugged me in a long embrace, as if for ever. Suddenly, he let go, running back to Ikaikorn. Then father, mother, number one son, number two son, and daughter bowed together as a family, as we waved goodnight.

EMPATHIES

41

Thursday morning. When we entered the Adjudication Hall, a robbery case was in session. The soft-spoken Citizen Adjudication Counselor (analogous to our defense attorney) was directing questions to the witness: "Did you recognize our Brother Kalaiswat beside the door?" "Yes, Brother Counselor." "But judging from the darkness of the place and your position at the time, it would have been extremely difficult for you to do so." Turning to the Regional Adjudication Counselor (analogous to our state prosecutor), "Would you not agree, my Brother Counselor?" The latter thought for a moment, then allowed that it might well have been the situation. Whereupon the counselors and the three members of the panel analyzed the merits of the case and all agreed upon a tentative disposition of the indictment.

"Brother Kalaiswat, before we make our suggestion, would you care to add a further comment?" the presiding adjudicator said to the defendant. "I have nothing further, Brother Adjudicator." "We feel that there is a likelihood that you are innocent of stabbing the attendant at the Saikung Museum and stealing the jade buddha. On the other hand, your own account of your activities and whereabouts was far from satisfactory. Perhaps, you had refrained from giving a full recital for a personal and valid reason. Yet, your recent general behavior toward your kind father and your brethren has not been very inspiring to the young. We feel therefore that you would be benefitted by a period of reflection on your past and future life. Brother Regional Counselor had initially proposed three years. We now all seem to feel that a year would be more reasonable. Do you have an alternative proposal, Brother Kalaiswat?" "No, Brother Adjudicator."

"Then a year at the succorance center it will be," pronounced the presiding Adjudicator. "We wish you well, Brother Kalaiswat."

42

I had always been bothered by the leniency of our courts back home toward criminals. But this Laian process strikes me as being all out of bounds. By the time I sat down at lunch as guest of the Adjudication Panel in its chambers, I was so worked up about their pampering of the robber that without the niceties of table talk between strangers, I launched into a vigorous exposition of our American prosecuting techniques.

The adjudicators were taken aback when I described the selective presentation of assorted facts in court and the conscious discrediting of witnesses against one's client even when one knows they are telling the truth. Enjoying the dramatic impact, I then recited some striking recent cases in which informants had been cleverly implanted by the government and electronic spying devices ingeniously installed, in which offenders had been bribed by the prosecutors with the promise of immunity if they would testify against their friends, and in which men had been coerced by national legislators under threat of imprisonment to betray their benefactors before Congressional committees. I showed how no stone was left unturned in the pursuit and the incarceration of our criminals. The Senior Adjudicator's eyes met mine at this point and I realized that I had gone too far.

Dropping his fork with its piece of stabbed steak, he rose from the table in a daze and gazed out of the window. "Have I been misleading the students all these years?" he mumbled to himself in French. "Was what I told them at the last commencement on the leadership of the American Bar toward adoption of our jurisprudence of reasonableness and compassion all an illusion? . . . What will they do when they find out? . . . Keep insisting that justice *must* have adversaries? . . . Must have *two* sides? . . . That the ultimate objective must be *dissolution* and *not* reconciliation? . . . What will the immense impact of that great nation's influence do to our younger people in Chianglai? . . . Will they come to distrust each other more and more . . . and love each other less and less . . . as time goes on?"

43

What had promised to have been a pleasant luncheon turned out to be a calamity. I started by thinking that the American way would make stimulating conversation. I ended by ruining everything. The stare of the Adjudicator's eyes kept haunting me, as I trudged slowly over to my next appointment.

I arrived at the Internal Peace Headquarters with a heavy heart, remorseful over what I had just done. "You go around without the least care for the tender sensibilities of other people. You shoot off your blabbering mouth. You tell everybody how *you* in America do it. Big deal! You smash ideals. You trample the pieces. You scatter smut. A goddam shit militant! That's all you are!" I looked at the floor in shame and sorrow.

When the Chief of Internal Peace (analogous to our Chief of Police) bounded into the reception foyer with a boisterous hello, he saw I was not up to it. Inviting me into the office, he inquired about my health. Should he call for a doctor? I was too depressed to talk at first. But feeling the need to tell my troubles, to confess my sins, as it were, I then recounted the regrettable experience. He listened with a sympathetic silence. When I finished and looked up, I noticed that his own eyes had turned red and misty. It appeared that he too just then realized that he is doomed to operate the justice of two sides and live as adversary to his brethren till the very day he leaves what he up to then must have thought to be the pinnacle of his professional prestige.

44

His briefing on police activities began with a description of the Laian ranking of offenses. Highest crimes are those that ravage Nature, such as injuring people, torturing animals, damaging trees and shrubs, and fouling air and waters. Infractions of the law involving only wealth and man-made things are classified as misdemeanors, provided there is an honest intent to repair the loss. Refusal to do so raises the offense to a high crime, not on the basis of the act against material goods per se, but of breaking faith with a brother in the communion of the One.

But the discussion dragged on without the slightest trace of enthusiasm on the part of either one of us. I broke it off after fifteen minutes and returned directly to the guest house.

Those sad eyes of the Adjudicator's just would not let go of me. "Please say it is not so!" they kept pleading.

45

I went straight into the kitchen, took a bottle of mei ju, and plopped into the easy chair in the living room. Then I kept guzzling gulps of the stuff. I banged my fist on the side table as I fell asleep.

Tremors shook me through and through, as I yelled for forgiveness. It was my aide awakening me from my nightmare and reminding me of the administrator's formal banquet.

After a quick shower, I cleared up considerably. I began to feel much better, as I looked forward to another one of those occasions for the spirit. I dressed in a hurry. Sprightly stepped into the car. And off we went.

46

All of the senior regional officials had been invited with their spouses. The women were delicately beautiful in their flowing silk gowns, brightly colored with designs of birds and flowers. The hall was permeated with a festive air. I was thoroughly enjoying myself as I chatted with the guests and exchanged delightful tidbits about our respective countries.

As I sat down to the right of Mahanouk, he passed on the information that the wife of Senior Adjudicator Duc has just phoned. She said her husband had quite unexpectedly come home about three in the afternoon and gone straight to bed without a word. She did not know what was ailing him but she had never seen him in so weakened a condition. She thought it could have been an intestinal disorder of some kind. Perhaps staph poisoning at lunch. She tried to call the doctor. But he would not let her do it. She extended their apologies for their absence.

My heart sank. I tried to act out my role of honored guest, adequately proposing and responding, I hope, to the thirty-two toasts. Truthfully though, I did not remember anything, except a vague impression of the Chief of Internal Peace at a nearby table, facing me directly and sitting with his eyes focused on his plate in order to avoid mine.

47

It was ten o'clock before I got up on Friday morning. I was awakened repeatedly by the aide. But I would only answer and fall right back to sleep. We finally showed up quite late at the Saikung Succorance Center. After three hours with a most enjoyable lunch with the residents, I got an inkling as to the significance behind the name.

There is no equivalent in Chianglai to our concept of imprisonment. Neither retribution by society nor the deterrence of potential criminals plays a major role in the sentencing of legal offenders. The main objective is the person's rehabilitation. The inmates are kept busy with specially designed routines, particularly vocational training for most and philosophical reflections for others. The machine shops are extremely well equipped for every kind of operations. They produce precision parts for the Saikung Armament Works. Many of the graduates of the center go there directly for employment. When some of the machines are idle, people on the outside are admitted as students. At the time of my tour, the latter accounted for a third of the enrollment. It was difficult for me to tell them apart from the others. The manager informed me that new students are also unable to do so. But by the time they get to learn each other's identities, they have become so used to working with their classmates that the knowledge does not make the slightest difference in their relationships.

About half of the instructors were between sixty-five and seventy-two years of age. Most of the older members work part-time. They appear to be more effective as a whole than the younger ones. They command greater respect because of their old age and they seem to diffuse a degree of calm wherever they are. Most important, they are better able to provide a broader based perspective on the human mutuality of caring, which gradually dawned on me as the overall atmosphere that the staff was subconsciously fostering in everything they do.

48

The operations of the center mirror the fairness, reasonableness, and basic faith in human goodness of Laian jurisprudence. Penalties for violations of the law are restricted to probational assignments and confinements in a succorance center. Monetary fines are never levied, since these are considered to be disproportionately harsh on poorer people. Nor is there a charge for lawyer and related fees for the same reason. Death is regarded as altogether too unreasonable to impose. The period of rehabilitation in a succorance center ranges from six months to six years. The six-month sentence represents the minimum time considered necessary to make a lasting improvement in one's salutary attitude toward his fellow creatures. The maximum reflects the view that fifteen percent of one's productive life should be the most that should, in fairness, be extracted for any single purpose. Within the succorance center, the programs are tailored to the specific needs of the individual, not only with respect to subject matter but also with respect to intensity. The latter is adjusted so as to attain the needed resolution of the individual's anxieties and a rejuvenation of his sense of meaningfulness in society within the allotted time.

Once the resident is on the mend, the visiting arrangements for his family and friends include weekends in adjacent parks, where they enjoy group picnics and the like. The outings are extremely popular with those without visitors as well, for they would always be invited along by the others. Most of the associations that begin this way grow into lifelong friendships. While the residents are serving out their terms, a portion of their former wages, minus expenses for their upkeep and repayments for the damages incurred, continue to be paid to their dependents. It is felt that the latter should not be made to suffer for the breadwinner's mistake. The most impressive stipulation in the exercise to me was the responsibility of the manager not only to train the resident in some marketable skill but also to find a job for him to which he will report for work after release, with a transition leave of thirty days. Apparently, the launching of an individual into the succeeding phase of his life is a commonly accepted practice among Laian employers. The necessity for the custom was explained to me as minimizing the disruptions to good living by hiatuses of loneliness and anxiety. The headmistress whom I had visited in Prakung, for example, sees to it that an acceptance into college or a concrete employment offer is available to everyone of her graduates.

When I showed astonishment at such coddling of criminals, the manager expressed astonishment at my astonishment. "Sir, don't we all fail at one time or another?" he spoke to me in a tone of voice that I gathered he must use with his students. "When we do, do we not hope some forgiving brother will assist us to recover? And, is this not one of the continuing and cogent reasons why men live together in society?"

49

The School of Art was last on our Saikung agenda. As we entered, some voices attracted our attention to a group of young people in animated conversation with arms gesticulating. Nearby in a courtyard sat a man motionless in transfixed silence in front of a narcissus blooming in the ground. A middle-aged lady approached us with a smile and introduced herself as the Elder Painter.

As she was describing the school's activities, I watched the thirty or so students outdoors. Every now and then one would engage another in a dialogue. Before long, more would join the pair. Soon a full-scale discussion would be underway. I remarked how struck I was with the aliveness of the place.

"The group is exchanging views on how the hills in landscapes should be treated to bring out the souls of trees," explained the Elder Painter. "This seems to be the way beginners invariably approach the subject. By talking. By empirically trying. Mostly by verbalizing till they come to realize that words are really poor means for the purpose. Only after they naturally converse with brush and eyes, instead of talk and mind do they become artists of talent, like the painter communing with the narcissus. This is what we try to put across. On rare occasions someone shows up who is in tune with the beyond. He is the mystical transmuter of what some Chinese call *ch'i*. How he is able to adorn what meets the eye with what moves the heart I can't say that I know. I suppose this cannot be explicitly taught. We can only feel and talk around the subject and then show his paintings to the pupils, while extending homage to the Master."

50

Our tour ended where the masterpieces of the renowned Naniphan were hung in the main hall.

I was fascinated by her animals. At first they looked like any other by an able artist. But as I was slowly passing the fourth painting, my mind seemed to have been left behind some place and my eyes remained obliviously focused on the animals themselves. Through some strange metamorphosis, their eyes began to speak, communicating in a new dimension, altogether strange yet somehow clear. I felt that I had apprehended what they were relaying in the new dimension and had replied, it seemed, in an intimate exchange. And everything was immersed in a kind of pervasive geniality.

Suddenly, I was brought back to earth from the engaging reverie. The bells of the ivy-covered towers of the Mission of Saint Francis just across the gulch were pealing the Angelus and announcing that the closing hour for the art museum had come.

51

Dao was waiting with two horses at the entrance of the Sonbang Park when I showed up on Saturday. He had flown from Terkung to join me for the weekend.

I was told that Dao would frequently come here to contemplate the future of the country. He would go on packing trips alone for days when there were strong divergencies among the senior officials over crucial issues. Nobody knows what he does, or where he goes while he is here. Invariably he would return to the capital with a proposal which would gain unanimous endorsement. Equally invariably, everyone would comment on its obvious simplicity.

"Do be careful, J. C. about hurting any of the little animals or scaring any of the big ones," Dao said as we started. "This is *their* home, after all, and we are only guests."

52

After reining our horses from the man-made paths into the green luxuriant growth, I appreciated the appropriateness of his warning. A swarm of Nature under hoofs—little green snakes and pythons, frogs and geckoes, mice and rabbits, orange grouse and rainbow pheasants, . . .

At the far end of the clearing was a herd of elephants meandering along. We changed our course at each encounter so as to avoid disturbing them. Along the way, we came across two-horned rhinoceroses, ox-like bantengs, tapirs, gibbons, hornbills, babblers, drongos, painted storks, mahseers, trout, . . . As I trailed behind Dao, he seemed so congenially a part of the setting that I began to get a glimmer of what he had been saying at the Terkung presentation about the Uncarved Unity. He moved along as naturally as the barking deers among the trees, as he kept up a running commentary: mother monkey teaching the young ones how to peel a mango, the stronger mouse allowing the weaker ones to eat first, the birds singing more effusively and joyfully during off-mating seasons, when they had no ulterior motives on their minds, . . .

As I marvelled at the towering peaks, the unending canopy of green, the teeming life beneath, and our two inconsequential human echoes of the vibrant vitality, I thought of those Oriental landscapes, which had appeared so bland to me in the museums back home. I simply must go back for another look—so I promised myself.

53

As we sat around the campfire after supper, I attempted to describe the pleasant sensation that had been perfusing through me all day. There I was so . . . free—which was not really what I had meant but was the closest word I could think of. It might well have been that I had felt that way because everything else around us was free. The grass was not mowed but was left free to grow the way it naturally does. The birds were not caged . . . the notion of cages distracted my line of thought. "I haven't heard a thing about zoos, Dao," I strayed off into another subject. "Is there a pretty one nearby?"

"There are no zoos in Chianglai," he stated in a matter-of-fact manner. "As you have just said, J. C., you feel so free. Why? Because all others here are also free. Not just the two of us. How can we be free if our own brother plants are clipped and our brother animals are caged? That is why Chianglai has only natural preserves and sanctuaries. No zoos."

"But you must admit that they are educational for children," I countered. "And besides, it certainly is quite innocuous as far as entertainment goes." Dao remained firm in his even tenor. "In our philosophy of life, we do not talk about education or entertainment in the same breath as our brother's freedom. That is why I say again that there can be no zoos in Chianglai. Only freedom."

54

When I awoke that bright Sunday morning, Dao was sitting on a grassy mound in an expanse of green repose. He was watching something on the ground a few feet away, most intently.

As he trotted back for breakfast, I inquired about what had been happening out there. It was a field mouse, he said, bringing forth a litter. Dao had been musing over how well it went, despite the absence of an obstetrician in attendance. Who would have assisted mother mouse, had she gotten into difficulty? To whom could she have appealed? Perhaps, there is a God, who took care of her. Perhaps, the field mouse did pray in her own way. But she certainly could not have approached God in the same manner as men do. He surmised that the kind of praying taught by ministers are superfluous to what God does anyway. He could not imagine that God requires His dependents to kneel and ask before He extends benevolent balm. Surely, He does not sit back until His creatures bend and beg before He blesses. Nor does He come to the support only of the articulate, or only of the aggressive in the fawning, or only of those represented by silken-tongued intermediaries. His benefits diffuse to all, without the imploring—just because God is good. "It should be the same with government," he concluded that there is a lesson here that he and his fellow government officials should learn. "The good government's beneficences too, diffuse to all—the unknown as well as the famous, the distant as well as the nearby, the retiring as well as the high-reaching—just because it is good."

As we resumed our horseback riding, neither Dao nor I spoke much. We just dissolved into the largeness of the wilderness. Words seemed so noisily discordant to the fine and filling feeling.

A SIX-POEM MUSICAL MIME

55

Dao went back to Terkung Sunday night. My aide and I flew on to Maikung. Maikung was the first of the completely planned metropolises in Chianglai. Its population of 350,000 is equilibrating at the programmed level.

There is no law that restricts the people as to where they may live. But manufacturing facilities and opportunities for gainful work are carefully controlled. Production plants, employing over 500 workers, for example, have not been approved for Maikung. Agricultural, research, and small industrial enterprises constitute the principal activities. Available employment opportunities in other places are extensively publicized and kept up to date. The costs for interview, retraining, and associated travel for the family are covered by the Regional Administration.

By means of such prompt communication of job openings and subsidies of related expenses the cities have been able to keep within a fifth of their planned densities.

56

Maikung's Center for Research was our initial call. It resembles one of our basic research institutions in America in that the staff enjoys considerable freedom in the choice of problems and approaches. But the flavor is distinctly Laian.

The organization is divided generally—nothing apparently is rigid in the center, everything is only generally structured—into a group involved in personal well-being and another in social well-being. The specialists in Heritage and in Ecology fall in the second group. Aside from these loose elements, the center is not administratively further subdivided. The investigators work in teams. These vary in size and composition in accordance with the nature of the task at hand. The members shape the problems to be studied, organize the teams, conduct the project, and ensure that the results are passed on to the right group for translation into practice. The director of the center does not manage in our sense of the word. He tries to foster a cooperative atmosphere and keep alive an open intellectual approach to inquiry. He does, however, have authority to hire and fire. Yet here, again, potential candidates are frequently suggested by the staff itself, which feels the need for certain expertise.

The procedure has been in effect for ten years. Everyone seems pleased not only with the spirit of the place but also with its contributions.

57

There are apparently no written guidelines on how the projects are to be initiated or concluded. Somehow, something gets set in motion. Somehow, something stops. Some of the projects are successfully completed. Others fade into abandonment.

After listening for a short while in each of three team discussions, I began to sense a vague common point of departure to which they all appear to subscribe intuitively. That point of departure orients the investigator in his attempts at making a significant contribution to the current human or social situation. Other experts are invited to form a team, as required. A full-blown project soon emerges.

The underlying philosophy involves the transforming of value into change and of change into value. Their fundamental questions seem to be: What is the next rate-governing step to be resolved in improving the well-being of the Laians? Operationally, how are these creative advances to be smoothly assimilated into Laian culture? And conversely, how can Laian values be expressed in day-to-day practices?

58

I expressed some reservations as to the amount of progress in the basic sciences that can be expected under such an orientation. "How can the researcher probe the technical frontiers if continually held back by prior notions of social ramifications? For who can anticipate the ultimate practical value of basic research?"

The director did not disagree with the desirability of chemists in the center being as professional as chemists elsewhere. But to him the bridge of human relevance should still be constantly borne in mind. If the chemist starts his thinking with this link in mind—and there is no rule in the center saying that he *must*—his work would probably possess a richer trans-scientific vector. It would suffuse his aspirations with beneficient significance at all times. Such an inspiration is quite different from those approaches that ignore the social consequences, letting them emerge, as they will, for good or for evil. At the center the chemist would usually first analyze the social needs of the people with several of his associates in other disciplines, such as economics and psychology. He would then proceed with a basic investigation of his own formulation. Having gone through the question of relevance, the translations of his findings into the social good becomes much more straightforward than would have been the case had he not done so. Prior deliberation of this nature would at the very least allow the chemist to say sincerely: "I planned this work to the best of my insight to pursue the potentialities of good within my talents and to the best of my conscience to avoid the potentialities of evil."

"Such a sequence may sound worthwhile for Chianglai's political objectives," I shrugged my shoulders. "But wouldn't it be bad for chemistry?" He did not think that it would necessarily be. "There are numerous outstanding chemists in your country and others who are busy conducting experiments in the mode you are recommending. They will continue to do so for some time to come. We do not believe that our few chemists, of rather average competence, can add much of significance in the style of your compatriots. Yet, even with our meager handful, we might still be able to invite attention to the possibility that *all* research can be intentionally a priori relevant to human welfare and be guided by the ensuing spirit. In any case, I believe that it can be made much more so than has been the practice in days gone by."

59

Maikung's farming complex is the largest in the country. Temperatures in the seventies, some eighty inches of yearly rainfall, and the rich alluvial soil offer excellent conditions. Rice fields stretch as far as our eyes can see.

I was perplexed by how the paddies were arranged, as I surveyed them from the plane while landing yesterday. It even seemed to violate the common-sense experience of contour planting. It appeared as if somebody had deliberately gone about designing an extremely complex jig-saw puzzle while half drunk. When I inquired into the reason, no one was able to offer an explanation that was even half-way convincing.

"Terkung ordered it this way," someone finally divulged the secret, after twenty minutes of polite apologetics. "No one gave any explanations, however."

60

The Director of the Laboratory for Agricultural Research was especially pleased to see me and said that he and his staff were most excited at the news of my visit. They had read my monograph on methods for preserving food, a subject of considerable interest to Laian farmers. "Would you be so kind as to address a few words to us," he added after our fourth cup of tea. "Just a few words, honorable sir, on any subject." I proposed a survey on the latest technological advances in America.

Nearly 700 were present at the hastily convened assembly at ten-thirty. I reviewed the field for two hours: low-cost systems for refrigeration, dehydration, pickling, meat sterilization using ionizing radiations, and so on. The questions were submitted on assorted bits of paper as the talk progressed. There was a steady stream, accumulating to a couple hundred when I got around to answering them. At three-thirty in the afternoon, with no breaks in between of any kind, there still were fifty left, and more kept drifting to the rostrum. The director finally decided to conclude the session: "We have been inspired not only by the outstanding achievements of you and your associates in America, but also by the abundant generosity of your self, which you shared so . . . so spontaneously. We thank you, esteemed sir, from the bottom of our hearts for these most valuable lessons." Then came a sustained applause from the enthusiastic audience.

I got to the men's room in the nick of time.

61

We had two hours of open time before the evening reception. So the aide and I relaxed and strolled along the elevated pathways of the rice fields, flushing paddy birds as we zig-zagged our way. The southwest monsoon rain had just begun recently and the black soil was amply wet for working. In two months the ditches and canals for irrigation would be filled with water. Now, it was plowing time. The water buffaloes were being ridden home by their companion-boys, in a serene procession on the twilight-hued horizon. One of them approached from the direction facing us and waited at the junction, so that we could pass.

I saluted with a smile. The boy smiled back. "Young brother," I addressed him, pointing to the water buffalo. "What's your friend's name?" "Good Brother, sir." "Did you give him the name?" "Yes, sir." "Why that name?" "He works hard with us. He never hurts the other boys. He never steps on other people's plantings. That's why I call him Good Brother." "What was the song you were just playing on your flute?" "The tiger song, sir." "Will you sing it for us?"

Whereupon, his face grew serious, as he sang with genuine feeling:

Brother tiger, brother tiger!
Oh please, do lower your roar.
Did you not promise, dear brother
You'll ne'er be angry any more?

Our good brother, the buffalo,
Will help us with our rice this spring.
When you roar, his horns dip low,
How can he then do his plowing?

62

After dinner, hosted by the manager of the cooperative, we attended a performance of a six-poem musical mime. Musical mimes are poetic operas, with ballet. The story and the mood are provided by the mime and music. While the poems describe the essential portions of the plot, their main role is to set the emotional high points in their recitative to musical accompaniment. In the orchestra, consisting of a mixture of indigenous and occidental instruments, the melody was mainly carried by a native free-reed horn and seven bamboo flutes.

The musical mime was entitled *The Canary's Tree-House*. It concerned a man lost in the woods. The more he dashed about, the more lost he became. He cursed the animals for leaving him. He shook his clenched fist at the darkened sky. He thrashed about the thicket angrily and crashed into a branch, knocking a canary's nest into the ground and scattering the eggs in all directions. As he staggered back, he stepped on one of them. The sight of squashed embryo beneath his toes brought on a sudden sense of sadness. He sat down in stunned remorse. He thought about the sweet songs that were once to have come from the embryo. He begged forgiveness from the parent birds, though they were nowhere to be seen, for bringing such a tragic ending to their child and to the trees and animals for depriving them of kinship that was to have been their's to cherish. He forgot about himself being lost and set about carefully rebuilding the canary's tree house, twig by twig, and finally lovingly replaced the four remaining eggs, one by one. As he leaned back against the tree and looked at the restored nest snugly fastened and secure, a smile appeared on him. The sun began to peek around the clouds. The animals came out. The birds burst out in song. Caught up in this flood of joy, the man jumped up and danced a beautiful *adagio*. As he ended with a bow of gratitude to the inhabiters of the forest for forgiving and rejuvenating him, he recognized the spot as that from which he had originally wandered off the trail. Escorted by his newly made friends, he stepped jubilantly homeward, as the curtain fell.

Although I enjoyed the musical mime very much, I was affected by it in a much more profound way. My urban personality will never be the same again. I kept wondering whether it was Minh's Sharingness at work again.

63

We spent Tuesday morning at the two agencies geographically located here but reporting directly to Saikung Headquarters. These were the Metropolis and the Ecology agencies.

Being manager of a metropolis in Chianglai seems more stressful than being the mayor of Los Angeles. A metropolis is not a separate politically independent unit. It is a geographical term, like a valley. It is an area where the population density of neighboring communities is so high that a large degree of common service and standardization would be needed for economy sake. The manager of a metropolis is thus first and foremost a coordinator, an ameliorator, an arbiter. As many as twenty-five communities might be involved in a metropolis about a million in population. There is no line authority from the national or regional chambers. He must rely primarily on reason, persuasion, and patience. When communities get too far out of line, so as to incur potential suffering by individuals in some other jurisdiction, however, he does not hesitate to call upon the Metropolis Agency in Maikung, which can then hand down an order in the name of the Senior Regional Administrator. The issuance of such an order carries an embarassing inference of unwillingness to work together for the greater public welfare. Community administrators try to avoid such a taint as much as possible. On the other hand, resorting to such a drastic action is also taken as an indication of inadequacy in the ability of the Manager of the Metropolis to get people working together for the common good. He is also extremely reluctant to invoke this ultimate leverage because it would bring anguish to his brethren.

It is no wonder that, as the Elder Doctor of the Agency told me at the dinner last night, the managers of metropolises have the highest incidence of heart attacks in Chianglai.

64

The Director of the Metropolis Agency was dubious about the likelihood of an urban center of over half a million providing a naturally enriching life for most of its residents under ordinary conditions. This can be attained with herculean effort on the part of the citizenry, if it is located by itself and surrounded by large areas of natural environment. Such natural external belts are stipulated in the master urban plan. The respective sizes are proportional to population densities. Furthermore, their extensions must course through the city in the form of interconnected woods and game preserves without discontinuities, which would inhibit the free migration of the animal inhabitants. Considerable pains are taken in this direction, such as the elevation of selected portions of the road net in the area. In this way the Laians remain in constant touch with the rest of living Nature. But the director has little optimism for an urban center with a population above two million. In such agglomerations life for most of the residents can only mean eternal compromisings of diversified disjunctions from Nature.

He recognized that a certain number of large metropolises is required for national and economic purposes. But extraordinary measures should be taken in these situations by the national authorities to relieve the stresses of urban living. "When does an atomic bomb explode?" he asked rhetorically. "When the packing density of neutrons is beyond the critical mass. Similarly with the packing density of human beings." Jumping to the blackboard, he derived a series of equations, showing how the human interfaces go up geometrically with the arithmetic increase in the population. He then took account of the increasing speed of communications, the decreasing mean free path in crowded urban settings, and the concomitant conversions of the personalities through impersonal sophistication and exploitive cunning. Out of these considerations, he obtained the relief factor for the geometric rise in psychic pressure actually imposed on the individual immersed within the densities of larger cities. He believed the figure lies between 1.2 and 3.6. This means, other factors being equal, that the open fields, parks, rivers, beaches, and the like must go up an additional 1.2 to 3.6 times with a doubling of the population, if one wishes to ensure a comparable level of good living. There is a crossover point, at which it would be theoretically impossible to furnish the requisite incremental natural buffers for people as a whole with further increases in population. This point was put at about two million.

"This threshold, however, applies to people with a rather high sense of brotherhood," he expressed a reservation. "Otherwise even a population of only two can be explosive!"

65

The director was such an interesting person with an analytical approach to social issues, so unusual among the Laians, that I overstayed my time. This left me only thirty minutes for the meeting with the Director of the Ecology Agency.

The outstanding feature of her concept is complete acceptance of the fact of change. Pollution, of course, ought to be controlled. But unlike many environmentalists in the United States, she considers it contrary to the ways of Nature to attempt to freeze her evolution at any point in time. This cannot be done in any case. The flora and the fauna are continually evolving. A given change in one sector should be welcomed, if it is compatible with that of the totality moving in the direction of the good. Accordingly, her agency deliberates at great lengths over the concomitant transitions, which disturb or foster the desired trend toward a progressively harmonious whole for all creatures—animals and plants, as well as human beings.

She expressed much disappointment when I said that I could not stay longer. She and her staff had been reading extensivley about the vigorous campaign in America and had hoped that I would teach them out of our experience as to how better to perform their mission, which she described as sensitivity to Nature's harmony and its embodiment in human affairs.

66

We had precious little time to drive out to the airport so our plane could reach Pnomkung by five. Our driver took us at his usual and moderate speed. We told him to press on the accelerator. Just as he did so, a mongoose ran across the street. The driver hit the brakes. Too late. The rear wheel ran right over.

Screeching halt. The driver got out. Looked and stood and softly sobbed. My aide leaned forward to tell him to get back into the car and speed on. I withheld his arm and shushed. The aide and I both sat back in respectful silence. But instead of coming back, the driver shuffled in the opposite direction. After borrowing a shovel from the Laian sitting on his doorstep, he returned and slowly searched around until he found a cool spot shaded by a spreading banyan. There he dug a hole, three feet deep, squared the sides and bottom. Breaking off four fronds from a nearby banana clump, he neatly wrapped the limp form, gently lowered it into the grave. He then meticulously smoothened out the fronds and shoveled in the earth. He stood beside the mound with head bowed for a minute. Finally he brought the shovel back, shook the man's hand as they both sadly bowed to each other, returned behind the wheel, and drove off at a moderate speed.

Not a word . . . from anyone.

A MILITARY COMMAND

67

As we started our descent for landing at the Pnomkung airport, I inquired about the regiment of troops down there. The pilot said it looked like some dignitary was being rendered military honors. The commander smartly strode up to our plane and introduced himself as Colonel-General Kosadwin, the Commanding General of the Eastern Sector. Clicking his hard heels, he stood erect and snapped a crisp salute. He then escorted me to the reviewing stand.

Orders to attention were barked out. The anthem followed. Kosadwin then accompanied me on his jeep around front and back of the formation. I was struck by the unevenness. About half appeared quite professional. But the other half was very unmilitary. After that, the band marched forward with a martial air that had the bag-pipey sounds of a Scottish fantasy. The soldiers trooped by in review. The first batallion goose-stepped in perfect cadence as it passed our stand. The second tramped by in waves. The third was awful. When the last platoon did an eyes-right, a soldier in the front line center banged his cheek against his rifle, loosening it from his grip. It bounced around the ground and sent three soldiers sprawling. Three more flying rifles. Ten more lurching bodies.

My insides were about to burst with roaring laughter. But I looked straight ahead with a strict military mien, as if everything was going perfectly. Kosadwin did the same.

68

In his introductory remarks at the briefing the next morning, Kosadwin made an overall statement about the country's strategy. Due to her mores and economy, the strategy can only be defensive. "Thus, internally you will observe that land use, economic structure, and routines of daily living gear themselves to a protracted fight against invaders," he elaborated. "Externally, our forces are designed for spoiling operations twelve kilometers beyond our northern border at the Sonbang Mountains, forty-five kilometers beyond our eastern border to the Baobang Mountains and five hundred some kilometers out to sea."

Then he offered a proposed agenda for my approval. First: organization and mission. Second: future planning. Third: strategic posture. Fourth: civilian auxiliaries. Fifth: equipment. I had no additional suggestions.

"My assistants can provide details, should you desire. Do you have any questions on the briefing so far, sir?" Kosadwin asked. "No? Then . . . Major! Proceed!"

69

"As General Kosadwin said, the country is divided into sectors: Eastern and Western," the young officer sharply pointed to the two halves on the wall map. "As Commanding General of the Eastern Sector, General Kosadwin is responsible for the defense of the area bounded by the Sonbang Mountains in the north, the Luangkong River in the east, the Wakong River in the west, and 500 kilometers beyond the southern coast, including the capital of our country, Terkung." More stabbings at the map. And so went an hour of statistics, mission statements, charts, and the like.

Sectors are in turn divided into three land combat corps and one sea corps. The air corps covers both land and sea. Logistic centers are responsibilities of the regional administrators, who administer materiel research and engineering, procurement, distribution, and maintenance, as well as personnel recruitment and pre-induction processing. The Defense Futurity Command is housed on the Pnomkung post but reports directly to the national commander of defense. It is responsible for studies of intelligence and human knowledge for military implications, formulation of future strategies and tactics, including paramilitary operations and contingency reactions, and the design of special equipment systems.

"We do not regard the military forces as the long-term guarantors of our national security. We must ultimately rely on the determination of the people to defend their land, their families, their memories, their way of life, and their posterity," Kosadwin emphasized the cornerstone of Laian strategy. "That's why we in the military give considerable weight to our impact on the civilian side. If what we do weakens it, then our myopic actions will be self-defeating." He described the various procedures to ensure awareness of this fundamental premise. For example, every third assignment of a career military man involves a tour of duty in a nonmilitary post of equivalent degree of challenge. In his own case, the assignments had included aide to Prakung's senior administrator, instructor at Maikung Succorance Center, and deputy manager of the Saikung Armament Works.

70

An estimate of the strategic situation was next presented by the operations officer. An attack from countries to the north is judged unlikely because of the impenetrable mountains and their nonexistent navy. Chances of invasion from the east are also relatively low. The next door neighbor is a third the size of Chianglai and is acculturated with a similar nonaggressive heritage. The country farther east, however, had historically been aggressively inspired, expanding her territory fifteenfold in the last eighty years. She has been infiltrating the adjacent neighbor with the so-called peaceful influences during the last thirty years. At the present time, she is switching from a cultural penetration to a kind of financial and industrial bridgehead. He believes she is now in a position to provoke a suitable incident to invoke high-sounding pretexts, like protecting her friends and national interests and dignity, at any time she cares to launch a military expansion. Since a friendship pact exists between the neighbor and Chianglai, however, it is doubtful that the other country, which is somewhat smaller than Chianglai, would risk a war without reliable allies, which she does not have at the present time.

"There is a greater danger from the sea. Our 1500 some kilometers of coastline are studded with fine sandy beaches. It would be physically impossible for us to station fixed defenses at every potential beachhead to repel invasions from the sea. Available intelligence suggests that Country X is eyeing this part of the world, particularly our weak neighbor to the east. Since X is aware of our existing military pact, she is preparing to attack both of us simultaneously. The analysis of her dissembling strategies of past conquests would suggest a thrust initially at Haikung on the southern coast, then north along the Wakong River for fifty some kilometers, northeast to cut the neighbor's main petroleum supply to the interior and her rice basin."

Based on such an estimate, Chianglai has given its sea forces top priority. The enemy must be discouraged from landing. "Should his army ever land, however, we shall then resort to tactics known as interstitial permeations and explosive punctures," the brigadier continued. "Our long-haul defensive tactics, sir, rely primarily on mobile units of batallion size making up the six or so divisions in the highlands, with about a score of regimental combat teams in augmentation, and civilian guerrillas. In this phase the dedication of the people, as General Kosadwin has just reiterated, will be the decisive factor."

71

He described their own preparedness for last-ditch fighting at some length. "From your extensive sampling of our country, you must have observed, sir, what might have appeared as inefficient layouts in the farmlands, wasteful duplication by communities, and other signs of apparently poor management. Undoubtedly, some have indeed resulted from deficiencies. But most of them have been intentionally implemented for paramilitary purposes. Our rice paddies are a case in point. They are laid out in a fashion to preclude an armor blitz across the country. We can then handle scattered tanks with mines and hand-held antitank missiles with greater ease."

Laian strategists assume that nuclear bombs will be used by the invader up to fifty kiloton yields. The size and distribution of Chianglai's metropolises have been planned, in part, for nuclear survival. Only two of the metropolises being planned exceed 500,000, four more down to 100,000, eight more down to 50,000. All the others will be less than 50,000. Furthermore, metropolises over 250,000 will be separated by at least a thousand and a half kilometers. All over 50,000 are defensively tunneled.

For the purpose of sustained guerrilla actions, the communities are to be biologically self-sufficient with the help of immediate next-door neighbors. Given weapon caches locally and larger inland stockpiles backed by networks of replenishment, Chianglai should be in a position to keep fighting for a very long time.

72

During supper in Kosadwin's quarters, conversation centered on the servicemen themselves.

The effective cadre of the armed forces is 75,000. These are the professionals. About two-thirds of them came through at least two military generations from the Sonbang Mountain tribal stock. Fine, tough, and disciplined. The others in the 327,000-man force, in Kosadwin's own words, "aren't worth a damn."

"I often wonder whether building up a first-class fighting machine in Chianglai with her present cultural orientations is a hopeless task," he gave vent to his frustrations. "Getting Laians mad enough to kill. They just don't want to. It's ingrained, I suppose. Of course, I understand quite well that Laians are brought up to be considerate and compassionate to their fellow creatures. And believe me, I do appreciate the goodness of our people. But you simply can't win wars, not even a defensive one, by being considerate and compassionate—as your own powerful Americans so well know."

73

Thursday at the Armory. Kosadwin showed the usual assemblage of materiel, including several light tanks and planes of the 1970 vintage.

He enthusiastically talked about their small arms. The machine guns, rifles, mortars, and recoilless weapons were invented by the staff of the Defense Futurity Command and produced in Chianglai. They were ingeniously adapted to the last detail for local use. The small arms nestle perfectly for most efficient packing in caches. Moving parts are simplified for easy maintenance by untrained personnel.

When I asked about the picture on the wall of what looked like one of the latest models of jet fighters, he snorted: "Got a squadron *free* a couple of years ago through military aid. They are fine planes and all that. But they're gobbling up all of my loose cash. War is simply pricing itself out of all sanity. A crazy business!"

74

The equipment for the navy was most impressive. There is no doubt about it. Navy gets the best.

A submersible appears to be the backbone of the fleet. It was also designed by the Defense Futurity Command and manufactured in Chianglai. It carries antiaircraft guns on port and starboard decks, protected trenches fore and aft for men with hand-held missiles, and below deck, four torpedoes. Reinforced against underwater charges. Able to be replenished from submerged supply points. Normal complement of ten men. Cruising range of some 2000 kilometers. When properly arrayed in tactical formations, it would be almost impossible for ships to penetrate to shore, without being exposed to at least three of these launchers.

Closer to shore, fast-moving gunboats bear the principal defense. Its main weapon is a guided missile, locking on the target ship. It flies about three feet above the ocean surface, guiding an underwater self-propelled hydrodynamically shaped mine. The warhead itself is not primarily an explosive but a small electronic beacon, which attaches firmly to the surface upon striking, and on which the mine homes. Fired at night, it is impossible to counter. During daylight, as the weaponeers would put it, the probability of hit is 0.9 and the probability of kill is 0.77.

AN ANCIENT LEGEND

75

Dao met us at the airport when we returned to Terkung Friday morning. He asked whether I would prefer to discuss my observations as we took a stroll or sit in some room where there was a blackboard. He appeared noticeably pleased when I chose the former. So the chauffeur dropped us off in town and the aide took our belongings to the steamboat for the night cruise down the Wakong River to Haikung.

We casually wended our way through friendly lanes of Laians. I had never felt as good before as I did then in seeing people smile and returning a smile of my own. When we left the central part of town and the endearing ties began to thin, a sense of loneliness grew over me.

Dao and I ambled along the grassy paths of Terkung Park. Before I knew it, I stumbled. Looking back, I did not see anything that could have tripped me—nothing, except possibly a tiny centipede. My foot must have refused to step on it.

76

As we moved along, I asked a string of questions, which had bothered me during the trip. My eyes must have expressed a puzzled disagreement at just about every other reply of his. For I found him patiently retracing sequence after sequence: basic values underpinning Laian culture, corollary attitudes, accommodations to practical constraints, and specific practices that emerged.

After he had clarified my doubts, at least to the point of my getting some appreciation of his view of things, he solicited my counsel on beneficent democracy that I might care to pass on, based on my own experience in government in general and my visit to Chianglai in particular. "I may be able to suggest a little here and there in special areas which I might have specially studied," I evinced a modicum of modesty which, I recall, was not at all my usual display. "But as for fundamental policies and procedures for wholesome governance for our brothers here in Chianglai, I am afraid the trip has made me very humble. When I got your invitation, Dao, I thought I had a number of basic ideas which would be of great help to you. But now . . . after two weeks of slow awakening . . . I realize that I do not have a thing of real value . . . not a thing."

I said nothing for a minute or so, then went on: "Back in the states, I had discussed the situation with a brilliant and close friend, Dr. Schwarz of the McKennie Company, our most respected management consulting firm. We spent three weekends, drawing up a framework of Chianglai's future development. I brought along ten copies of the plan and of six reports I had prepared myself, as well as two books by the leading scholars of political science and public administration in America. I had intended to present them to you at this time, together with some embellishing remarks in the light of my experience here. But I had torn them all into little pieces and threw the worthless scrap into the trash can . . . after the big banquet . . . in Saikung."

77

As I struggled with the noodles slipping through my chopsticks, Dao sat on the grass, looking up respectfully into the eyes of the noodle vendor standing nearby. The scene was that of an eager pupil at the feet of his revered master. After lunch, I commented that the gentleman must have been saying some very interesting things. "And most instructive to *me*," Dao added.

The vendor had covered a range of subjects. Particularly critical were his remarks on the government's attitude toward the private family-size enterprises. There is no one to whom he, as a small-time entrepreneur, can appeal for advice and help. To him, this means that the government is planning to eliminate his kind through neglect. "If this happens," said he, shaking his thin finger at Dao, "tragedy will come to Chianglai." The country will have lost her sense of reasonableness. Without this reasonableness, society succumbs to competitive savagery. "Is the small desire of people like me not a reasonable one?" the man implored. "We do not exploit others. Our income is not excessive—only a fourth more than factory workers. But my wife and I work much longer hours. And do we not bring worthwhile and timely service and, I hope, some joy to you and your good brother?" The noodle vendor confessed that being a Cantonese immigrant, he could not claim as deep an association with Chianglai as his next door neighbor, a wood carver from a long line of woodcarvers. Besides, peddling lunches is not the kind of skill men take pride in passing on to their sons. "But when I go by the carver's little shop," the vendor's eyes lit up, "I say to myself: '*There* is Chianglai—roots ten thousand years long.' " Then a frown of sadness. "Surely, all of us should understand at least this much. No official, not even Honorable Senior Administrator Nam himself, can point to his high office and say that. This is why I feel so sad about the government's unreasonable treatment of family-size entrepreneurs. I arrived in Chianglai when I was twelve. I have come to love my Laian brothers. But I am afraid for them. Because when the roots are cut, the flowers will wilt and the plant will die." This was, according to Dao's account, what the noodle vendor had said.

Dao then slowly lapsed into his meditative silence, which I had learnt to respect back in the days of Montparnasse. He remained motionless for over five minutes with his dreamy half-closed eyes soliciting something beyond the realm of space and time. Slowly they opened wide. He quickly scribbled down a few notes. After that, he was his charming self again and we resumed our walk.

78

As we headed for the docks, the thought of leaving these people of whom I have become so much a part somehow filled me with a vague and depressing apprehension. Dao suspected I was troubled about something and encouraged me to talk about it. As I did, it gradually became clear that one of my underlying fears was based on the absence of anything written which will protect their rights for the future, after the fine people like Dao and Nam are gone. There was no Constitution. There was not even a Trans-Socialist Party. No explicit guarantees against a terrible dictatorship. I could almost see that dreadful day approaching.

"What gives rise to man's beneficence? Something written?" Dao answered the questions himself. "Surely not so, J. C. Can beneficence arise only at a particular point in the flow of history? Say, on the date some piece of paper is signed? the day some church was founded? Surely not so. Perhaps some document can serve as a reminder of the dangers of the totalitarian oppression of the masses, the democratic exploitation of minorities, and the religious persecution of the unbelievers in orthodoxy, J. C. But will it protect anyone against the misguidance of idealism, the conceit of the intellect, the vanity of wealth, the fraudulence of fame, the callousness of militancy, the camouflage of cunning, and the obtuseness of power?"

He thought for a second, then continued. "Do you not remember what Administrator Nam said when you asked about his main preoccupation? Something about nurturing a stability of trust and a sinking of deep anchorage into the heritage of Laians. Something about an intuitive oneness in our love of land, sky, people . . . trees and animals . . . mountains and paddies . . . tiny pebbles and little ferns . . . Well . . .

there and *only* there lies lasting surety. Where *else,* J. C.?" As I stepped on the gangplank, I felt that I was beginning to grasp what he had been saying. But it then eluded me again. And everything was as murky as ever.

79

Moon above mangrove. Boat moving with the tide. Scene serene.

Peering into that tranquility, I wondered: Is there freedom out there? Certainly, not our kind. . . . Why are they so happy then? . . . Can it be that our kind is really not necessary for a person to be happy? . . . No, that just can't be! . . . Then, why is there such widespread anguish back home . . . and suffering . . . so much more than out there? . . . Perhaps, it's what we have let our freedom do to us . . . or what we haven't done with it. . . . Perhaps, it's what they have not let their kind of freedom do to them . . . or what they have done with it. . . . What makes them tick in any case? . . . The thought brought to mind Dao's self-reflection at the monument of Keikitran and Eleevan: "If you can really feel the spirit of that bronze sculpture, you will grasp . . . what makes Chianglai tick."

"Dao," I broke the quiet. "Who is Keikitran? . . . and, who is Eleevan?" So Dao told me the legend of Keikitran and Eleevan.

80

Keikitran had always been the favorite son of the God Akuatran. He was a youth of boundless energy. The humdrum uniformity of heavenly perfection often bored him. On occasion, he would sneak off to his secret garden by a winding river on a tiny planet. He enjoyed the way the birds and animals would say hello to him, the way the flowers would smile, and the way the trees would wave. And everybody was spontaneous and cheerful. Keikitran used to remove the little burrs and thorns imbedded in his furry friends. He would feed his feathery friends with delicious berries from his hands. And he would freshen his green leafy friends with crystal water. He acquired experiences that were new to him. Like kindness. Never did he know of kindness in his father's home, for everything was perfect. Nobody needed any help. Soon, he felt much closer to his leafy, feathery, and furry friends than to his godly relatives above. The plants and animals, the winds and waters, earth and sky were full of joy when Keikitran would come and visit. One day, as the godling was conversing with his friends, he heard an anxious chirping from the bushes. "Keiki! Keiki! Help! Help!" Up he jumped and dashed across the pathway. There stood the excited bird, beside the still form of a kitten—black, with a white cravat, a white streak down the chest and belly, and white chin and paws. A boulder had dislodged itself, rolled down the path, and crushed the kitten's front right paw. It was a pitiful and gory sight. Keikitran did not know what to do—so strange was the experience, for never had he witnessed such suffering before in heaven. For the first time, he appreciated what compassion was. He did what best he knew how, sitting by the kitten's side and gently stroking him. He split a dried gourd, filled it with the goat's milk, and placed it right beside the kitten. But the kitten did not move. And all the animals stood by in silent sadness. The sky was dark; the winds were still. For three days, no one said a word. But early on the fourth, a feeble meow was heard. As everyone continued to observe with keen anticipation, the kitten slowly opened his green eyes and meowed again, but this time, loud and cheery. Keikitran obtained some fresh milk from the goat. The kitten lapped it up and purred. It then leaned backward, raised the injured paw, and licked it. The swelling soon subsided. The bluish color turned healthy red. The valley burst into a song of joy. The sun shone through. The breeze blew blissfully again. So overjoyed was Keikitran that for the first time in his entire life, tears came to his eyes. Before long, the kitten was its former self, except for a partial twisting of the paw and the cracking of a claw. The bird then named the kitten Eleevan.

Keikitran and Eleevan became the closest of friends. On the following trip, Keikitran invited his furry friend to live with him in heaven. But the Chancellor of Laws would have no part of it, for it had been clearly written in the Goddom Rule 17: "Only perfect beings shall enter The Great Goddom of Akuatran." And Eleevan did not come close to qualifying. Its right paw and claw did not meet Goddom standards. Keikitran went to his father. But it was no use. Even Akuatran Himself could not escape the Law of Goddom. For perfection brooks no deviation whatsoever—neither from Akuatran nor Eleevan.

Keikitran, however, was determined to remain together with his furry friend. Since Eleevan was not permitted in the heavenly sphere, Keikitran would stay where both of them could live. So he left The Great Goddom of Akuatran together with his lovely bride, Eeonna. They arrived a million some years ago and settled in his secret garden in a place, now known as Terkung and became the primal ancestors of Laians. This is why Chianglai has come to be known as The Land of Keikitran and Eleevan.

A BLURRED VISION

81

"Au revoir!" As I turned into the plane at the Haikung airport, Dao called out: "About your answers to my two key questions at the Terkung briefing, J. C.—yes or no?"

"To the first one . . . about everyone trying his best, my answer is—yes," I yelled back above the whining engines. "As to the second . . . about Chianglai succeeding within our lifetime—I don't know." We both waved fondly at each other, as films of tears blurred my vision. I drew back into the cabin hesitatingly and padded slowly down the aisle.

I leaned back in the reclining seat and wiped my watery eyes. Reflecting on my last words, I thought that perhaps the answer to the second question should also have been—yes. But what heathen doctrines! Even if I did feel kindredly disposed toward them and even if I do wish them well, how can I, a true American, admit to their success? I'm sure he understands. And yet . . . I'm not so sure . . . my view of Dao was blurred, and blurred by something from within myself, an unknown thing beyond my own control. In any case, I'm glad that I did meet him half-way. That's the least that I—for old time's sake—can do.

SELECTED BIBLIOGRAPHY

Alain (Émile Chartier). *Alain on Happiness.* Translated by R. D. Cottrell and J. E. Cottrell. New York: Ungar, 1973.

Allport, G. W. *The Nature of Prejudice.* Reading: Addison-Wesley, 1954.

Amory, C. *Man Kind?* New York: Harper & Row, 1974.

Arnold, A. *The Light of Asia.* New York: Pauper, 1946.

Aurelius, M. *Meditations.* Translated by G. Long. In: *Harvard Classics.* Edited by C. W. Eliot. New York: Collier, 1909.

Bailey, F. G. *Gifts and Poisons.* Oxford: Blackwell, 1971.

Barmash, I. *The Self-Made Man.* New York: Macmillan, 1969.

Battalia, O. W. and J. J. Tarrant. *The Corporate Eunuch.* New York: Crowell, 1973.

Beston, H. *The Outermost House.* New York: Viking, 1969.

Bhagavad-Gita. Translated by S. Prabhavananda and C. Isherwood. Hollywood: Rodd, 1947.

Buckley, J. C. and H. Schmidt. *The Retirement Handbook.* New York: Harper & Row, 1971. Fourth Edition.

Campbell, J. *The Hero with a Thousand Faces.* New York: Pantheon, 1949.

Cawelti, J. G. *Apostles of the Self-Made Man.* Chicago: University of Chicago, 1965.

Cicero, M. On old age. Translated by E. S. Shuckburgh. In: *Harvard Classics.* Edited by C. W. Eliot. New York: Collier, 1909.

Chew, P. *The Inner World of the Middle-Aged Man.* New York: Macmillan, 1976.

Chuang Tzu. *Complete Works of Chuang Tzu.* Translated by B. Watson. New York: Columbia University, 1968.

Coblenz, S. A. *The Long Road to Humanity.* New York: Yoseloff, 1959.

Coleman, L. L. *Freedom from Fear.* New York: Hawthorn, 1959.

Coomaraswamy, A. K. *The Bugbear of Literacy.* London: Dobson, 1947.

Djilas, M. *The Unperfect Society.* Translated by D. Cooke. New York: Harcourt, Brace & World, 1969.

Emerson, R. W. Essays: Self-reliance, The over-soul, and Compensation. In: S. Commins and R. N. Linscott, Ed. *The Social Philosophers.* New York: Random House, 1947.

Epictetus. *The Discourses and Manual.* Translated by P. E. Matheson. Oxford: Oxford University, 1916.
The Fitness of Man's Environment. Smithsonian Institution Annual Symposium, February 16–18, 1967. Washington, D. C.: Smithsonian Institution, 1968.
Fromm, E. *To Have or To Be.* New York: Harper & Row, 1976.
Gaylin, W. *Feelings.* New York: Harper & Row, 1979.
Gumpert, M. *The Anatomy of Happiness.* New York: McGraw-Hill, 1951.
Hazo, R. G. *The Idea of Love.* New York: Praeger, 1967.
Heilbroner, R. L., M. Mintz, C. McCarthy, S. J. Ungar, K. Vandivier, S. Friedman, and J. Boyd. *In the Name of Profit.* Garden City: Doubleday, 1972.
Heller, R. *The Great Executive Dream.* New York: Delacorte, 1972.
Hesse, H. *Magister Ludi.* Translated by M. Savill. New York: Ungar, 1949.
Holbrook, D. *The Masks of Hate.* Oxford: Pergamon, 1972.
Howell, J. T. *Hard Living on Clay Street.* New York: Anchor, 1973.
Huxley, A. *The Perennial Philosophy.* New York: Harper, 1945.
Huygen, W. and R. Poortvliet. *Gnomes.* New York: Abrams, 1977.
Jalal al-Din, Rumi. *Mathnawi.* Translated by R. A. Nicholson. Leiden: Brill, 1925.
James, W. *The Varieties of Religious Experience.* New York: Mentor, 1958.
Jennings, E. E. *The Executive in Crisis.* East Lansing: Michigan State University, 1965.
Kiley, J. C. *Self-Rescue.* New York: McGraw-Hill, 1977.
Krishnamurti, J. *The First and Last Freedom.* London: Gollancz, 1954.
Krutch, J. W. *The Voice of the Desert.* New York: Sloane, 1955.
Lao Tzu. *Tao Te Ching.* Translated by G.-F. Feng and J. English. New York: Vintage, 1972.
Lavelle, L. *The Meaning of Holiness.* Translated by D. O'Sullivan. New York: Pantheon, 1956.
Lewis, C. S. *The Four Loves.* New York: Harcourt, Brace, 1960.
Lin Yutang. *Translations from the Chinese.* Cleveland: World, 1963.
Lubbock, J. *The Use of Life.* Freeport: Books for Libraries, 1972.
MacIver, R. M. *The Pursuit of Happiness.* New York: Simon and Schuster, 1955.
Milgram, S. *Obedience to Authority.* New York: Harper & Row, 1974.
Miller. H. *The Colossus of Maroussi.* Harmondsworth: Penguin, 1950.
Mindess, H. *Laughter and Liberation.* Los Angeles: Nash, 1971.
Montaigne, M. E. de. *Essays.* Translated by S. Hughes. New York: New American Library, 1970.
Moskin, J. R. *Morality in America.* New York: Random House, 1966. Revised Edition.
Moustakas. C. E. *Loneliness.* Englewood Cliffs: Prentice-Hall, 1961.
Naranjo, C. *The One Quest.* New York: Viking, 1972.
Nasruddin Hoca. Translated by: I. Shah. *The Subtleties of Mulla Nasruddin.* London: Cape, 1973.

Nicolson, H. *Good Behaviour*. Garden City: Doubleday, 1956.

Nietzsche, F. *Thus Spoke Zarathustra*. Translated by R. J. Hollingdale. Harmondsworth: Penguin, 1961.

Olson, R. G. *The Morality of Self Interest*. New York: Harcourt, Brace, 1965.

Panchatantra. Translated by A. R. Ryder. Chicago: University of Chicago, 1956.

Picard, M. *The World of Silence*. Translated by S. Godman. Chicago: Regnery, 1952.

Pomerance. B. *The Elephant Man,* New York: Grove, 1979.

Reisman, D., N. Glazer, and R. Denny. *The Lonely Crowd*. New Haven: Yale University, 1953.

Rescher, N. *Unselfishness*. Pittsburgh: University of Pittsburgh, 1975.

Ross, N. W., Ed. *The World of Zen*. New York: Vintage, 1960.

Rubin, Z., Ed. *Doing unto Others*. Englewood Cliffs: Prentice-Hall, 1974.

Russell, B. *Bertrand Russell Speaks His Mind*. New York: Hard Books, 1960.

Saadi. The *Gulistan*. Translated by E. Rehatsek and edited by W. G. Archer. London: Allen and Unwin, 1964.

Sayles, L. R. *Leadership*. New York: McGraw-Hill, 1979.

Scheler, M. *The Nature of Sympathy*. Translated by P. Heath. New Haven: Yale University, 1954.

Selye, H. *Stress without Distress*. Philadelphia: Lippincott, 1974.

Silver, S. M. *How to Enjoy This Moment*. New York: Simon & Schuster, 1967.

Siu, R. G. H. *The Tao of Science*. Cambridge, MIT, 1958.

Smith, H. C. *Sensitivity to People*. New York: McGraw-Hill, 1966.

Solomon, R. C. *The Passions*. Garden City: Anchor, 1976.

Suzuki, D. T. *Zen and Japanese Culture*. New York: Pantheon, 1959.

Tagore, R. *The Religion of Man*. New York: Macmillan, 1931.

Tawney, R. H. *The Acquisitive Society*. New York: Harcourt, Brace, 1920.

Tolstoy, L. *What Men Live By*. Translated by J. Hill. New York: Pauper, n. d.

Uris, A. *The Frustrated Titan*. New York: Van Nostrand, 1972.

Witcutt, W. P. *The Rise and Fall of the Individual*. London: S. P. C. K., 1958.

Wolman, B. B. *Victims of Success*. New York: Quadrangle, 1973.

Wu Ch'eng-en. *Monkey*. Translated by A. Waley. New York: Day, 1943.

INDEX